Gender, Sexuality, and the Law

This volume examines the role of law as a tool for advancing women's rights and gender equity in local, national, and global contexts.

Many feminist scholars note a marked failure of law to achieve goals connected to women's rights and gender equality. Despite its limitations, law provides aspirational norms that can be mobilized to hold institutions accountable and to provide material benefit to those excluded from systems of power. In conversation with each other, the chapters in this volume help to advance understanding of both the limitations and the potential of law as a tool for advancing democratic participation, rights, and justice around issues related to gender and sexuality. Contributors acknowledge, to varying degrees, that law has important symbolism and may be used as a lever to mobilize change. At the same time, some offer cautionary notes about the potential downside risks and unintended consequences of relying upon law in pursuit of women's rights and gender equity.

Collectively, the chapters in this volume explore the disjuncture between the promise and expectation of legal reform and the lived experience of those laws by people intended as the beneficiaries of legal change.

This book was originally published as a special issue of *Global Discourse.*

Debra L. DeLaet is the David E. Maxwell Distinguished Professor of International Affairs at Drake University, Des Moines, USA. She is the author of several books, numerous articles, and book chapters on human rights, global health, and global gender issues.

Renée Ann Cramer is a Professor of Law, Politics, and Society at Drake University, Des Moines, USA. Since 2004, she has been engaged in ethnographic and participant observation field work with homebirth midwives, advocates for midwifery, and families who have had out-of-hospital births.

I0894971

Gender, Sexuality and the Law

Gender, Sexuality, and the Law

Edited by
Debra L. DeLaet and Renée Ann Cramer

Routledge
Taylor & Francis Group
LONDON AND NEW YORK

First published 2019
by Routledge
2 Park Square, Milton Park, Abingdon, Oxon, OX14 4RN

and by Routledge
605 Third Avenue, New York, NY 10017

First issued in paperback 2020

Routledge is an imprint of the Taylor & Francis Group, an informa business

British Library Cataloguing-in-Publication Data
A catalogue record for this book is available from the British Library

ISBN 13: 978-0-367-73084-0 (pbk)
ISBN 13: 978-0-367-21923-9 (hbk)

Typeset in Myriad Pro
by codeMantra

Publisher's Note

The publisher accepts responsibility for any inconsistencies that may have arisen during the conversion of this book from journal articles to book chapters, namely the possible inclusion of journal terminology.

Contents

Citation Information

The chapters in this book were originally published in the journal *Global Discourse*, volume 8, issue 3 (September 2018). When citing this material, please use the original page numbering for each article, as follows:

Introduction
Introduction: gender, sexuality, and the law
Debra L. DeLaet and Renée A. Cramer
Global Discourse, volume 8, issue 3 (September 2018) pp. 383–386

Chapter 1
Lost in legation: the gap between rhetoric and reality in international human rights law governing women's rights
Debra L. DeLaet
Global Discourse, volume 8, issue 3 (September 2018) pp. 387–404

Chapter 2
What's at stake in the treaty reporting process? Cuba and the United Nations' convention on women's rights
Lisa Baldez
Global Discourse, volume 8, issue 3 (September 2018) pp. 405–421

Chapter 3
Gender politics and geopolitics of international criminal law in Uganda
Annie Bunting
Global Discourse, volume 8, issue 3 (September 2018) pp. 422–437

Chapter 4
Spaces of international gender justice: a reply to Baldez and DeLaet
Annie Bunting
Global Discourse, volume 8, issue 3 (September 2018) pp. 438–440

Chapter 5
Tacking between the global and the local: a reply to DeLaet and Bunting
Lisa Baldez
Global Discourse, volume 8, issue 3 (September 2018) pp. 441–443

Chapter 6

What's law got to do with it?: A reply to Baldez and Bunting
Debra L. DeLaet
Global Discourse, volume 8, issue 3 (September 2018) pp. 444–447

Chapter 7

Attempting international normative change in gender and the law: a reply to DeLaet, Baldez and Bunting
Darby Matt
Global Discourse, volume 8, issue 3 (September 2018) pp. 448–451

Chapter 8

'The stigma of Western words': asylum law, transgender identity and sexual orientation in South Africa
B Camminga
Global Discourse, volume 8, issue 3 (September 2018) pp. 452–469

Chapter 9

Gender, sexuality and the right to a non-projected future: a reply to Camminga
Elizabeth Mills
Global Discourse, volume 8, issue 3 (September 2018) pp. 470–472

Chapter 10

Gender, sexuality and the limits of the law
Elizabeth Mills
Global Discourse, volume 8, issue 3 (September 2018) pp. 473–484

Chapter 11

Wo/andering about walls: a reply to Elizabeth Mills
B Camminga
Global Discourse, volume 8, issue 3 (September 2018) pp. 485–487

Chapter 12

The problem of visibility in LGBT human rights: a reply to Camminga and Mills
Phoebe Clark
Global Discourse, volume 8, issue 3 (September 2018) pp. 488–492

Chapter 13

The limits of law in securing reproductive freedoms: midwife-assisted homebirth in the United States
Renée Ann Cramer
Global Discourse, volume 8, issue 3 (September 2018) pp. 493–509

Chapter 14

Mothers do not make good workers: the role of work/life balance policies in reinforcing gendered stereotypes
Sarah Cote Hampson
Global Discourse, volume 8, issue 3 (September 2018) pp. 510–531

Chapter 15

Embedded exclusions: exploring gender equality in Peru's participatory democratic framework
Stephanie McNulty
Global Discourse, volume 8, issue 3 (September 2018) pp. 532–549

Chapter 16

Gender, the workplace and the limits of the law: a reply to Cramer and Cote Hampson
Stephanie McNulty
Global Discourse, volume 8, issue 3 (September 2018) pp. 550–552

Chapter 17

Law's promises and its limits: a reply to Cramer and McNulty
Sarah Cote Hampson
Global Discourse, volume 8, issue 3 (September 2018) pp. 553–555

Chapter 18

Process is insufficient: a reply to Cote Hampson and McNulty
Renée Ann Cramer
Global Discourse, volume 8, issue 3 (September 2018) pp. 556–560

Chapter 19

Policymaking for gender equality: a reply to Cramer, Cote Hampson, and McNulty
Sara Feldman
Global Discourse, volume 8, issue 3 (September 2018) pp. 561–565

Notes on Contributors

Lisa Baldez is a Professor of Government, and of Latin American, Latino and Caribbean Studies at Dartmouth College, USA. Her research examines the extent to which formal institutional rules shape the possibilities for achieving gender equality.

Annie Bunting is an Associate Professor in the Law & Society program at York University, Toronto, Canada. Her research expertise includes socio-legal studies of marriage and childhoods; feminist international law; and culture, religion, and law.

B Camminga is a Postdoctoral Research Fellow at the African Centre for Migration and Society at Wits University, Johannesburg, South Africa. Their research focuses on knowledge production and concepts of the everyday in relation to the needs of transgender and gender-transgressive asylum seekers from Africa.

Phoebe Clark is a Teaching Assistant and Graduate Student in the Department of Geography at the University of Washington, Seattle, USA.

Sarah Cote Hampson is an Assistant Professor in the School of Interdisciplinary Arts and Sciences at the University of Washington Tacoma, USA. Her research focuses on public policy in the US from a socio-legal perspective. She also studies gender, race, and ethnicity in US electoral politics.

Renée Ann Cramer is a Professor of Law, Politics, and Society at Drake University, Des Moines, USA. Since 2004, she has been engaged in ethnographic and participant observation field work with homebirth midwives, advocates for midwifery, and families who have had out-of-hospital births.

Debra L. DeLaet is the David E. Maxwell Distinguished Professor of International Affairs at Drake University, Des Moines, USA. She is the author of several books, numerous articles, and book chapters on human rights, global health, and global gender issues.

Sara Feldman is majoring in Law, Politics, and Society and History, with a minor in Sociology and Politics, and concentration in Women's and Gender Studies, at Drake University, Des Moines, USA.

Darby Matt is studying International Relations/Law, Politics, and Society at Drake University, Des Moines, USA.

Stephanie McNulty is an Associate Professor of Government at Franklin and Marshall College, Lancaster, USA. She is a Latin Americanist with expertise in participatory governance, gender, decentralization, and development.

Elizabeth Mills is a Senior Lecturer in International Development in the Department of Anthropology at the University of Sussex, Brighton, UK. Her recent ethnographic research has explored women's embodied accounts of HIV and AIDS biomedicines in South Africa and Brazil.

INTRODUCTION

Introduction: gender, sexuality, and the law

Debra L. DeLaet and Renée A. Cramer

This issue of *Global Discourse* is the product of a multidisciplinary scholarly collaboration focused on questions related to gender, sexuality, and the law. As editors, we sought to foster a scholarly collaboration that integrated principles of gender equity into the process of developing this issue. This collaboration began with a workshop held at Drake University during October 2018.[1] We invited scholars representing multiple disciplines from different global regions. Contributing scholars also are at different stages in their academic career. We are pleased that our efforts to diversify contributing scholars has helped produce a special issue with a rich set of contributions, though we acknowledge that the special issue would offer an even more valuable perspective had we succeeded in recruiting an even more diverse set of contributing scholars from a broader range of disciplinary backgrounds and geographic regions. Much work remains to be done to ensure broad, inclusive scholarly discussions about gender, sexuality, and the law.

Throughout the research process, we asked contributors to engage in robust, productive scholarly exchange. At our fall workshop, we placed papers in research clusters focused on specific dimensions of gender, sexuality, and the law. Research Cluster 1, with papers by Baldez (2018a, 2018b), Bunting (2018a, 2018b) and DeLaet (2018a, 2018b) focus primarily on international law as a mechanism for addressing women's rights and gender equity. The papers by Camminga (2018a, 2018b) and Mills (2018a, 2018b) in Research Cluster 2 explicitly examine global issues related to sexuality and gender equity. In Research Cluster 3, papers by Cramer (2018a, 2018b), Cote Hampson (2018a, 2018b) and McNulty (2018a, 2018b) focus on national law and policies related to gender equality. Although all participants in the workshop offered feedback on each paper, scholars in each research cluster took primary responsibility for reviewing and providing critiques of the other papers in their cluster. We asked contributors to put their pieces in conversation with each other, explicitly identifying and engaging in discussion around common themes, points of tension or disagreement, and lingering questions raised by each article considered collectively. The productive nature of these purposeful efforts to foster scholarly dialogue is evident in the articles and replies published here. We also sought to model a scholarly process with an emphasis on equity by including undergraduate students in the scholarly collaboration. Numerous Drake students participated in the fall workshop at Drake and had opportunities to observe the scholarly conversations and to offer their own critiques to the presented papers. A select few of these written student replies are included in the special issue.

This special issue represents the culmination of the scholarly discussions we began at the workshop at Drake in October 2017. Subsequent to our in-person discussions at the workshop, we continued to engage in discussions and to offer feedback on questions related to gender, sexuality, and the law. Although each contributor offers different conclusions about the relative value of the law, the contributions here reflect synergy about the challenges of exclusively relying on a top-down conception of the law as a tool for pursuing social and political change around women's rights and gender equity. The rule of law is an essential part of functioning democracies, and reliance on law and legal claims-making is standard practice for advocates in international and domestic contexts across a range of issues. However, it is not at all clear that formal legal rules and venues are the best places for human rights and equity to be achieved.

For women's rights and gender equity in particular, reliance on formal legal rules may be problematic, as law itself is critiqued as patriarchal, hierarchical, and rigidly formal in ways that do violence to women's claims, as well as the claims of LGBTQ people. Indeed, many feminist scholars note a marked failure of law to achieve the goals laid out in legislation, international treaties, and constitutional articulations of rights.

Yet, rights and law are important – incredibly so – and often useful in given contexts. They provide aspirational norms that can be mobilized to hold institutions accountable and to provide material benefit to those excluded from systems of power. The fundamental questions, then, involve how, and when, formal law is useful for attaining gender equity in international and domestic law. And, when is it limited in utility? The contributions to this special issue offer divergent answers to these questions. In conversation with each other, the pieces help to advance our understanding of both the limitations and the potential of law as a tool for advancing democratic participation, rights, and justice around issues related to gender and sexuality.

The first three articles in this issue examine international law as a potential mechanism for advancing women's rights and gender equality. Within this cluster of articles, the first article, by Debra DeLaet (2018a), points to the failure of international human rights law (with a specific focus on the *Convention on the Elimination of Discrimination against Women*) to generate systemic change globally. In her examination of Cuba's participation in the *Convention on the Elimination of Discrimination against Women* in the next article, Lisa Baldez (2018a) offers a relatively more positive assessment of the potential for international human rights law to transform human rights outcomes Baldez when states participate in treaty reporting processes. Annie Bunting (2018a), in the third article in this cluster, examines Ugandan victim survivors' views on the prosecution of crimes against humanity at the International Criminal Court. Bunting offers a mixed perspective, whereby international criminal trials may provide political space for meaning-making and historical documentation even if they do not provide for restorative justice, healing, or gender equality.

The second set of pieces in this special issue focus specifically on gender, sexuality, and the law. In their examination of asylum law, transgender identity, and sexual orientation in South Africa, B Camminga (2018a) considers the tensions that arise when a person is seen as transgender or presumed to be transgender while not self-identifying as transgender during the process of asylum-seeking. Elizabeth Mills (2018a) focuses on embodied experiences of inequality under the wall through an examination of the ways in which international discourses and institutions shape domestic legal frameworks governing gender and sexuality, particularly in determining which bodies are made visible, effaced, or entirely ignored.

The final articles in this issue closely examine the law and policy-making in domestic contexts.

In her examination of midwife assisted homebirth in the United States, Renée Cramer (2018a) points to the limits of law in securing reproductive freedoms due to the gap between doctrine and legislation, and implementation as well as the contingent and constitutive relationships between law and transformational change. Sarah Cote Hampson's (2018a) piece, the next in this research cluster, looks at 'family friendly' policies in the United States, such as maternity leave, and concludes that these policies create and reinforce stereotypes that exacerbate rather than alleviate tensions around work/life balance. In the final piece, Stephanie McNulty (2018a) examines state-mandated participatory budgeting in Peru and concludes that the political spaces meant to empower all citizens actually (re)produce fundamental gender inequities.

Each of the articles in this special issue point to the limitations of the law as a tool for generating transformative change in support of women's rights and equality. Yet, contributors acknowledge, to varying degrees, that law has important symbolism and may be used as a lever to mobilize change. At the same time, other pieces offer cautionary notes about the potential downside risks and unintended consequences of relying upon law in pursuit of women's rights and gender equity.

The scholarly conversation in this special issue indicates that several fundamental questions remain. What is the role of law in creating social change? Are the role and efficacy of law different in the particular cases related to gender and sexual equality? If so, why? Are pragmatic approaches to gender equality too piecemeal to be effective? Does law meet its promise most fruitfully, in incremental and gradual approaches that allow cultural change to catch up to more progressively-minded policies? Or, does culture more usefully lead in areas where transformational change is desired – creating a groundswell for better practices, that law later formalizes?

Clearly, law alone is insufficient to drive change in support of the expansion of women's rights and gender equity. Yet, the authors in this issue offer divergent viewpoints about the extent to which law is necessary or potentially beneficial towards these aims and whether alternative strategies that circumvent formal law are more promising. In doing so, these articles demonstrate the usefulness of having practitioners, scholars, and those impacted by policies in conversation with each other, especially as part of a process of clarifying goals and assessing results. They point to the promise of additional research on how those meant to benefit from law and policy are impacted by particular rules and laws. And, these articles indicate a disjuncture between policy-makers and legislators, and the on-the-ground reality of the policies and laws in action. In the disjuncture between the promise and expectation of legal reform, and the lived experience of those laws, scholars might also find creative approaches and workarounds implemented by the people, whose hopes may have been disappointed by legal change.

It is quite likely that law is more than one thing, to all of those involved in using it to achieve gender and sexual equality. Indeed, these articles show us that law is a tool, a lever, a symbol, a word to mobilize around, a strategy to mobilize with, a disappointment, and, a victory.

Note

1. The editors are grateful for generous support from the following Drake bodies that made the workshop possible: Nelson Institute for International Affairs, the Slay Fund for Social Justice, the program in Women and Gender Studies, the College of Arts and Sciences, and the Maxwell Professorship in International Affairs.

Disclosure statement

No potential conflict of interest was reported by the authors.

References

Baldez, L. 2018a. "What's at Stake in the Treaty Reporting Process? Cuba and the United Nations' Convention on Women's Rights." *Global Discourse*. doi: 10.1080/23269995.2018.1520009

Baldez, L. 2018b. "Tacking between the Global and the Local: A Reply to DeLaet and Bunting." *Global Discourse*. doi: 10.1080/23269995.2018.1520012

Bunting, A. 2018a. "Gender Politics and Geopolitics of International Criminal Law in Uganda." *Global Discourse*. doi: 10.1080/23269995.2018.1520010

Bunting, A. 2018b. "Spaces of International Gender Justice: A Reply to Baldez and DeLaet." *Global Discourse*. doi: 10.1080/23269995.2018.1520011

Camminga, B. 2018a. "The Stigma of Western Words': Asylum Law, Transgender Identity and Sexual Orientation in South Africa." *Global Discourse*. doi: 10.1080/23269995.2018.1521045

Camminga, B. 2018b. "Wo/Andering about Walls: A Reply to Elizabeth Mills." *Global Discourse*. doi: 10.1080/23269995.2018.1521105

Cramer, R. 2018a. "The Limits of Law in Securing Reproductive Freedoms: Midwife-Assisted Homebirth in the United States." *Global Discourse*. doi: 10.1080/23269995.2018.1521122

Cramer, R. 2018b. "Process Is Insufficient: A Reply to Cote Hampson and McNulty." *Global Discourse*. doi: 10.1080/23269995.2018.1521165

Cote Hampson, S. 2018a. ""Mothers Do Not Make Good Workers: The Role of Work/Life Balance Policies in Reinforcing Gendered Stereotypes." *Global Discourse*. doi: 10.1080/23269995.2018.1521129

Cote Hampson, S. 2018b. "Law's Promises and Its Limits: A Reply to Cramer and McNulty." *Global Discourse*. doi: 10.1080/23269995.2018.1521148

DeLaet, D. 2018a. "Lost in Legation: The Gap between Rhetoric and Reality in International Human Rights Law Governing Women's Rights." *Global Discourse*. doi: 10.1080/23269995.2018.1520006

DeLaet, D. 2018b. "What's Law Got to Do with It? A Reply to Baldez and Bunting." *Global Discourse*. doi: 10.1080/23269995.2018.1520014

McNulty, S. 2018a. "Embedded Exclusions: Exploring Gender Equality in Peru's Participatory Democratic Framework." *Global Discourse*. doi: 10.1080/23269995.2018.1521137

McNulty, S. 2018b. "Gender, the Workplace, and the Limits of the Law: A Reply to Cramer and Cote Hampson." *Global Discourse*. doi: 10.1080/23269995.2018.1521142

Mills, E. 2018a. "Sexuality and the Limits of the Law." *Global Discourse*. doi: 10.1080/23269995.2018.1521099

Mills, E. 2018b. "Gender, Sexuality and the Right to a Non-Projected Future: A Reply to Camminga." *Global Discourse*. doi: 10.1080/23269995.2018.1521051

Lost in legation: the gap between rhetoric and reality in international human rights law governing women's rights

Debra L. DeLaet

ABSTRACT

This article weaves together insights from political science, human rights scholarship, feminist legal theory, and other critical perspectives to explore the limits of global legalism as a primary mechanism for promoting women's rights. Specifically, it examines international human rights law governing women's rights to consider the limitations of law as a mechanism for improving the status of women globally. Although its development has been prolific, formal international human rights law is characterized by a significant gap between aspirational rhetoric and the reality of limited implementation and enforcement. This gap between rhetoric and reality demonstrates the limitations of a universalistic legal framework as a mechanism for promoting significant gains for women's equality and rights. The article investigates the limitations of international human rights law as a tool for promoting women's rights through a close examination of human rights treaty systems, specifically the *Convention on the Elimination of Discrimination Against Women*.

Introduction

This article weaves together insights from political science, human rights scholarship, feminist legal theory, and other critical perspectives to explore the limits of global legalism as a primary mechanism for promoting women's rights. Global legalism represents an approach to global problems that seeks solutions rooted in formal law and institutions. In the area of human rights, global legalism favors the creation of universal legal norms and international institutions as the key component of human rights promotion (Hafner-Burton 2013, 10). Global legalism tends to treat the codification of human rights treaties as an inherently positive development irrespective of whether or not they produce systemic improvements globally. The critical perspective developed in this article challenges global legalism and suggests that the codification of formal law is insufficient to mobilize systemic progress in the advancement of women's rights or human rights in general.

International human rights law has explicitly codified equal rights for women in the political, economic, and social spheres. Nevertheless, gender-based violence and gendered sociocultural inequities remain deeply embedded in societies across the globe. Human rights treaties prohibit legal barriers to women's access to the full array of political, economic, and social rights. Yet, cultural change does not necessarily follow the removal of legal barriers to equal rights. Equal political rights under the law, at either the international or national level, do not produce equal representation for women (Ellerby 2017, 109–113). Human rights treaties and national policies guaranteeing the right to work for women do not necessarily transform the informal gender barriers that result in women working in more vulnerable, lower-paid sectors of the economy (134–138). International or national laws criminalizing violence against women will not necessarily overcome the toxic masculinity that drives men to commit violence or the gender biases that hinder women from reporting sexual assault (169–179). In short, the formal guarantee of legal equality does not necessarily challenge pervasive and deep-seated gender norms that produce structural inequalities.

As a result, global legalism is an insufficient tool for producing the political and cultural changes necessary for the progressive realization of women's rights as human rights. Formal law at either the national or international levels may not overcome the 'stickiness' of cultural norms. The extent to which formal law will produce social transformation depends extensively on cultural and political transformation at the local level. Because the benefits of formal law are limited, there should also be limitations on the investment of financial resources and political capital in global norm generation and institutionalization relative to investments in local initiatives intended to produce sociocultural transformation.

This manuscript investigates the limitations of international human rights law as a tool for promoting women's rights through a close examination of international human rights treaties, particularly the *Convention on the Elimination of Discrimination Against Women*, as well as the monitoring bodies and institutions associated with these treaties.

The progressive development of international legal norms governing women's rights

Women's rights in international human rights law

The *International Covenant on Civil and Political Rights* (ICCPR) and the *International Covenant on Economic, Social and Cultural Rights* (ICESCR) formally establish women's rights as human rights.[1] As the core legal treaties in the international human rights regime, these binding legal documents codify an expansive list of universal human rights and represent the broadest articulation of human rights norms in international law. In articulating this broad set of rights, both the ICCPR and the ICESCR adopt an equal rights approach in their treatment of women's rights.

The ICCPR includes a non-discrimination clause indicating that states may not discriminate on the grounds of biological sex in addition to other protected categories, including race, language, religion, political opinion, and national origin (Article 2, Par. 1). It also calls upon States Parties to 'undertake to ensure the equal right of men and women to the enjoyment of all civil and political rights set forth in the present

Covenant' (Article 3). The treaty specifies that any derogation from treaty obligations during a time of public emergency, as allowed under specific conditions, may not be based on discrimination on the grounds of biological sex or other protected categories (Article 4, Par. 1).

The ICESCR also includes a non-discrimination clause precluding discrimination on the grounds of biological sex and other categories (Article 2, Par. 2) and calls upon States Parties to 'undertake to ensure the right of men and women to the enjoyment of all economic, social and cultural rights set forth in the present Covenant' (Article 3). The treaty calls for equal pay for equal work and calls upon states to guarantee equal work conditions for women and men (Article 7). Although both the ICCPR and the ICESCR primarily reflect an equal rights approach to women's rights, they also incorporate a small number of provisions that articulate particular rights for women under specific conditions. The ICCPR specifies that the death penalty may not be carried out against pregnant women (Article 6, Par. 5). The ICESCR identifies calls for special protection for mothers before and after childbirth and calls for paid leave or adequate social security benefits for working mothers (Article 10, Par. 2).

Growing out of these broad-based human rights treaties, the international human rights regime has steadily expanded via the development of specialized human rights treaties that have fleshed out human rights norms and created monitoring bodies and other human rights machinery in particular issue areas. These specialized treaties differ in regard to whether they explicitly incorporate an equal rights framework or simply imply that the enumerated rights cover all persons, including women. The *International Convention on the Elimination of All Forms of Racial Discrimination* (CERD) makes reference to the obligation to observe fundamental human rights without distinction based on discriminatory grounds, including on the grounds of biological sex, in its Preamble. The *Torture Convention* (UNTC) does not include provisions specifically referencing women's rights; nor does it contain a non-discrimination clause. The *Convention on the Rights of the Child* (CRC) includes a non-discrimination clause (Article 2). Apart from a clause calling upon states to ensure appropriate pre- and post-natal care for mothers (Article 24, Par. 2d), the CRC does not otherwise make reference to biological sex or gender in its provisions.

States have created a range of mechanisms to implement the international human rights regime, including the norms governing women's rights. Foremost, each human rights treaty creates an associated treaty-monitoring body with responsibilities for monitoring state compliance and progress toward fulfilling the fundamental rights codified in particular treaties. The UN human rights system includes seven treaty-monitoring bodies, one for each of the major treaties that constitute the international human rights regime: (1) the Human Rights Committee (ICCPR); (2) the Economic, Social and Cultural Rights Committee (ICESCR); (3) the Committee Against Torture (UNTC); (4) the Committee on the Elimination of Racial Discrimination (CERD); (5) the Committee on the Elimination of Discrimination Against Women (CEDAW), discussed in detail below; (6) the Committee on the Rights of the Child (CRC); and (7) The Committee on the Rights of Persons with Disabilities (CRPD). The international human rights regime establishes only a weak monitoring system that is implemented via these bodies. The monitoring process, which is set out in each respective treaty, typically calls for states to submit regular reports to the associated treaty-monitoring body. The committees then review submitted reports based on constructive dialogue with state parties through which the treaty-monitoring bodies make suggestions or recommendations about how states may fulfill their treaty obligations. The treaty-monitoring bodies may only make non-binding recommendations that do not have the force of law, and states commonly do not follow these recommendations.

Ultimately, the international human rights regime tends to defer to state sovereignty, limiting its capacity to generate substantial and meaningful change. This reality means that international norms governing women's rights – whether encompassed in an explicit or implicit equal rights framework in general human rights treaties or expressed as particularized women's rights in specific provisions of general treaties – are not accompanied by meaningful enforcement mechanisms that would allow for the law to serve as a significant lever for advancing women's rights and women's equality. Thus, the progressive development of international treaty-based norms governing women's rights are of symbolic importance, may contribute to concrete changes in specific domestic contexts, but have not produced systemic improvements to the status of women across the globe.

The UN convention on the elimination of all forms of discrimination against women

The limitations of relying on international human rights law to promote women's rights are illustrated by an examination of the *UN Convention on the Elimination of All Forms of Discrimination Against Women* (CEDAW), adopted by the UN General Assembly in 1979 and entering into force in 1981. Unlike other core treaties in the international human rights regime, CEDAW goes beyond a strictly equal rights framework and articulates a range of rights that are particular to women. To be sure, CEDAW makes clear that women, without discrimination, are entitled to the same set of fundamental human rights as men. To this end, many of CEDAW's provisions serve to reaffirm that women have a right to the equal enjoyment of human rights protections that have been codified in other treaties. CEDAW reaffirms women's right to legal protection under the law (Article 2), to all forms of political participation (Article 7), to education (Article 10), and to work (Article 11).

Although it reaffirms equal rights for women, CEDAW also contains provisions that articulate particular rights for women on the grounds that they are necessary to redress the longstanding and pernicious effects of institutionalized gender inequities and to recognize the unique needs of women in particular issue areas, especially as relates to maternity (Ellerby 2017, 78; Merry 2006b, 75).

Article 4 is a critical provision in this regard. It specifies that temporary special measures adopted by States Parties '… aimed at accelerating de facto equality between men and women shall not be considered discrimination as defined in the present Convention.' Subsequent clauses in this provision also indicate that states shall discontinue these measures '…when the objectives of equality of opportunity and treatment have been achieved.' More specifically, Article 4 specifies that state policies '…aimed at protecting maternity shall not be considered discriminatory.' This particular right for women is elaborated in Article 11 (Par. 2) that calls upon States Parties to introduce maternity leave 'with pay or with comparable social benefits.' The same paragraph asks states to prohibit the dismissal of employees due to pregnancy, maternal leave, or marital status. CEDAW contains an additional provision that asserts women's right to prenatal and postnatal care (Article 12, Par. 2).

Whereas Articles 4 and 11 provide for particular rights for women in recognition of both the historic barriers to women's equality and the unique needs of women, CEDAW goes further than other core treaties in the international human rights regime in seeking to challenge social and cultural norms that emphasize differences between men and women and resultant gender inequalities. Specifically, Article 5 (Par. a) calls upon states to '… modify the social and cultural patterns of conduct of men and women, with a view to achieving the elimination of prejudices and customary and all other practices which are based on the idea of the inferiority or the superiority of either of the sexes or on stereotyped roles for men and women.' Interestingly, this provision is in tension with Articles 4 and 11 which, by protecting maternity but not parental rights, reinforce traditional and gender-stereotyped roles for women.

The Committee on the Elimination of Discrimination Against Women is the treaty-monitoring body with oversight responsibilities for CEDAW. Like the other treaty-monitoring bodies, it provides only a weak system of monitoring and enforcement. The committee receives and reviews reports from States Parties and may seek to improve states' human rights records via constructive dialogue. It may further make non-binding recommendations that do not have the force of law. The Optional Protocol to CEDAW also allows individuals and non-governmental organizations to submit complaints to the committee and mandates the Committee to initiate inquiries into grave or systematic violations of rights. These provisions are only in effect when accepted by the state party in question. Also, it is notable that the Committee does not have any authority for rendering or enforcing binding judgments in such circumstances. Critics have noted that implementation mechanisms for CEDAW are even more limited than the weak enforcement mechanisms of human rights treaties in general; this was especially the case prior to the adoption of CEDAW's Optional Protocol in 1999 (Byrnes and Conners 1996; Byrnes 1994).

Despite the absence of provisions for strong enforcement, the CEDAW process – built on constructive dialogue and cooperative interactions between the Committee and state parties – creates a pathway by which global norms may shape national policies on women's rights Merry (2006b) notes the important cultural work that gets done in the CEDAW review process: 'It articulates the principles of gender equality and state responsibility and demonstrates how they apply to the countries under scrutiny. The process of ratification, preparing reports, and presenting and discussing reports fosters new cultural understandings of gender and violence' (72–73). By establishing norms and creating institutional spaces in which global actors engage around these norms, CEDAW provides opportunities for states and non-governmental organizations to pressure governments to shift policy related to the status of women.

Case studies of particular countries demonstrate that this process can produce meaningful cultural and political change (Baldez 2018, 2014; Merry 2006b, 72–102). Notably, recent research has shown that CEDAW ratification has been positively correlated with improvements in women's rights, especially in the case of political rights. Recent research has shown that CEDAW may generate positive effects for women's rights and equality when ratification triggers sociopolitical dynamics *within* individual countries that help to override embedded cultural norms that are antithetical to women's rights (Englehart and Miller 2014).

Although change is possible, it is far from guaranteed. Existing case studies on the CEDAW monitoring process demonstrate variation across states in regard to their commitment to participating in the CEDAW review process. The vast majority of the world's states have ratified CEDAW, notable exceptions including the United States, Iran, Somalia, and the Sudan (Office of the High Commissioner for Human Rights). States that have ratified CEDAW frequently have attached reservations asserting that they will not be bound by specific provisions. Many state members of the CEDAW regime have failed to submit required reports, in a timely fashion or at all (Merry 2006b, 83–84). State that actively participate in the CEDAW review process also manifest varying levels of commitment to implementation in different issue areas (Baldez 2018). As the subsequent section shows, CEDAW remains insufficient to produce systemic advances in the global status of women.

Necessary but insufficient: why law is not enough

The fact that women's rights have achieved a place of prominence in the international legal order has great symbolic and aspirational importance. Improving the status of the world's women is perhaps the single most important thing that can be done to increase the wellbeing of all persons and to promote economic and social development at the population level in countries across the globe (Sen 2001). Because of international law's potential as a powerful normative and discursive framework, its codification of norms recognizing fundamental women's rights raises the profile of women's equality and generates possibilities that state and non-state actors will leverage these norms in pursuit of policy changes that would improve the status of women. According to Hudson, Bowen and Nielsen, 'While law cannot dictate practice and often stands impotent before it, law is nevertheless generally regarded as a strong normative factor capable of modifying practice over time, and importantly, of establishing state and community ideals' (Hudson, Bowen, and Nielsen 2011, 456). In this view, law – both domestic and international – serves as an essential normative framework which makes the promotion of women's rights possible.

International human rights law has given women's rights normative force. In turn, state and non-state actors can leverage these norms to pursue change in domestic settings. Further, international laws and institutions can play an important role in transforming cultural norms related to women's rights in particular societies (Merry 2006a). State participation in treaties governing women's rights has helped to produce concrete benefits in specific countries (Baldez 2018, 2014; Warner 2010). Data on treaty participation and various indicators of women's equality also show that the ratification of international treaties on women's rights, most prominently the Convention on the Elimination of Discrimination against Women, is correlated with improvements in the status of women (Simmons 2009).

Progress on specific indicators suggests that global norms governing women's rights may have contributed to improvements in the status of women across the globe. According to UN Women, significant gains in women's rights have followed the adoption of the Beijing Declaration and Platform for action. The *Progress of the World's Women*

2015–2016 report identifies the following areas of global progress: higher access to education for girls, higher rates of women working, more women in elected office and leadership positions, the greater prominence of violence against women in policy agendas across the globe, and more equitable property and marriage laws (UN Women 2015).

Despite the positive contributions of international human rights law in advancing norms articulating women's rights, the gap between the aspirational nature of global norms and the status of women's rights across the globe remains vast. Women continue to be underrepresented in national governing bodies and international organizations. Women constitute a majority of the world's population living in poverty and encounter institutionalized economic inequities in countries at every level of economic development. The prevalence of violence against women can be characterized as a global epidemic. Rape continues to be systematically deployed as a weapon of war, and sexual slavery remains a prevalent feature of the global political landscape (Ellerby 2017, 37–41).

In evaluating the potential contributions of global legalism to improving the status of women, it can be difficult to disentangle the specific role of international human rights treaties and institutions. On the one hand, available data indicates that state participation in international human rights regimes tends to produce, on average, better human rights outcomes (Simmons 2009). The correlation between state participation in CEDAW and improved outcomes for women's rights is robust (Englehart and Miller 2014). Further, positive trends in national law and policy governing women's rights correlate with the progressive development of international human rights law. In recent decades, there has been a steady increase in national legislation focused on increasing the political representation of women, improving women's economic rights, and prohibiting violence against women. These national legislative advancements have produced legal protections for women that should not be discounted (Ellerby 2017, 25–37).

On the other hand, available evidence suggests that the transformative potential of international human rights treaties is limited. Treaty participation may make it somewhat more likely that states – under specific conditions – will take steps that have the potential to improve human rights. Notably, states will *not* comply with treaty obligations vis-à-vis human rights unless doing so converges with their interests, as defined by state elites (Simmons 2009, 122). Moreover, it is not clear that the positive relationship between human rights treaty participation and improved outcomes in the status of women is a causal one. A global assessment of human rights enforcement suggests limited state compliance with treaty obligations even when treaty regimes have almost universal participation (Posner 2012). Global trends indicating improvement in the status of women also correlate with other broad economic and political developments, including the growth in the number of liberal democracies across the globe (829). Whether or not states comply with treaty obligations depends to a very large extent on domestic political contexts and the extent to which domestic actors and legal institutions embrace the legal norms codified in the relevant treaty (Slaughter and Burke-White 2006; McGuiness 2006).

States participate in treaty regimes to pursue a range of potential political and economic benefits, including enhanced political legitimacy, bilateral or multilateral aid, or foreign investment. State parties to human rights treaties may reap such benefits even without substantial compliance to a treaty's provisions (Hafner-Burton 2013; Merry 2006b, 79). In fact, some studies have found an inverse relationship between participation in human rights treaties and human rights outcomes (Hafner-Burton 2013, 74–75;

Hathaway 2004, 201–204). Thus, a state's ratification of treaties that codify women's rights does not necessarily signal its commitment to protecting equal rights or improving the status of women.

Furthermore, available data also suggests that international human rights law has been more likely to contribute to meaningful advances in countries that already provide basic legal protections for fundamental human rights and where the worst abuses are the least likely to occur (Hafner-Burton 2013). According to Hafner-Burton, the international human rights regime has a much worse record of generating change in settings where the most egregious human rights violations tend to occur and in countries without socio-legal systems that are already supportive of basic human rights. When progress has been achieved, it has normally been the result of domestic political and legal processes.

Thus, the effectiveness of international human rights law in translating norms into outcomes hinges significantly on specific domestic political contexts. Scholarship on the process of treaty monitoring and implementation in particular countries sheds light on the factors that determine whether or not participation in treaties that govern women's rights will contribute to improvements in the status of women (Baldez 2014; Merry 2006b, 92–100). The critical role that national governments play in implementing international treaties demonstrates that statist dynamics are central in determining the impact of global human rights norms. Solutions to vexing human rights challenges are located – for better or worse – primarily within states.

Further, the prevalence of patriarchal cultural values that transcend state borders limit the effectiveness of either international treaties or national legislation as tools for advancing women's rights. Neither international human rights law nor domestic policy are sufficient to overcome the gender biases and sociocultural barriers that hinder progress in the attainment of rights and equality for women in specific countries (Warner 2010). International human rights law emphasizes a liberal conception of rights which prioritizes giving women equal access to fundamental human rights but does not challenge biased gender norms that perpetuate discrimination and violence against women. The persistence of patriarchal values in countries across the globe ultimately acts as primary barriers to progress for women (Ellerby 2017).

Tension regarding contending perspectives on the sociocultural norms that shape gender inequities is central to the question of why formal law is limited as a mechanism for advancing women's rights. Cultural differences, especially around gender, are often invoked as an obstacle to change vis-à-vis women's rights as human rights (Merry 2006b, 90–98). International human rights laws can produce unintended and counterproductive effects when they generate backlash and resistance to the 'Western' values that these treaties ostensibly represent (Massoud 2011). For example, violence against women perpetrated by the Taliban and the Islamic State of Iraq and Syria (ISIS) has been driven in part by resistance to Western projections of power in the Middle East. Fundamental tension between global norms and local contexts has manifested in CEDAW review processes in ways that have resulted in retrenchment rather than progress on national laws and policies related to women's rights and equality (Merry 2006b, 103–133).

The international human rights regime also risks elevating the influence of states with poor human rights records. States with no intention of upholding their treaty-based human rights commitments may, nonetheless, ratify human rights treaties. In doing so, they achieve potential symbolic gains as they participate on the same level as states with stronger human rights records in international human rights institutions, where they may play the role of human rights detractors. The often-prominent role of detractor states, along with the enforcement failures of the international human rights regime, ultimately may serve to delegitimize the objective of global human rights promotion (Hafner-Burton 2013, 196–197). Other critics of global legalism have suggested that the international human rights bureaucracy operates largely in service of protecting or expanding its own interests, in the form of funds, access, and influence, and that they may 'colonize local claims to his end' (Hopgood 2013, 172).

Notably, it is the socio-legal context in a particular country that drives the relationship between formal law and outcomes. State ratification of a human rights treaty does *not* necessarily alter the domestic political landscape in dramatic ways or make a state more likely to pursue policies intended to fulfill treaty-based human rights obligations. Rather, treaty participation is more likely to produce human rights protections in societies where the sociopolitical conditions are, relatively speaking, already more conducive to the promotion of human rights (Hafner-Burton 2013, 11). Social and political factors produce the conditions for legal transformation, not vice versa. To the extent that the persistence of patriarchal values in a wide range of social and political systems represents the core barrier to progress on the status of women across the globe, the systematic evidence suggests that formal law is not a sufficient tool for challenging gender-based violence and inequity.

International law is produced via diplomacy. States are the primary actors that drive the process of international treaty making, and state elites are inevitably influenced by the prevailing sociocultural norms in the societies they govern. Thus, states have created international human rights treaties that do not include effective enforcement mechanisms by which the aspirational norms that they contain might be forcibly implemented. Treaties require the express consent of states to attain the status of law and reflect negotiated compromises among state parties rather than being generated by impartial or neutral arbiters of legal norms. Not surprisingly, international human rights law ultimately retains a statist bias that defers to the value of state sovereignty and to the preferences and interests of states, especially powerful states. Too often, these state preferences and norms reflect patriarchal cultural values that undermine the status of women across the globe.

Feminist legal theory, critical perspectives, and the limitations of the law

This section applies insights from feminist legal theory and other critical perspectives to explain why formal international human rights treaties and institutions have proven to be an insufficient tool for producing systemic and sustainable improvements to the status of the world's women. The critiques developed in this section identify challenges that emerge when formal law (national or international) is relied upon at the expense of localized efforts to generate sociocultural change, with particular focus on how these challenges manifest in the CEDAW treaty regime.

Law as a potential site of marginalization or sublimation

Critical feminist legal theory cautions that contesting gendered inequities and discriminatory social practices at the site of the law risks transforming feminism more than the law itself (Fineman and Thomadsen 1991, xii). Advocacy for women's equality for women has transformed the face of international human rights law, and women's rights are firmly embedded in the international legal system. The core treaties in the international human rights regime make clear that women are entitled to fundamental human rights, and CEDAW recognizes particular women's rights as human rights. Feminism *has* transformed the law. However, the law has been transformed more in form than function.

Despite meaningful progress in some countries, pervasive and persistent gender-based violence and inequities across the globe demonstrate that codifying equal rights for women is insufficient to leverage change. Incorporating women as legal bearers of international human rights does not alter the fundamentally statist nature of international law. States ultimately create, interpret, and implement international law. Not surprisingly, state interests and preferences fundamentally influence the substantive content of human rights treaties and the nature of implementation and enforcement processes (Hafner-Burton 2013, 44–66).

Even when international and national laws codify equal rights for women, these legal provisions are insufficient to overcome informal barriers and gender biases that impede the realization of women's rights in practice (Ellerby 2017). The Committee on CEDAW has issued a general recommendation acknowledging gender biases as an obstacle to women's rights and calling upon states to take steps to eliminate these biases. Nonetheless, gender norms that serve as barriers to equity are especially difficult to change, even in countries with relatively progressive records on the status of women (Merry 2006b, 75).

Given the symbolic importance of international law and the aspirational potential of international norms governing women's rights, the fact that the law has limited effects in practice may not seem to be a significant matter. Nevertheless, efforts to advance the status of women globally via formal international law have pitfalls that need to be carefully weighed. Historically, international human rights law has reinforced a public-private dichotomy that has downplayed human rights issues that are of particular concern to women (Aolain 2011, 286–287; Ellerby 2017, 175–176). The human rights regime has traditionally been concerned primarily with violations committed by states, such as torture, repression, and freedom of speech. Even in the sphere of economic, social, and cultural rights, international human rights law focuses largely on state obligations to undertake steps to advance these rights. International human rights law has been less concerned with abuses perpetrated by private actors, including gender discrimination and violence against women, or with state failure to appropriately address these violations. As a result, international human rights law has historically downplayed rights violations that are especially likely to be experienced by women.

CEDAW challenges this dichotomy more than previous treaties in articulating norms that point to the centrality of gender biases in the private sphere. Yet, formal law cannot be relied upon to dramatically transform the private sphere even when it incorporates provisions that assert legal norms purported to trump cultural values that prevail in particular societies. The codification of normative aspirations cannot force cultural change, and transformations that advance women's equality and rights often emerge out of localized politics rather than formal legal initiatives directed by states or international organizations (Merry 2003).

Some feminist legal scholars have expressed skepticism about the value of special treaties like CEDAW that mark off women's rights as deserving of particular protection. Hilary Charlesworth articulates a compelling version of this perspective:

> [t]his dilemma pervades modern international legal responses to the unequal position of women: the attempt to improve women's lives through general laws can allow women's concerns to be submerged in what are deemed more global issues; however, the price of creating separate institutional mechanisms for women has been the building of a 'women's ghetto' with less power, resources, and priority than the 'general' human rights bodies. (Charlesworth 2005, 1)

This dilemma seems even more pronounced when one considers the weak enforcement model that characterizes international human rights law.

Some feminists argue that the hierarchical, adversarial, and statist nature of international legal institutions not only fails to improve the status of women but is, in fact, antithetical to underlying feminist goals (Binion 1995). Instead, critical feminist perspectives suggest that alternative approaches may be more likely to lead to genuine transformation of the socio-economic structures and dynamics that impede equality for women in their daily lives. Gayle Binion has favored a 'responsibility model' that would emphasize human needs rather than human rights and would work more closely with women's organizations and feminist activists in particular locations rather than devoting so many resources to the formation of abstract international law (Binion 1995). Similarly, Michele Alexandre has put forward a 'feminism-in-action' approach that would emphasize working with women, in particular and localized contexts, to advance the status of women. To this end, she favors the mobilization of organic grassroots movements rather than a reliance on formal and distant international law or institutions (Alexandre 2011, 99–100).

Law as a site of statist politics

Feminist legal theorists consistently highlight the socially and politically constructed nature of law at all levels. Rather than providing an 'objective' framework that exists outside of politics, law reflects and reinforces existing discourses and structures of power (Fineman and Thomadsen 1991, xiv). In this way, formal law can perpetuate inequities and injustices even when, on the surface, it incorporates norms that appear to codify equality. A reliance on formal law to advance human rights risks reinforcing the oppressive elements of state sovereignty in the name of seeking the state's endorsement for particular rights claims and prompting the regulatory as much as the emancipatory dimensions of the law (Golder 2015, 91–93). Wendy Brown argues that rights discourse can evoke rights-limiting constructions of identities associated with the categories in which rights are being claimed. In this way, the pursuit of women's rights via formal legal mechanisms can reinforce gender-based inequities by encoding gendered power structures and hierarchies in the law (Brown 2000). According to Alexandre:

> When dominant groups are confronted with laws mandating that they accommodate groups they have previously subjugated, they evade such laws by creating a legal system

> where formal equality obscures the effects of that subjugation and perpetuates at the same time as it legitimates the historic and existing contexts of inequality. (Alexandre 2011, 101)

Lawmaking at the international level does not escape this dynamic. In this case, states are the dominant actors that construct laws acquiescing to political demands for new legal norms in ways that ultimately defer to their own preferences and interests.

The state-centric nature of international human rights law serves as an impediment to it being used to leverage fundamental changes to inequitable economic structures (including gender bias in employment and wage disparities among men and women), political systems, and cultural norms that will be essential for dramatically improving women's rights in diverse societies across the globe. If a state does not believe that a particular treaty reflects its interests, it will not sign or ratify that treaty. Alternatively, it will sign and ratify the treaty with reservations that dilute the force of the law in practice. In general, states will not advance international laws that are deemed to fundamentally threaten state sovereignty. Thus, the gap between aspirational rhetoric and statist realities in international human rights law is at some level inevitable.

CEDAW illustrates the ways in which the statist nature of international human rights law manifests in ambivalent language, legal loopholes, ill-defined state obligations, and a lack of concrete enforcement mechanisms. In calling for states to 'embody the principle of the equality of men and women in their national constitutions' or other legislation (Article 2) as a means of eliminating discrimination against women, CEDAW defines neither 'equality' nor 'discrimination' with precision. To be sure, CEDAW provides a definition of discrimination in Article 1 that prohibits sex-based distinctions that would prevent women from fully enjoying their fundamental human rights. However, cross-cultural consensus on the precise meanings of these terms in practice does not exist. For example, French legal prohibitions against wearing the niqab – the full veil worn by some Muslim women – have been upheld by the European Court of Human Rights. Proponents of these prohibitions see them as a mechanism for protecting the full equality of women in French society. However, critics contend that French law undermines the equality of women who prefer to wear the veil by inhibiting their ability to participate fully in public life in ways that are consistent with their religious views. CEDAW does not provide definitional clarity that can be used to settle cross-cultural disagreements of this nature.

This ambivalence leaves open the question of whether states are called upon to promote equality of opportunity or equal outcomes and whether discriminatory outcomes are consistent with the treaty so long as a state formally adopts equality of opportunity. Subsequently, CEDAW authorizes temporary special measures intended to accelerate de facto equality but asserts that they shall be discontinued 'when the objectives of equality of opportunity and treatment have been achieved' (Article 4). At one level, this clause implies that the equality is defined in terms of equality of opportunity, but the reference to equality of treatment demonstrates that the clause does not resolve the ambivalence. We know that CEDAW calls for equality and for the elimination of discrimination against women, but we do not ultimately know what these treaty provisions require of states.

CEDAW also includes loopholes and ill-defined state obligations that limit the extent to which it can be used to hold states accountable for promoting women's rights. For example, as previously mentioned, Article 4 authorizes states to adopt temporary special measures to accelerate de facto equality between men and women that should not be considered discriminatory. However, CEDAW does not *obligate* states to do so. Given that many of the human rights violations and inequities faced by women are deeply embedded in sociocultural structures with longstanding effects, mere recognition of equality of opportunity will not be sufficient to override these barriers. However, it is unlikely that a sufficient number of states would have signed onto CEDAW if it had incorporated more clear-cut obligations. Indeed, it is notable that CEDAW is one of the treaties in the international human rights regime to which the largest number of state reservations have been made (De Pauw 2013).

The CEDAW monitoring and review process also illustrates the statist nature of international human rights law. The Committee does not have any authority for rendering or enforcing binding judgments. The Committee has initiated a more active approach in identifying non-compatible reservations made by states parties (De Pauw 2013). Nevertheless, the Committee still does not have the power to implement or enforce treaty provisions within states. In the end, the primarily non-adversarial approach to treaty-monitoring induces state participation in CEDAW but results in a form of self-policing whereby any progress on the advancement of CEDAW norms will come as a result of the voluntary participation of states.

All of these factors – ambivalent language, legal loopholes, ill-defined state obligations, and weak enforcement mechanisms – are reflective of the fundamental paradox of international human rights law. Formal international law is produced via a diplomatic and political process that produces a soft form of law characterized by weak enforcement. Such compromises are essential to induce states to join human rights treaties. States have very little to lose by joining these treaties; given how they are watered down, the barriers to joining can be low. Yet, because the treaties retain aspirational norms, states may gain legitimacy by becoming parties to them. This paradox may help explain why international human rights law sometimes generates unintended consequences, such as when an increase in human rights violations correlates with growth in the number of states that have ratified international human rights instruments (Hafner-Burton 2013, 74–75). Ellerby (2017) succinctly summarizes this dilemma: 'States may be a major catalyst for changing rules and regulations but they may also take these ideas and use them in ways activists do not intend or for reasons other than justice' (205).

Law as a site of reflection rather than transformation

Hudson, Bowsen, and Nielsen, argue that '…contestation over law is often a critical first step in changing practice' (Hudson, Bowen, and Nielsen 2011, 456). Although they acknowledge that legal transformation may not be sufficient, they suggest that changes to the law may be necessary to generate cultural and social change. Further, they assert that the law may be the site where change needs to be initiated. Conversely, a critical feminist perspective suggests that the law will be more likely to reflect prevailing ideologies and cultural perspectives held by majorities in a given society than to precipitate change (Fineman and Thomadsen 1991, x). This view of the law as a mirror rather than a catalyst challenges notions that change must begin with the law, even if law cannot alone produce desired cultural, political, or social changes.

Even when the law incorporates potentially transformative norms and aspirations, it tends to be structured in ways that reflect and reinforce existing power structures and dynamics within and across societies. International human rights law is diminished by a gap between aspirational rhetoric and the reality of a statist body of law that waters down potentially transformative norms through ambivalent language, legal loopholes, ill-defined obligations, state reservations, and weak enforcement mechanisms. At times, this paradox has been interpreted by feminist scholars through a lens that combines a degree of wishful thinking with a pragmatic acknowledgement of the political constraints that characterize the international legal order.

For example, Keller asserts that 'CEDAW has helped advance women's rights worldwide' and that it '…can be a powerful tool to promote gender equality' (Keller 2004, 35). At the same time, she acknowledges that reservations made by some ratifying states '… effectively gut the provisions of the treaty, often on the basis of religious or cultural norms' and that 'true acceptance and actual implementation of the rights and protections contained therein have yet to be achieved by many states parties' (35). Keller, nonetheless, concludes that advocates for women's rights and equality should still encourage states to ratify, without reservation, CEDAW as a necessary if imperfect first step.

At first glance, it may seem indisputable that proponents of women's rights should advocate for state participation in CEDAW as a necessary if insufficient step toward the realization of women's rights and equality. However, this view cannot be accepted uncritically. To the extent that international law reflects prevailing sociocultural norms, it may reproduce rather than challenge dynamics that perpetuate women's inequality. The law has constitutive power – it creates roles and subject positions rather than merely codifying aspirational norms (Golder 2015).

CEDAW's codification of rights particular to women, especially rights related to maternity (Articles 4 and 11), is instructive. By explicitly codifying maternity rather than parental leave, CEDAW reifies conservative constructions of traditional gender roles as pertaining to parenting (DeLaet 2013, 120–123).[2] In doing so, CEDAW reinforces traditional roles and subject positions for women in the realm of parenthood that may make it more difficult to challenge conservative constructions of gender roles and identities in other realms. Indeed, CEDAW explicitly acknowledges the tension between providing particular rights based on traditional gender roles and the need to challenge these roles in efforts to advance women's rights and equality. In Article 5 (Par. b), CEDAW calls for family education recognizing maternity as a *social* function (emphasis added) and underscores the 'common responsibility of men and women in the upbringing and development of their children.' Despite Article 5's recognition of maternity as a social function and the acknowledgement of parenting as a shared responsibility among men and women, CEDAW codifies maternity as a social function by providing only for maternity leave. In this way, CEDAW's provisions codifying differential rights for women are constitutive; they reinforce inequitable roles and subject positions rather than articulating transformative standards.

Supporters of the CEDAW approach contend that differential treatment, in matters related to maternity as well as other issues, remains an appropriate method to promote genuine equality of opportunity in contexts in which women face deeply-embedded structural and socioeconomic barriers to equality. The tension between these perspectives on particular rights for women under CEDAW reveals a lack of consensus among feminist scholars regarding the relative benefits and costs of relying on international law as a mechanism for advancing women's rights.

In the face of such limitations, Alexandre suggests that innovative, localized grassroots movements may prove better mechanisms for advancing the status of women globally (Alexandre 2011, 105–109). Likewise, Ni Aolain argues that a universalistic formal legal framework tends to reflect 'Western' norms and fails to adequately account for particular local contexts. In her view, non-legal frameworks may be more attentive to culturally-specific gender discourses and power structures and, thus, may represent a more appropriate site for initiating social and political change (Aolain 2011, 281–286). In a non-feminist variation of this argument, Hafner-Burton argues in favor of the concept of localization, a process in which local actors, especially 'norm entrepreneurs', must play a central role in vetting and translating human rights norms in politically and culturally appropriate ways for progress to occur (Hafner-Burton 2013, 151–163).

In these non-statist constructions, the first steps for initiating change begin not *within* the law, but outside of it. Critical theorists further clarify the ways in which politics precede the law rather than depicting law as a constraining force above politics.

For example, Golder describes the ways that Michel Foucault's work, typically viewed as antithetical to liberal rights discourse, might be used to argue in favor of human rights while simultaneously criticizing universalistic frameworks by mobilizing aspects of the human rights framework in service of critical change and contestation (Golder 2015, 51). To this end, human rights as legal norms are constituted by human rights discourse and activism rather than being rooted in philosophical or formal legal foundations (90).

In all of these formulations, action that is explicitly political and firmly embedded in local contexts is assumed to be more likely to produce change than monitoring mechanisms relying on states to report up to treaty-monitoring bodies with no power to compel compliance (Merry 2003, 2006b). Such distinctions may seem minor, and, arguably, feminist legal scholars, critical scholars, and practitioners committed to advancing the status of women should not spend time deliberating the most appropriate mechanisms for promoting a global agenda for women so long as they agree on ultimate goals.

However, global resources for promoting human rights goals are scarce. In this context, it very much matters how we prioritize global women's initiatives. At the same time that it produces limited concrete benefits, international human rights law involves the expenditure of significant resources – for example, on bureaucratic bodies with only limited and weak capabilities for norm dissemination and monitoring and on international conferences that generate ever-more international norms without the backing of genuine enforcement power (Hafner-Burton 2013, xv; Posner 2012, 831). Although funds spent on these institutional mechanisms are small in comparison to many other state expenditures for less worthy causes, these monies might otherwise be spent on women's rights initiatives in localized contexts that may have a higher likelihood of changing social and cultural structures that underpin global gender inequities.

The range of possibilities is broad. Survivors of human rights abuses may be more likely to obtain justice via restorative mechanisms or psychosocial processes than trials (DeLaet 2006). Therapeutic initiatives that emphasize the healing of survivors of human rights abuses, including trauma therapy, the provision of direct services, and reparations to survivors, may empower and give agency to survivors in ways that reduce gender barriers to survivor participation in justice and peace initiatives (DeLaet, Golden, and

Laveta, forthcoming). Local norm entrepreneurs may be better equipped than distant bureaucrats to determine how to use scarce resources in strategic and effective ways in an effort to enhance human rights protections in particular societies (Hafner-Burton 2013, 82). Families may be a more fertile site for the transformation of cultural values than governmental bureaucracies (Mackie 1996). Diverting funding from global bureaucracies to local initiatives that work within communities to foster change may be more likely to produce transformative outcomes. Such local initiatives might include the development of community-based advocacy, the development of women's shelters, and training on gender violence and gender inequity across a range of professions, including police, health care professionals, and educators would be warranted (Merry 2006a). Human rights education at the local level may play an essential role in transformative change (Bajaj 2015). Advocacy directed at local governing structures may also be more likely to produce meaningful political change in specific communities (Smith 2017; Gilhool 2006).

Conclusions

The progressive development of international human rights law governing women's rights should be celebrated for its symbolic importance and for the potential that states and non-state actors may be able to leverage global norms to transform domestic political contexts. Even though women across the globe continue to experience pervasive and persistent inequities, the international human rights regime has 'shifted the goalposts for what is acceptable and also motivated foreign policy on human rights' (Hafner-Burton 2013, 2). Despite the significant gap between aspirational rhetoric and a reality of limited implementation and enforcement, actors committed to advancing the status of the world's women can mobilize global norms governing women's rights in their efforts. The incorporation of women's rights into international human rights law has been associated with positive outcomes.

Yet, feminist legal scholars must remain attentive to the limitations of formal law in translating legal norms into effective governance in practice, especially in the service of rights, social justice, and equality for women and other marginalized groups. The gap between aspirational rhetoric and politically grounded legal realities can be especially pronounced at the global level. Feminist legal scholars and women's rights activists should not rely exclusively on the international human rights regime, which remains statist at its core, to advance the agenda of women's rights. Formal law is not sufficient to drive change. Nor can law be relied on, in isolation, as an effective initial step toward change. The law is not neutral; nor is it above and beyond politics. Rather, formal law remains firmly embedded in particular political contexts at the local, national, and international levels. Any successful effort to generate social and cultural change in these particular contexts will need to engage deeply and directly with a broadly defined politics that precedes and transcends the law.

This perspective does not represent a rejection of the symbolic importance of the law so much as a recognition of the limits of what law alone can accomplish. Universal human rights laws are already firmly in place. They represent an incredibly important development in the articulation of aspirational norms. Although domestic political actors may leverage these norms in their human rights advocacy, efforts to implement these norms in an effort to progressively realize human rights in practice will need to rely far more on non-legal tools. The law alone is not enough.

Notes

1. Both Covenants were adopted by the UN General Assembly and opened for signature in 1966. Each entered into force in 1976.
2. Although the General Comments issued by the Committee on the Elimination of Discrimination Against Women generally call for the recognition of the equal status of men and women as well as parents, the committee has not issued any comments that would challenge the ability of states to prioritize maternity rather than parental leave.

Disclosure statement

No potential conflict of interest was reported by the author.

References

Alexandre, M. 2011. "The New Faces of Feminism: Feminism-In-Action and Organic Feminists in a Post-Feminist Era." In *Transcending the Boundaries of Law: Generations of Feminism and Legal Theory*, edited by M. A. Fineman, 97–110. New York and London: Routledge.

Aolain, F. N. 2011. "Learning the Lessons: What Feminist Legal Theory Teaches International Human Rights Law and Practice." In *Transcending the Boundaries of Law: Generations of Feminism and Legal Theory*, edited by M. A. Fineman, 281–289. New York and London: Routledge.

Bajaj, M. 2015. "Human Rights Education: Imaginative Possibilities for Creating Change." *Teachers College Record* 117 (10).

Baldez, L. 2014. *Defying Convention: U.S. Resistance to the UN Treaty on Women's Rights*. Cambridge: Cambridge University Press.

Baldez, L. 2018. "What's at Stake in the Treaty Reporting Process? Cuba and the United Nations Convention on Women's Rights." *Global Discourse*. doi:10.1080/23269995.2018.1520009

Binion, G. 1995. "Human Rights: A Feminist Perspective." *Human Rights Quarterly* 17 (3): 509–526. doi:10.1353/hrq.1995.0022.

Brown, W. 2000. "Suffering Rights as Paradoxes." *Constellations* 7: 208–229. doi:10.1111/cons.2000.7.issue-2.

Byrnes, A. 1994. "Towards More Effective Enforcement of Women's Rights through the Use of International Law and Procedures." In *Human Rights of Women: National and International Perspectives*, edited by R. J. Cook, 189–227. Philadelphia, PA: University of Pennsylvania Press.

Byrnes, A., and J. Conners. 1996. "Enforcing the Human Rights of Women." *Brooklyn Journal of International Law* 21 (3): 679–797.

Charlesworth, H. 2005. "Not Waving but Drowning: Gender Mainstreaming and Human Rights in the United Nations." *Harvard Human Rights Journal* 18 (1): 1–18.

De Pauw, M. 2013. "Women's Rights: From Bad to Worse? Assessing the Evolution of Incompatible Reservations to the CEDAW Convention." *Merkourios: Utrecht Journal of International and European Law* 29 (77): 51–65.

DeLaet, D. L. 2006. "Gender Justice: A Gendered Assessment of Truth-Telling Mechanisms." In *Telling the Truths: Truth Telling and Peace Building in Post-Conflict Xocieties.*, edited by T. A. Borer, 151–179. Notre Dame: University of Notre Dame Press.

DeLaet, D. L. 2013. *The Global Struggle for Human Rights: Universal Principles in World Politics*. 2nd ed. Stamford, CT: Cengage.

DeLaet, D. L., S. Golden, and V. Laveta. Forthcoming. "Therapeutic Justice for Survivors of Human Rights Violations and Wartime Violence." In *Gender, Global Health, and Violence: Feminist Perspectives on Peace and Disease*, edited by C. Confortini and T. Vaittinen. Lanham: Rowman & Littlefield.

Ellerby, K. 2017. *No Shortcut to Change: An Unlikely Path to a More Gender-Equitable World.* New York: New York University Press.

Englehart, N. A., and M. K. Miller. 2014. "The CEDAW Effect: International Law's Impact on Women's Rights." *Journal of Human Rights* 13 (1): 22–47. doi:10.1080/14754835.2013.824274.

Fineman, M. A., and N. Thomadsen, eds. 1991. *At the Boundaries of Law: Feminism and Legal Theory.* London and New York: Routledge.

Gilhool, G. 2006. "Local Human Rights Initiatives." *Peace and Freedom* 66 (1): 15.

Golder, B. 2015. *Foucault and the Politics of Rights.* Stanford, CA: Stanford University Press.

Hafner-Burton, E. M. 2013. *Making Human Rights a Reality.* Princeton, NJ: Princeton University Press.

Hathaway, O. A. 2004. "The Promise and Limits of the International Law of Torture." In *Torture: A Collection*, edited by S. Levinson, 199–227. Oxford: Oxford University Press.

Hopgood, S. 2013. *The Endtimes of Human Rights.* Ithaca, New York: Cornell University Press.

Hudson, V. M., D. L. Bowen, and P. L. Nielsen. 2011. "What is the Relationship between Inequity in Family Law and Violence against Women? Approaching the Issue of Legal Enclaves." *Politics & Gender* 7 (4): 453–492. doi:10.1017/S1743923X11000328.

Keller, L. M. 2004. "The Convention on the Elimination of Discrimination against Women: Evolution and (Non)Implementation Worldwide." *Thomas Jefferson Law Review* 27 (35): 35–43.

Mackie, G. 1996. "Ending Footbinding and Infibulation: A Convention Account." *American Sociological Review* 61 (6): 999–1017. doi:10.2307/2096305.

Massoud, M. F. 2011. "Do Victims of War Need International Law? Human Rights Education Programs in Authoritarian Sudan." *Law and Society Review* 45 (1): 1–32. doi:10.1111/j.1540-5893.2011.00426.x.

McGuiness, M. E. 2006. "Exploring the Limits of International Human Rights Law." *Georgia Journal of International and Comparative Law* 34: 393–421.

Merry, S. E. 2003. "Rights Talk and the Experience of Law: Implementing Women's Human Rights to Protection from Violence." *Human Rights Quarterly* 25 (2): 343–381. doi:10.1353/hrq.2003.0020.

Merry, S. E. 2006a. "Transnational Human Rights and Local Activism: Mapping the Middle." *American Anthropologist* 108 (1): 38–51. doi:10.1525/aa.2006.108.1.38.

Merry, S. E. 2006b. *Human Rights & Gender Violence.* Chicago: University of Chicago Press.

Posner, E. A. 2012. "Some Skeptical Comments on Beth Simmons's Mobilizing for Human Rights." *New York University Journal of International Law and Politics* 44: 819–832.

Sen, A. 2001. "The Many Faces of Gender Inequality." *The New Republic*, September 27. 35–40.

Simmons, B. A. 2009. *Mobilizing for Human Rights: International Law in Domestic Politics.* New York: Cambridge University Press.

Slaughter, A.-M., and W. Burke-White. 2006. "The Future of International Law is Domestic (Or, the European Way of Law)." *Harvard International Law Journal* 47 (2): 327–352.

Smith, J. 2017. "Local Responses to Right-Wing Populism: Building Human Rights Cities." *Studies in Social Justice* 11 (2): 347–368. doi:10.26522/ssj.v11i2.1394.

UN Women. 2015. "Progress of the World's Women 2015–2016: Transforming Economies, Realizing Rights." Accessed July 16 2016. http://progress.unwomen.org/en/2015/

United Nations Office of the High Commissioner for Human Rights. 2017. "Status of Ratification: The Convention on the Elimination of Discrimination against Women." Accessed October 13 2017. http://indicators.ohchr.org

Warner, A. 2010. *Recognizing Rights Promoting Progress: The Global Impact of CEDAW.* International Center for Research for Women. Accessed July 16 2016. http://www.icrw.org/publications/recognizing-rights-promoting-progress.

What's at stake in the treaty reporting process? Cuba and the United Nations' convention on women's rights

Lisa Baldez

ABSTRACT

What impact do U.N. human rights treaties have on the countries that ratify them? Most of the scholarly literature on this topic focuses on ratification, with little attention to the ways that the process of reporting can shape compliance. Ratification commits countries to a regular process of documenting and defending the extent to which they comply with a particular treaty. Many countries participate faithfully in the reporting process, devoting significant resources to it and subjecting themselves to vigorous review by the committees that oversee compliance. What is at stake in the reporting process? What can we learn from taking seriously the content of the exchanges between government officials and committee experts? This article examines Cuba's engagement the Convention on the Elimination of All Forms of Discrimination Against Women (CEDAW) across eight reporting cycles, from 1982 to 2016. Cuba has adopted many changes, but has strenuously resisted the CEDAW Committee's assessment of its progress on critical aspects of violence against women policy.

The United Nations (U.N.) Convention on the Elimination of All Forms of Discrimination Against Women, known as CEDAW, has been ratified by 189 countries, nearly every U.N. member nation.[1] What impact has CEDAW had on women's rights? An extensive scholarly literature examines the effect of ratification of the convention on various aspects of the status of women. Some studies argue that CEDAW has positive effects, leading to increases in women's life expectancy (Gray, Kittilson, and Sandholtz 2006), higher rates of women in elective office (Kenworthy and Malami 1999), increases in the ratio of girls to boys in primary and secondary education, access to family planning and employment opportunities for women (Simmons 2009) as well as the adoption of women's rights policy (Htun and Weldon 2018). Others find that CEDAW ratification has no impact on women's rights (Paxton 1997; True and Mintrom 2001). Regardless of the kinds of correlations they establish, nearly all of these studies focus on treaty ratification as the key explanatory variable.[2]

Ratification of a treaty is a critical and ostensibly necessary step that a country must take if a treaty is to affect domestic policy – but ratification is also merely the first of many steps that a country takes in its efforts to comply with CEDAW. The reporting process is an important and often overlooked component of the treaty process. Ratification commits countries to a rigorous and continuous process of reporting their compliance with the convention. Many countries participate faithfully in the reporting process, devoting significant resources to it and subjecting themselves to vigorous review by the committee that oversees compliance. Nonetheless, scholarly research devotes scant attention to this process (but see Creamer and Simmons 2015).

This article delves into the details of the reporting process in an effort to understand the significance of what happens there. What is at stake in the reporting process? What can we learn from taking seriously the content of the exchanges between government officials and committee experts? Is the reporting process as epiphenomenal to ratification as its omission from this literature would suggest?[3] The literature on international norms predicts that we will see convergence over time between international and domestic law. Repeated interactions between a treaty body and a government should socialize government delegations and elicit shared understandings of global norms over time. To what extent does engagement in the reporting process contribute to these effects?

This article examines Cuba's engagement with the committee that oversees CEDAW over more than three decades. I examine the interactions between the members ('experts') of the CEDAW Committee and the government delegation of a single country – Cuba. I review the reporting process over time, from Cuba's first report in 1982 to the follow-up from its most recent report in 2016, in order to evaluate the degree to which it has led to greater convergence between government policy and global women's rights norms. My analysis focuses on violence against women, just one of the many issues covered by the treaty.[4]

There are reasons we should expect to see Cuba conform with these expectations, and reasons why we might see it diverge from them. Cuba has been deeply invested in the U.N. as a source of legitimacy since the dissolution of the Soviet bloc. Moreover, Cuba has long viewed itself as a global leader in the promotion of equality between men and women. Given Cuba's long-term and deep commitment to the human rights regime within the U.N., we should expect to see a particularly strong level of convergence between Cuban law and international norms of human rights. Cuba has strong incentives to demonstrate that it is complying with those norms, in order to challenge accusations coming from critics in the U.S.. On the other hand, the domestic political situation in Cuba lacks the characteristics that many have defined as making adoption of treaty norms more likely: it is a stable authoritarian regime with a weak civil society, conditions that Simmons (2009) suggests mitigate against treaty impact. Adoption of policy on violence against women is also low in countries that lack a strong, autonomous women's movement (Weldon 2002; Htun and Weldon 2018).

This analysis of the exchanges between Cuban government officials and the experts on the CEDAW committee over the 38 years in which Cuba has been a state party to the convention suggests Cuba's record is mixed. Cuba has engaged fully in the reporting process, it has raised the priority of violence against women policy at the domestic level and it has adopted some new policies in response to the CEDAW Committee's recommendations. Nonetheless, it has resisted the CEDAW Committee's assessment of its progress on critical aspects of violence against women policy. Two issues in particular – the sufficiency of

Cuba's methods for collecting statistical data on the incidence of domestic violence and the degree to which Cuban law provides adequate protection for victims – remain points of intense contention between the Cuban government and the CEDAW Committee.

CEDAW and violence against women

Violence against women did not emerge as a priority issue for the global women's movement until the 1980s (Keck and Sikkink 1997). The formal text of CEDAW makes no mention of violence against women or sexual violence, reflecting the understanding of women's rights that prevailed when the treaty was drafted in the 1970s. As violence against women began to emerge as a key aspect of women's rights, the CEDAW Committee incorporated it into the reporting process by means of the General Recommendations, a formal mechanism that allows the Committee experts to provide guidance to governments about how to implement the convention. The Committee first addressed the issue of violence against women in 1989, with General Recommendation No. 12. This statement recommends to States parties that their reports include information on legislation, support services and statistical information. It is no more than half a page long and contains very general instructions. The Committee soon realized it needed to provide more specific guidance so in 1992, it published a second General Recommendation on violence against women. GR No. 19 was the most extensive and detailed set of guidelines that the Committee had created on any issue up to that point. GR No. 19 explains the logic of the 'close connection between discrimination against women, gender-based violence, and violations of human rights and fundamental freedoms' and recommends action in 24 specific areas. From 1992 to 2017, GR No. 19 defined the standard against which the CEDAW Committee assessed the *de jure* and de facto status of violence against women. In 2017, the Committee issued an additional General Recommendation (No. 35) to provide 'further guidance' on gender-based violence, which will be relevant Cuba in the future. The CEDAW Committee thus did not initially request information on violence against women but starting in 1992, the experts have routinely asked specific questions about the measures that states have adopted to combat violence against women.[5]

Methodology

CEDAW member countries initiate the reporting process by preparing a report that assesses the *de jure* and de facto status of women and submitting it to the CEDAW Committee. The Committee, a group of 23 experts elected by the States parties to the convention, then prepares a *List of Issues* highlighting its main concerns and the countries prepares a written response to those questions. A government delegation then travels to the Office of the High Commissioner on Human Rights in Geneva to present the report and to engage the experts on the CEDAW Committee in a face-to-face discussion known as a *constructive dialogue*. Nongovernmental organizations (NGOs) are invited to submit 'shadow reports' that highlight issues not raised by the government and correct misleading information. Many NGOs also attend CEDAW sessions. The CEDAW Committee then prepares a set of *Concluding Observations* assessing the overall level of implementation and recommending future action. In recent years, the Committee has required States parties to submit a written follow-up as well. States parties to the convention engage in this process every 4 years.

In terms of participation in the reporting process, Cuba has been a model CEDAW member. Since it ratified CEDAW in 1980, Cuba has met all its reporting obligations. It presented its first periodic report before the Committee in 1982. It presented its second and third periodic reports in 1996, taking advantage of a change in U.N. policy that allowed countries to present multiple reports simultaneously. Cuba appeared before the Committee in 2000 to present its fourth report. It submitted its fifth and sixth reports in 2006 and its seventh and eighth reports in 2013. The documentation for these sessions, all of which is available online on the OHCHR website. This analysis also examines the report from a visit to Cuba by the Special Rapporteur on Violence Against Women in 1999, as well as the Cuban government's response to that report, materials that informed subsequent CEDAW sessions.

Cuba's U.N. strategy

Cuba's close engagement with the U.N. and its historic commitment to women's rights make it an interesting case in which to examine the impact of CEDAW ratification. Exercising leadership with the U.N. is a key component of Cuba's foreign policy (Dominguez 2001; Alzugaray 2015). Since the collapse of the Soviet Union, Cuba has sought to forge a coalition of support within the U.N. to establish global leadership and to counter U.S. hostility. The General Assembly, the Economic and Social Commission, and the Human Rights Council have been important arenas for Cuban influence within the U.N. In each of the past 25 years, the U.N. General Assembly has voted to condemn the U.S. embargo against Cuba. Cuban delegates have been elected to the Human Rights Council (and the Commission on Human Rights before that) many times. Cuba was the first country to sign CEDAW and the second to ratify it. A Cuban delegate has served on the CEDAW Committee for all but 6 years of its existence, more than any other country. Cuba has regularly submitted its periodic reports for all the treaties it has ratified in a timely manner.

A couple of factors motivate Cuba's U.N. strategy. Part of the rationale is to limit U.S. power and to build an international coalition of support that could limit possible U.S. interference in Cuban affairs. After the collapse of the Soviet Union, with no prospects for a replacement benefactor, Cuba 'focused on building up a diplomatic defense that might restrict the United States' freedom of action against Cuba' (Kapcia 2011, 185). While the U.S. may never have seriously considered invading Cuba, 'many Cubans genuinely feared invasion, mindful of the ease with which U.S. troops had been sent to Panama in 1989' (187). Defending its human rights record – and preventing other countries from criticizing it – also motivates Cuba's U.N. strategy. Anti-Castro organizations in the U.S. routinely accuse the Cuban government of egregious violations of human rights. The U.N. is one arena in which Cuba can counter these claims, challenge U.S. policy and rally international support (Dominguez 2001). Cuba institutionalized these commitments to the international arena by amending Article 12 of its 1992 Constitution to explicitly commit Cuba to the 'principles proclaimed in the United Nations Charter' (Dominguez 1996, 301).

Cuba's embrace of international human rights norms is not merely defensive. Cuba portrays itself as one of the world's premier guarantors of economic and social rights and defends its record on standards of women's rights, health, education, employment and housing. Cuba has been a leader in global efforts to challenge neoliberalism. As Alzugaray (2015, 192) asserts, 'At the United Nations and other international forums, the Cuban government has insisted on challenging the neoliberal and hegemonic world order and adopting an autonomous policy.' For Cuba, this has meant 'challeng[ing] the existing world order and propos[ing] alterative solutions to global problems such as underdevelopment, trade, finance, production, disarmament and so forth' (181). The revolutionary government of Cuba has also consistently portrayed itself as a world leader in achieving women's equality and as being in full compliance with CEDAW. The government stakes its legitimacy in part on support for women's equality. Cuba embraced women's rights more than a decade earlier than most countries. The creation of the Federation of Cuban Women in 1975 established Cuba's reputation as being in the vanguard of state-led feminism.

In sum, participation in the U.N. is a central component of Cuban foreign policy and the stakes of demonstrating its commitment to global human rights norms are high. This leads me to expect that Cuba would readily comply with policy recommendations presented by any U.N. committee or commission. This expectation is in line with the scholarly literature on human rights norms, which suggests that, over time, participation in the human rights regime will lead to greater compliance and acceptance of global norms.

Cuba's initial engagement with the CEDAW committee

Cuba submitted its initial CEDAW report in 1982 and presented it at the second session that the CEDAW had held, in 1983. In accordance with the 'invisible' status of violence against women in the convention at that time, Cuba did not mention the issue in its initial report and the CEDAW Committee did not ask about it during the constructive dialogue. What is noticeable in the transcripts of this first session is the high praise that committee experts from Communist countries had for Cuba's 'considerable achievements in equality between the sexes' and the Cuban delegation's 'candor,' 'frankness and modesty' in describing the obstacles it faced in doing so. Experts from other regions of the world asked more challenging questions about things such as contradictions between laws, artistic freedom and the criminalization of prostitution (United Nations General Assembly 1984, 4).

Cuba submitted its second and third periodic report in 1992 and provided a slightly revised version in 1995. That report heeded the instructions for reporting on violence against women established by GR No. 12, explaining that the Penal Code was sufficient to address violence against women and that separate legislation was not necessary:

> The crime of spousal assault is not treated separately. This is because the levels of violence between couples do not amount to a social phenomenon. Factors favourably influencing this situation are the educative effect of the Family Code, and formal and sex education, which includes the new concept of marriage based upon love and mutual respect. (Committee on the Elimination of Discrimination Against Women 1992, 13)

Cuban officials sought to persuade the CEDAW experts that domestic violence was a minor problem in comparison to the impact of the U.S. trade embargo on Cuban women. In her opening statement to the committee, Ms. Ferrer Gomez, head of the Cuban delegation, framed the issue of violence against women in terms of the embargo, which Cubans refer to as the blockade.[6] As she asserted,

> In 1990, when Cuba had been attempting to re-enter the world economy and the cold war was allegedly at an end, the United States government had stepped up the blockade in an attempt to bring the Cuban people to its knees. The blockade was the worst form of violence that could be inflicted on Cuba's women; it was a deliberate aggression that violated the most elementary rules of international law and the principles of the Charter of the United Nations. (Committee on the Elimination of Discrimination Against Women 1996b, 2)

Ferrer Gomez acknowledged that violence of women did exist in Cuba but was less common than in other countries 'because Cuban women had a high level of self-esteem and also because Cuban society had traditionally rejected such violence.' Moreover, because it was rare, it was not considered a 'social problem' in Cuba (Committee on the Elimination of Discrimination Against Women 1996b, 2).

The four main claims that Cuba made about violence against women in these early sessions would be repeated in exchanges with the CEDAW Committee in the decades to come. First, violence against women was rare in Cuba and thus did not warrant legal reform. Second, it was rare because state policy guaranteed economic and social inequality, the main causes of violence against women. Third, to the extent that it did occur, it was adequately addressed by the existing penal code. Fourth, CEDAW did not adequately account for the impact of the U.S. trade embargo as a form of violence against women.

In the questioning that took place during the constructive dialogue, several committee members challenged these claims. One of the experts, Ms. Aouij from Tunisia, noted that 'the report made no mention of violence against women,' ostensibly referring to a lack of statistical data (Committee on the Elimination of Discrimination Against Women 1996b, 3). Ms. Bustelo Garcia del Real, an expert from Spain, noted that more data would confirm whether or not violence against women existed and, if so, 'how it could be combatted' (Committee on the Elimination of Discrimination Against Women 1996b, 3). Ms. Schöpp-Schilling, from Germany, was more forthright, saying that 'it was impossible to believe that there was no domestic violence in Cuba. The Cuban authorities should address what was a painful issue for any society' (Committee on the Elimination of Discrimination Against Women 1996b, 3). Despite these criticisms, Ms. Ferrer Gomez held her ground, clarifying that

> she had not meant to imply that domestic violence did not exist in Cuba, merely that it was not as serious a problem as in some other countries. There was no tradition of domestic violence in Cuba, and it was not generally condoned by society. Where it did occur, however, steps were being taken to remedy the problem. (Committee on the Elimination of Discrimination Against Women 1996b, 5)

Perhaps not surprisingly, the Committee commented on domestic violence in the Concluding Observations. Among the 'Principal subjects for concern,' it was noted 'with some scepticism that domestic violence was reported to be infrequent and that it was not considered to be a social problem' (Committee on the Elimination of Discrimination Against Women 1996a, 28). Among its 'suggestions and recommendations,' the committee instructed that 'surveys and studies should be undertaken to determine the extent and impact of violence against women, in particular domestic violence, even if unreported, and to take steps in accordance with general recommendation 19' (Committee on the Elimination of Discrimination Against Women 1996a).

Fourth periodic report

By the time the Cuban government submitted its fourth periodic report in 1999, it had heeded the Concluding Observations and had taken several steps to address violence against women. Per Committee instructions, the report described these efforts in a separate section on violence against women. It had created the National Group for the Prevention and Treatment of Violence in the Family, an inter-agency task force that included the Ministries of Education, Public Health, and Internal Affairs, the Institute of Forensic Medicine, the Office of the Public Prosecutor of the Republic, the National Center for Sex Education (CENESEX), the University of Havana, the Cuban Institute for Radio and Television (ICRT) and the People's Supreme Court. The purpose of this group was to create a national plan for action and coordinate policy across society.

The Council of State amended the Penal Code to address spousal and family violence – but did not adopt standalone legislation. The reformed code 'introduces as an aggravating circumstance in crimes of violence "the person of the spouse" and the notion of kinship between the perpetrator and the victim' (Committee on the Elimination of Discrimination Against Women 1999, 6). The Cuban delegation maintained that the Penal Code 'contained all the elements necessary to protect women from violence' (19). The government had adopted new laws in other areas, such as salary inequities for pregnant women, divorce and adoptions, so it was not resistant to adopting new laws per se. Other measures the government adopted included

- Training for government officials (including the police, Ministries of Health and Justice, the State Procurator's Office and the Radio and Television Institute) as well as 'community workers and specialists'
- Production of 'educational kits' used to guide discussions in local branches of the Federation of Cuban Women
- Study of court cases, Cuban legislation and VAW in other countries
- Treatment at 'FMC women and family counselling centres'
- Analysis of 20 earlier studies 'produced mainly between 1994 and 1998, although some go back to 1991' (21).

The periodic report indicated that this research identified myriad causes of domestic violence, including

> jealousy, lack of respect for the possessions of others, emotional conflicts and difficulties of communication in the couple and the family, low self-esteem on the part of women, unwanted children, rejection of children and other disabled members of the family, parental irresponsibility and insufficient education in the performance of family roles, machismo, alcoholism, economic problems, overcrowding and promiscuity, low cultural standards, frustration, insufficient training in accepting others with problems, mental disturbances, and ideological, political and religious conflicts. (Committee on the Elimination of Discrimination Against Women 1999, 21)

All of the factors listed in this paragraph highlight character flaws on the part of individual people. GR No. 19 acknowledges that individual behavior often lies at the heart of violence against women, particularly 'traditional attitudes regarding the subordinate role of women.' Nonetheless, it focuses *primarily* on structural causes of violence against women, such as poverty and unemployment. The solutions it proposes focus on action at the state level, not reform of individuals. CEDAW obligates governments to take 'all appropriate measures' to eliminate violence as a form of discrimination and to protect victims. The Cuban government considers itself to have already taken all appropriate measures to achieve these aims, by virtue of guaranteeing work, housing, food, healthcare, education and policies that ensure gender equality. From the perspective of the Cuban government, it has done all that can be done in terms of government action – so any remaining problems lie with individual shortcomings among people whose consciousness is underdeveloped.

The report also provided some statistical information, which was reported in the following way:

> "An analysis of these [133] cases of violence indicated the following basic features:
> (a) Violence by men against women: 75 cases (56.4 per cent)
> (b) Violence by women against men: 6 (4.5 per cent)
> (c) Violence by mothers against children: 35 (26.3 per cent)
> (d) Violence by fathers against children: 14 (10.5 per cent)". (Committee on the Elimination of Discrimination Against Women 1999, 21)

To put these data in context, consider that the World Health Organization estimates that on average, 1 in 3 women will be the victim of physical or sexual violence committed by an intimate partner or a non-intimate partner (World Health Organization 2017). Given that Cuba's population at the time was around 11 million, we should expect that approximately 3.6 million women would be victims of violence. The Cuban figures depart significantly from global averages (and do not sum to 100%).

Visit of Special Rapporteur on violence against women to Cuba

In the period between Cuba's submission of its fourth periodic report in September 1999 and its appearance before the CEDAW Committee in June 2000, the government hosted a visit by the Special Rapporteur on Violence against Women. The U.N. Commission on Human Rights created the Special Rapporteur in 1994 to integrate the issue of violence against women into all of the human rights mechanisms. The Special Rapporteur conducts country visits in order to gather information, recommend policy and focus attention on urgent cases of alleged violence against women (United Nations Office of the High Commissioner for Human Rights, n.d.). This was the first time the Cuban government had invited any United Nations human rights official to visit the country (United Nations Commission on Human Rights 2000b, 3). Radhika Coomaraswamy, who served as Special Rapporteur from 1994 to 2003, visited Cuba 7–12 June 1999.

The Cuban government appeared to have expected that this visit would provide evidence of Cuba's unassailable record of achievement on women's rights. The fact that the government extended this invitation at all is testament to Cuba's confidence. The Cuban government gave Coomaraswamy extraordinary access to high-ranking government officials; she met with Fidel Castro himself. She was taken to local-level government offices and organizations to get a sense of women's status at the grassroots level. The government anticipated – wrongly, it turns out – that the visit would showcase the country's achievements before the international community.

Coomaraswamy submitted her report to the Commission on Human Rights in February 2000. The report acknowledged Cuba's unique and strong commitment to women's rights: 'The Cuban revolution has resulted in a great deal of benefit for women. This was a conclusion that was rarely contested by any party, group or individual the Special Rapporteur spoke to' (United Nations Commission on Human Rights 2000a, 4). Her report corroborated the views that government officials had presented to CEDAW earlier:

> There was a perception among official circles that violence against women was not a problem in Cuba. The Special Rapporteur was informed that the statistics for reported cases were low and that women were economically independent and so did not tolerate domestic violence. It was argued that the ideological tenets of socialism prevented recourse to violence, unlike in capitalist countries. These perceptions condition Cuban approaches to violence against women. Despite the best efforts of women's organizations, the legislature, especially, was adamant that nothing need be done with regard to violence against women and that no new legislation was necessary. The judiciary was also satisfied that the present position was adequate. (United Nations Commission on Human Rights 2000a, 4)

She acknowledged the 'significant impact' of the embargo and called upon the U.S. government to end it – but also asserted that 'the counter-argument is that the situation is not a product of the embargo but of economic mismanagement by the central Government' (United Nations Commission on Human Rights 2000a). The report strongly criticized Cuba's record, characterizing the government's insistence that violence against women is not a problem as 'disconcerting' (United Nations Commission on Human Rights 2000a, 5). It identified mistreatment of female dissidents as a form of violence against women and called attention to problems in Cuba's treatment of prostitution, sexual harassment, data collection and the treatment of 'women whose political views are not acceptable to the Government' (United Nations Commission on Human Rights 2000a).

The Special Rapporteur's statements prompted a strongly worded condemnation from the Cuban government, in a *note verbale* submitted to the Commission on Human Rights. First, Cuba maintained that the Special Rapporteur's report was unduly influenced behind the scenes from the U.S. government, the Central Intelligence Agency, the 'Cuban mafia' in Miami and human rights groups funded by the U.S. Second, the report claimed that Coomaraswamy raised issues in the report about which she had not inquired during her visit, despite having had ample opportunity to do so, thus denying the government the chance to respond. Moreover, she did not give Cuba adequate time to respond to her report before she submitted it to the Commission on Human Rights. Finally, her report and her criticisms of Cuba denied Cuba's right to define human rights in a way consistent with socialist principles. Cuba's response to the claims made by the Special Rapporteur illustrates the degree to which the government was willing to go to defend its record (United Nations Commission on Human Rights 2000b).

The CEDAW session at which Cuba presented its fourth periodic report took place in June 2000, a year after the visit of the Special Rapporteur and a few months after the publication of her report. During the constructive dialogue, CEDAW Committee members focused particular attention on the absence of domestic violence legislation and the lack of sufficient statistical data. Committee expert Ivanka Corti (from Italy) requested, for example, that the 'delegation should explain more clearly how domestic violence was dealt with in the Cuban legal system' (Committee on the Elimination of Discrimination Against Women 2001, 4).

In their responses to queries from the Committee, members of the Cuban delegation demonstrated little understanding of the distinctive nature of domestic violence as opposed to other forms of violence. They considered violence of men toward women to fall in the same category as violence of women against men, and parents against children. When asked about legal penalties for violence against women, Ms. Miranda from Cuban delegation affirmed that 'any person who used violence on another person was subject to two or more years imprisonment,' threats of violence punishable by one year, and punishment for violence to pregnant woman 'was more severe' (Committee on the Elimination of Discrimination Against Women 2001, 4). Ms. Beretervide from Cuban delegation said violence in general was lower than it had been prior to the revolution, when 'it had not been uncommon for people to be murdered in the street, tortured or simply to disappear' (Committee on the Elimination of Discrimination Against Women 2001). These comments are striking in their departure from global norms of discourse surrounding violence against women.

Cuban government officials pointed to international factors to explain limitations in domestic policy. In response to a request about the visit of the Special Rapporteur, Cuban delegate Mr. Reyes Rodríguez characterized her report as 'extremely subjective and showed utter disregard for due process' and 'was based on the stereotypes peddled in the international press and had been subject to political manipulation' (Committee on the Elimination of Discrimination Against Women 2001, 10). Cuban officials again cast the issue of violence against women in terms of the embargo and U.S. policy toward Cuba. When asked about data on violence of mothers toward children, for example, Ms. Diaz from Cuban delegation responded that this kind of violence was rare but might be related to psychological stress caused by the embargo (Committee on the Elimination of Discrimination Against Women 2001, 5).

The Committee appeared to be unmoved by these claims. The Chair concluded the session with a warning that 'the delegation should be aware of the Committee's continuing concerns in such areas as domestic violence and violence against women' (Committee on the Elimination of Discrimination Against Women 2001, 10). The Concluding Observations drew attention to the issue, 'not[ing] with concern' the lack of legislation on violence against women and sexual harassment, insufficient statistical data and lack of information on government services for victims. It 'calls upon the government' to determine the extent of violence against women, 'invites the government' to raise public awareness of the issue and to 'increase the availability of support measure for women victims of domestic violence' (Committee on the Elimination of Discrimination Against Women 2000, 75).

Fifth and sixth periodic reports

Cuba submitted its next periodic report in 2006. In the report, in its responses to the list of issues posed by the CEDAW Committee, and in its interventions during the constructive dialogue, Cuba described the specific details of the Penal Code that pertained to domestic violence, the scope of research that had been undertaken on the topic, and services available to victims. The report indicated that the government had improved data collection efforts by developing 'quantitative and qualitative indicators' of court dossiers for crimes related to domestic violence ('assault, homicide, murder and rape') and setting up a registry to track visits to local offices of the Federation of Cuban Women (Committee on the Elimination of Discrimination Against Women 2006a, 33). Despite these changes, the data actually provided in the report do not differ from previous efforts, with the exception that this report included data for 3 years where the previous one had only included data for a single year. Cuba provided data on the incidence of domestic violence, in terms of cases reported to the government in 1998, 2001, 2002 and 2005 (with no explanation for the missing years and with an incorrect total for 2005). The data showed an upward trend in the number of cases of men committing violence against women, from 75 cases in 1998 to 333 cases in 2005, reported in a table that looks just like Table 1 (35).

The Cuban government again attributed limitations in its policies on this issue to the U.S. embargo, which it described as 'the most brutal manifestation of violence against Cuban women' (Committee on the Elimination of Discrimination Against Women 2006c, 2). In the CEDAW session later that year, the committee experts pushed members of the Cuban delegation to provide information on legal reform, prompting the government to reply that it prioritized 'caring for victims and members of their families, and on treating perpetrators' over legislative change:

> Whether or not criminal law provides protection in the event of violence is immaterial in this regard; the important thing is to ensure than society as a whole gets involved, in a structured manner, in prevention and rehabilitation activities. (Committee on the Elimination of Discrimination Against Women 2006b, 4)

Cuban government officials demonstrated a higher level of sophistication about the issue of violence against women and a more nuanced critique of the approaches suggested by the Committee. In response to a request for information about shelters for victims, for example, a member of the Cuban delegation stated,

> In our view, the best way to protect women victims of violence is to isolate the aggressor, since otherwise there would be a double victimization upon separating the women and, in most cases, their children, from their familiar living environment and conditions, places of work or study, and relationships with family, neighbors and friends. (Committee on the Elimination of Discrimination Against Women 2006b, 4)

This perspective diverges from the standards articulated in GR No. 19 but does reflect a thoughtful alternative. Cuban delegate Ms. Coker-Appiah framed its decision not to adopt a domestic violence law in terms of awareness of limitations of similar legislation in other Latin American countries:

> Cuba had taken part in an in-depth study of domestic violence in Latin America and the Caribbean, which had found that, even in countries that had separate laws on domestic violence, the problem persisted because the laws were not being enforced. The Cuban Government had therefore decided to focus on strengthening existing legal provisions and ensuring their enforcement, as the most effective way of addressing domestic violence. (Committee on the Elimination of Discrimination Against Women 2006b, 28)

Table 1. Domestic violence in Cuba.

	1998	2001	2002	2005
Violence – men against women	75	151	329	333
Violence – women against men	6	5	27	21
Violence – fathers against children	14	54	28	16
Violence – mothers against children	35	40	19	53
Total	**130**	**250**	**403**	**461**[a]

Table 2. FMC public welfare records – cases of violence.

	2006	2007	2008
Violence – men against women	315	266	327
Violence – women against men	30	43	25
Violence – fathers against children	6	31	12
Violence – mothers against children	209	178	184

Source: Committee on the Elimination of Discrimination Against Women (2011, 19).

While weak enforcement may not be a sufficient reason to avoid adopting a law, this perspective does accurately reflect the situation in many Latin American countries.

The Concluding Observations provided to Cuba in 2006 reflect a markedly more direct, detailed and pointed tone than in previous years. About half of the recommendations reflect the diplomatic language of the earlier recommendations – 'express concerns,' 'request additional information' and 'recommend the adoption of measures' to address particular issues. But several of the recommendations are framed in exhortatory language and request specific changes to existing legislation. The Committee called for more information not just about the existence of legislation on domestic violence but 'the content of these provisions and their effective enforcement,' as well as the definition of domestic violence, scope of support for victims and the results of efforts to assess the impact of the measures that the Cuban government claimed to have adopted. It also pointed out Cuba's failure to comply with recommendations made in the previous reporting cycle (Committee on the Elimination of Discrimination Against Women 2006d).

Seventh and eighth periodic reports

A similar line of argument took place during Cuba's most recent session, held in 2013 – but the Cuban government devoted far more space to reporting the efforts it had taken with regard to violence against women. In its response to questions submitted by the Committee prior to the session, the Cuban government reiterated the argument that domestic violence is a minor issue relative to the way that the embargo affects women:

> The available statistics and research demonstrate that the primary forms of violence in the country are domestic (primarily psychological and emotional) violence and, to a lesser degree, nonmarital rape. Without a doubt, the policy of embargo and aggression implemented by the Government of the United States of America against Cuba for more than 50 years is the manifestation of violence that has most affected Cuban women; those policies also constitute the primary obstacle to the nation's economic development. (Committee on the Elimination of Discrimination Against Women 2013a, 22)

It reported that 'a look at the figures shows an increase in such requests [for assistance from the FMC] as a result of the effort that has been made to raise awareness of the problem' (Committee on the Elimination of Discrimination Against Women 2013a). As with the previous report, the data on reported cases do not begin to come close to global averages and, contra the government's assertions, do not reveal an increase over time (see Table 2).

Despite Cuba's efforts to address violence against women, and to provide additional information about those efforts, the CEDAW Committee did not acknowledge any of these efforts as 'positive aspects' of progress toward full compliance. The Concluding

Observations that the Committee wrote in 2013 attribute the persistence of violence and underreporting to 'the prevalence of discriminatory social and cultural norms and the denial by the State party of the existence of different types of violence' (Committee on the Elimination of Discrimination Against Women 2013b, 6). The Concluding Observations urged Cuba to 'adopt a comprehensive law,' 'develop a national strategic plan and ensure that it is fully implemented,' 'provide mandatory training' for political officials, 'provide free legal aid' and create shelters, and 'collect statistical data and undertake studies' (Committee on the Elimination of Discrimination Against Women 2013b).

The Cuban government found this round of Concluding Observations sufficiently unacceptable as to warrant a response outside of the formal reporting process. It submitted a document to the CEDAW Committee to 'express its views and concerns on the concluding observations' (Republic of Cuba 2014, n.p.). The document states that some of the Concluding Observations 'reflect ignorance of the Cuban reality,' addresses issues that 'were not even covered in the interactive dialogue with the delegation' and makes no 'mention of the impact of the blockade on Cuban women' (Republic of Cuba 2014). It refutes the Committee's assessment of Cuba's policies regarding violence against women and several other issues. A year later, in 2015, the Cuban government issued a formal response to the Concluding Observations that defended its existing policies with regard to 'State machinery for the advancement of women,' drafting a National Plan of Action and 'enhanc[ing] the collection, analysis and dissemination of comprehensive data,' three areas that the Committee has called upon Cuba to make significant reforms. A year after that, in 2016, a member of the CEDAW Committee replied to Cuba's claims by maintaining that it considered the measures in question to be either partially or not implemented.

Discussion

This analysis of the exchanges between Cuban government officials and CEDAW committee experts suggests that the impact of the reporting process on Cuba's policy toward violence against women is mixed. It has reshaped Cuban discourse to a certain extent and shared views have emerged in some areas. There has been evolution on issues that Cuba and CEDAW disagreed upon early on – but the evolution has been a sharpening of conflict over how to interpret Cuba's record. Cuba has steadfastly defended actions that defy the guidance of the Committee – and the Committee has insisted on the adoption of certain provision in increasingly pointed terms over time. Two issues stand out as particularly conflictual. The Committee has consistently urged Cuba to adopt a standalone law penalizing violence against women and better methods for collecting data about the incidence and treatment of violence against women. Cuba has energetically resisted the Committee's recommendations, maintaining that the existing penal code provides adequate protection for victims and that its methods of gathering data are sufficient. Moreover, because the available data suggests that rates of violence against women are low in Cuba, the government maintains that additional reforms are unnecessary.

There are two things to be explained here: why Cuba has not adopted these policies and why does Cuba resist the CEDAW Committee so strenuously? One potential explanation for the limited impact on policy outcomes reflects the broader literature on violence against women. In the absence of a strong, independent women's movement, adoption of violence against women policy is less likely. The Cuban government has maintained that the Federation of Cuban Women does constitute an autonomous women's movement, but the fact that the head of that organization serves as a member of the Council of State and chairs a legislative committee reflects a different understanding of autonomy from the one that scholars have highlighted. In the absence of independent pressure from women's organizations at the domestic level, the urgings of the CEDAW Committee will only go so far.

That said, there is evidence in the documentation of the CEDAW process that the Cuban government has increased the priority of this issue and has taken steps to comply with some of the standards stipulated in General Recommendation No. 19, the standard for violence against women policy, such as training for public officials, services for victims and public information campaigns. The degree to which these commitments have actually been implemented on the ground cannot be determined from a review of the CEDAW documentation, in part because the Cuban government has provided little information about the assessment of these measures. A more thorough assessment of what policies have and have not been put into action would require fieldwork in Cuba itself.

What accounts for Cuba's resistance? Why has the Cuban government provided such strongly worded refutations of the Committee's assessment of Cuba's record? What is at stake in the dynamics of the process itself? One explanation suggests that Cuba's participation in the CEDAW process is one aspect of its broader foreign policy, in which the U.N. is an important arena for building allies and maintaining legitimacy in the face of hostile U.S. policy. Another explanation for Cuba's efforts to defend its record is that the standards by which the CEDAW committee evaluate the compliance of States parties to the convention have increased over time. In Cuba's first CEDAW session in 1984, the experts made comments, asked questions and probed for more information about what policies and laws the Cuban government adopted, or planned to adopt, but demurred from recommending that the government adopt specific policies. Over time, the CEDAW Committee has grown bolder, highlighting Cuba's limitations, making more pointed requests, plumbing apparent contradictions and calling attention to lacunae in periodic reports. The CEDAW Committee has challenged Cuba on these claims with building intensity over the 38 years since Cuba ratified the treaty. The Cuban case thus provides evidence to support the view that the CEDAW process has gained strength and clarity over time (Baldez 2014).

This study generates many questions about the reporting process but can only provide suggestive answers to those questions. In order to generate more solid claims, the findings of this research must be subjected to additional study through conversations with experts on the CEDAW Committee and Cuban government officials who participated in the process, as well as examining the degree to which certain policies were implemented on the ground in Cuba. This research raises questions that warrant further analysis: how does the status of violence against women compare to that of other aspects of compliance with CEDAW? How does Cuba's engagement with the CEDAW Committee compare to its interactions with other human rights treaty bodies? How does Cuba's experience in the U.N. human rights regime compare to that of other countries? How is the action that takes place during the reporting process connected to what happens at the domestic level in Cuba? To what extent does the Cuban government publicize CEDAW back home? These questions are the subject of future research.

Notes

1. CEDAW is one of nine treaties overseen by the U.N. Office of the High Commissioner on Human Rights. The other treaties are the International Convention on the Elimination of All Forms of Racial Discrimination (CERD), International Covenant on Civil and Political Rights (ICCPR), International Covenant on Economic, Social and Cultural Rights (ICESCR), Convention against Torture and Other Cruel, Inhuman or Degrading Treatment or Punishment (CAT), Convention on the Rights of the Child (CRC), International Convention on the Protection of the Rights of All Migrant Workers and Members of Their Families (CMW), International Convention for the Protection of All Persons from Enforced Disappearance (CED) and the Convention on the Rights of Persons with Disabilities (CRPD).
2. One exception is Htun and Weldon (2018), which examines the impact that withdrawing a reservation to CEDAW has on various aspects of women's rights policy. The question of what accounts for the contradictory findings in CEDAW research warrants further research, but is beyond the scope of this article.
3. The data contained in human rights reports and the evolution of the reporting process have been at the center of recent debates about how to measure progress in human rights (Fariss 2014; Cingranelli and Filippov 2018).
4. This article uses the term 'violence against women' because that is the term that the CEDAW Committee used during the period under study here. The term 'gender-based violence' is more widely used today.
5. The text of all of the General Recommendations is available on the CEDAW website, at https://www.ohchr.org/EN/HRBodies/CEDAW/Pages/CEDAWIndex.aspx.
6. Documentation of the CEDAW sessions typically refers to individuals by Mr., Ms., and Mrs.

Disclosure statement

No potential conflict of interest was reported by the author.

References

Alzugaray, C. 2015. "Cuba's External Projection: The Interplay between International Relations Theory and Foreign Policy Analysis." In *Handbook of Latin America in the World*, edited by J. I. Dominguez and A. Covarrubias, 180–196. New York and London: Routledge.

Baldez, L. 2014. *Defying Convention: U.S. Resistance to the U.N. Treaty on Women's Rights*. Cambridge, New York: Cambridge University Press.

Cingranelli, D., and M. Filippov. 2018. "Letter: Are Human Rights Practices Improving?" *American Political Science Review*. (Online). https://www.cambridge.org/core/journals/american-political-science-review/article/are-human-rights-practices-improving/972B4F471231AFC7908A4DA951020340. June.

Committee on the Elimination of Discrimination Against Women. 1992. *Second and Third Periodic Reports of States Parties: Cuba*. United Nations.

Committee on the Elimination of Discrimination Against Women. 1996a. *Report of the Committee on the Elimination of Discrimination Against Women (Fifteenth Session)*. United Nations.

Committee on the Elimination of Discrimination Against Women. 1996b. *Fifteenth Session: Summary Record of the 295th Meeting*. United Nations.

Committee on the Elimination of Discrimination Against Women. 1999. *Fourth Periodic Report of Cuba*. United Nations.

Committee on the Elimination of Discrimination Against Women. 2000. *Report of the Committee on the Elimination of Discrimination Against Women: Twenty-Second Session and Twenty-Third Session*. United Nations.

Committee on the Elimination of Discrimination Against Women. 2001. *Summary Record of the 474th Meeting. Consideration of Reports Submitted by States Parties under Article 18 of the Convention (Continued): Fourth Periodic Report of Cuba*. United Nations.

Committee on the Elimination of Discrimination Against Women. 2006a. *Consideration of Reports Submitted by States Parties under Article 18 of the Convention on the Elimination of All Discrimination Against Women: Combined Fifth and Sixth Periodic Reports of States Parties: Cuba*. United Nations.

Committee on the Elimination of Discrimination Against Women. 2006b. *Responses to the List of Issues and Questions for Consideration of the Combined Fifth and Sixth Periodic Report: Cuba*. United Nations.

Committee on the Elimination of Discrimination Against Women. 2006c. *Summary Record of the 739th Meeting (Chamber A): Consideration of Reports Submitted by States Parties under Article 18 of the Convention: Combined Fifth and Sixth Reports of Cuba*. United Nations.

Committee on the Elimination of Discrimination Against Women. 2006d. *Concluding Comments of the Committee on the Elimination of Discrimination Against Women: Cuba*. United Nations.

Committee on the Elimination of Discrimination Against Women. 2011. *Consideration of Reports Submitted by States Parties under Article 18 of the Convention on the Elimination of All Forms of Discrimination against Women Combined Seventh and Eighth Periodic Reports of States Parties: Cuba*. United Nations.

Committee on the Elimination of Discrimination Against Women. 2013a. *List of Issues and Questions with Regard to Consideration of Periodic Reports: Cuba; Addendum: Replies of Cuba to the List of Issues to be Taken up in Connection with the Consideration of its Seventh and Eighth Periodic Reports*. United Nations.

Committee on the Elimination of Discrimination Against Women. 2013b. *Concluding Observations on the Combined Seventh and Eighth Periodic Reports of Cuba*. United Nations.

Creamer, C. D., and B. A. Simmons. 2015. "Ratification, Reporting, and Rights: Quality of Participation in the Convention against Torture." *Human Rights Quarterly* 37: 579–608. doi:10.1353/hrq.2015.0041.

Dominguez, J. I. 1996. "Cuba in the International Community in the 1990s: Sovereignty, Human Rights and Democracy." In *Beyond Sovereignty: Collectively Defending Democracy in the Americas*, edited by T. Farer, 297–315. Baltimore: Johns Hopkins University Press.

Dominguez, J. I. 2001. "Cuban Foreign Policy and the International System." In *Latin America in the New International System*, edited by J. S. Tulchin and R. H. Espach, 183–206. Boulder and London: Lynne Rienner Publishers.

Fariss, C. J. 2014. "Respect for Human Rights Has Improved over Time: Modeling the Changing Standard Of Accountability." *American Political Science Review* 108 (2): 297–318. doi:10.1017/S0003055414000070.

Gray, M. M., M. C. Kittilson, and W. Sandholtz. 2006. "Women and Globalization: A Study of 180 Countries, 1975–2000." *International Organization* 60 (2): 293–333. doi:10.1017/S0020818306060176.

Htun, M., and S. L. Weldon. 2018. *The Logics of Gender Justice: State Action on Women's Rights around the World*. Cambridge, New York: Cambridge University Press.

Kapcia, A. 2011. "Defying Expectations: The External Profile and Activism of the Cuban Revolution." In *Latin American Foreign Policies*, edited by G. L. Gardini and P. Lambert, 179–195. New York: Palgrave Macmillan.

Keck, M. E., and K. Sikkink. 1997. *Activists beyond Borders: Advocacy Networks in International Politics*. Ithaca, NY: Cornell University Press.

Kenworthy, L., and M. Malami. 1999. "Gender Inequality in Political Representation: A Worldwide Comparative Analysis." *Social Forces* 78 (1): 235–268. doi:10.1093/sf/78.1.235.

Paxton, P. 1997. "Women in National Legislatures: A Cross-National Analysis." *Social Science Research* 26: 442–464. doi:10.1006/ssre.1997.0603.

Republic of Cuba. 2014. *Opinions of the Government of the Republic of Cuba on the Document CEDAW/C/CUB/CO/7–8 Containing the Concluding Observations of the Committee on the Elimination of Discrimination against Women (CEDAW) for Cuba Combined Seventh and Eighth Reports*. United Nations.

Simmons, B. A. 2009. *Mobilizing for Human Rights: International Law in Domestic Politics*. Cambridge, New York: Cambridge University Press.

True, J., and M. Mintrom. 2001. "Transnational Networks and Policy Diffusion: The Case of Gender Mainstreaming." *International Studies Quarterly* 45 (1): 27–57. doi:10.1111/isqu.2001.45.issue-1.

United Nations Commission on Human Rights. 2000a. *Integration of the Human Rights of Women and the Gender Perspective: Violence Against Women, Report of the Special Rapporteur on Violence against Women, Its Causes and Consequences, Ms. Radhika Coomaraswamy, Submitted in Accordance with Commission on Human Rights Resolution 1997/44: Addendum, Report on the Mission to Cuba*. United Nations.

United Nations Commission on Human Rights. 2000b. *Integration of the Human Rights of Women and the Gender Perspective: Violence Against Women, Note Verbale Dates 8 March 2000 from the Permanent Mission of Cuba to the United Nations Office at Geneva Addressed to the Office of the High Commissioner for Human Rights*. United Nations.

United Nations General Assembly. 1984. *Report of the Committee on the Elimination of Discrimination Against Women: Volume I (Second Session)*. United Nations.

United Nations Office of the High Commissioner for Human Rights. n.d. *Special Rapporteur on Violence Against Women, its Causes and Consequences*. United Nations.

Weldon, S. L. 2002. *Protest, Policy and the Problem of Violence against Women*. Pittsburgh: University of Pittsburgh Press.

World Health Organization. 2017. "Violence Against Women." http://www.who.int/news-room/fact-sheets/detail/violence-against-women.

Gender politics and geopolitics of international criminal law in Uganda

Annie Bunting

ABSTRACT

This paper explores the views of victim survivors – both men and women – on the current prosecution of Dominic Ongwen at the International Criminal Court (ICC) for crimes against humanity, including the crime of forced marriage. This case will be used as the central story around which the potential and limitations of international criminal law for gender justice will be explored. The Ongwen case has blurred the lines between victims and perpetrators of child soldiering and has generated much debate within and outside the continent. It has resuscitated the contestation and controversies surrounding the ICC regime in Uganda and Africa more broadly. The reflections I share in this paper come out of a collaborative research project I direct called 'Conjugal Slavery in War: Partnerships for the study of enslavement, marriage and masculinities' (CSiW 2015-2020). While Uganda and the Ongwen case will be central to this paper, our research project includes partners working with survivors of conflicts in the Democratic Republic of Congo, Liberia, Sierra Leone, Rwanda and northern Nigeria. We collected well over 250 interviews with women who were abducted for forced marriage. Using interview data from Uganda, as well as court records, this paper explores in-depth the geopolitics and gender politics of prosecuting conjugal slavery as an international crime.

Introduction

> I feel like that is just a waste of time: Remanding Dominic Ongwen, has it stopped Kony from staying in the bush? Kony is still abducting people, he is still continuing with the fight; he has not yet stopped. If the government is wasting money on Ongwen, why don't they use the money to build the capacity of [those] who were just innocently abducted and taken in the bush? Keeping Ongwen and Kwoyelo there will not change anything on anyone. Even if Ongwen die from there, it will not change anything. So if I am to say, what they should do is to take Ongwen before the victims to be forgiven because he was arrested for killing people. Because that would not even make the person killed by Ongwen rose from the death. (Lily Amono, Interview with Gladys Oroma, Uganda, October 2017)[1]

Lily Amono lives in northern Uganda. She was kidnapped by the Lord's Resistance Army (LRA) in 1992 at the age of nine and was forcibly married to an LRA 'medical officer' (Interview with Gladys Oroma, 2017). She spent more than 10 years in LRA captivity.

Some 6 years after her release, Amono asks how international criminal cases help victim survivors of the LRA–Ugandan government war, including victims of gender violence. The International Criminal Court (ICC) Prosecutor in 2005, following a referral by the Ugandan government,[2] unsealed arrest warrants against five suspects from the LRA which had been engaged in almost two decades of drawn out conflict with the Government of Uganda.[3] The arrest warrants issued by the ICC were for Joseph Kony and four top LRA commanders, including Dominic Ongwen. Following the deaths of Raskia Lukwiya and Okot Odhiambo, the cases against them were closed. Only Ongwen[4] currently stands trial in The Hague, with Kony and Vincent Otti still at large. As the Ongwen trial proceeds, it is important to reflect on whether the space of international justice has the potential to advance gender equality, provide an effective response to impunity, and create a meaningful historical record of gender violence. Given the history of women's groups' advocacy in favor of the establishment of the Court (Halley 2008) and the current controversies surrounding the ICC (Clarke, Knottnerous, and de Volder 2016), what does the Ongwen trial reveal about international gender justice? Has the ICC lived up to its promise of enlisting international law in the quest for greater gender justice?

As DeLaet (2018, this issue) and Baldez (2018, this issue) explore in their work, international law offers some promise to victims of mass human rights violations. In addition to women's rights violations being brought to the attention of international human rights bodies (CEDAW in particular), cases can reach international criminal courts and tribunals. Unlike the human rights regimes and monitoring mechanisms that are centered on the state and state action (DeLaet 2018, this issue) where governments engage in constructive dialogue with monitoring committees (Baldez 2018, this issue), international criminal law is focused on individual perpetrators – those most responsible as architects of atrocities or genocide. Thus, in addition to the issues raised by DeLaet and Baldez about the limits of international human rights law, international criminal law poses distinct challenges for gender justice (Ni Aoláin 2014). As Karen Engle (2018) argues, the 'dominant strategic response to sexual violence in conflict is increasingly penal in nature, often with an unspoken (and unproved) assumption that deterrence will result from bringing perpetrators to justice' (134). The limitations of criminal law include the dilemmas feminists identify in national jurisdictions (risks of revictimization of witness victims; reinforcing gendered and racist stereotypes; legitimizing the carceral state) as well as the particular global dynamics of international courts (geopolitics of the ICC; its distance from the communities in which the gender violence took place; and lack of meaningful reparations for survivors, to name a few). In this paper, I explore some of these limits as well as the potential of criminal law for victim survivors of crimes against humanity and war crimes. While I argue that international criminal trials do not offer meaningful restoration/healing nor comprehensive gender equality, they can be spaces of important meaning-making and documentation of the historical record. I think about the role of international criminal law and legal prosecution, therefore, as being about *spaces of justice*: the criminal trial can open up a space for public discourse, national memorialization, gender debates and claims for reparations and social repair.

International criminal law's reticence to address gendered crimes in post-World War II prosecutions has given way over the years to formal recognition and prosecution of several sexual- and gender-based crimes by contemporary international criminal courts and tribunals (Askin 2003, 288–303; 2004, 1; Mouthaan 2011, 777–781, 784–785; Campanaro 2001, 2559–2569). The recognition and progress in prosecuting gender crimes has been largely due to agitations by feminist scholars, practitioners and coalitions of nongovernmental organizations who have worked tirelessly to ensure accountability for victims of gender-based violence (Copelon 2000). The presence of female investigators and judges with expertise in gender issues also played a role in their sensitivity to evidence of gender violence and its subsequent prosecution by contemporary international tribunals and courts (Engle 2005, 781–784; Halley 2008; Mouthaan 2011, 782). This activism led to the first prosecution of and conviction for rape as a crime of genocide in international criminal law before the International Criminal Tribunal for Rwanda (ICTR) in the 1998 decision of *Prosecutor v. Akayesu*. The work of the international ad hoc and hybrid criminal tribunals – the ICTR, International Criminal Tribunal for the former Yugoslavia (ICTY), Special Court for Sierra Leone (SCSL) and the ICC – has brought substantial legal recognition to the practices of sexual- and gender-based violence, the recruitment of child soldiers and abduction of forced spouses in war.

Abduction for forced marriage in the conflict situations of Uganda and Sierra Leone[5] led to developments in international criminal law. The Special Court for Sierra Leone tried the offence of sexual slavery and also defined the crime of forced marriage for the first time in international law in the AFRC case in 2008.[6] While often referred to as sexual slavery, research and witness testimony before the international courts and tribunals make clear that the practice of forced conjugal association involves more than sexual servitudes (Bunting and Ikhimiukor 2018). The Rome Statute of the ICC codifies several gender-based violence offences in contrast to the enabling statutes of international criminal tribunals that preceded its establishment in 1998[7] (Kapur 2016, 74). The ICC and tribunals' jurisprudence on sexual- and gender-based crimes has led to advancements in the area of international criminal law. Over the past 20 years, through successive prosecution of gender-based crimes, the types of gendered harms recognized as crimes in international criminal law have expanded considerably. Adjudication of these crimes against humanity and war crimes also provides an important, yet limited, body of evidence of the experiences of the victims of these crimes.

The prosecution of sexual violence and gender-based crimes by international criminal courts and tribunals draws attention to these crimes committed across different conflict situations. In addition, the prosecution of sexual- and gender-based violence in international criminal law helps to place in context the lived realities of women and girls, inviting feminist inquiry into the connections and disruptions of gender inequalities and patriarchal practices between times of relative peace and armed conflict. From the testimonies of witnesses and victims given in proceedings as well as empirical work carried out in different conflict sites, a clearer understanding is garnered of the gendered nature of harms women and girls suffer as well as the roles they assume in armed conflict (Sankey 2016). As Doris Buss (2011) states,

> international criminal cases have generated substantial 'official' and scholarly knowledge about the gendered effects of conflict. The judgements and transcripts from international courts, such as for Rwanda, Yugoslavia, and Sierra Leone, provide a rich source of information on women's experience of conflict that compliments an equally productive stream of social-science research from within and outside the academy. Further, it is likely this explosion of scholarship on, and official recognition of gendered experiences of conflict, has influenced related developments in mainstreaming gender in post-conflict peace building. (414–415)

International criminal prosecution of these offences and jurisprudence to date, however, has simplistically cast males as perpetrators and females as victims of gender violence. The ICC, in its prosecution and recognition of gender-based crimes, has also largely addressed female victim survivors at the expense of exploring men's experiences of gender violence. This important limitation of international criminal law to date is explored below.

The ICC regime also encapsulates novel provisions absent in the statutes of the Yugoslavia and Rwanda Tribunals and the Special Court. The ICC statute codifies rights for victims of crime and for the first time creates a system of restorative justice in concert with the punitive nature of criminal proceedings. Under this enhanced role for victims within the international criminal justice system, victims of crimes including sexual- and gender-based violence have been given an opportunity to tell their story before the court, have their harms acknowledged and also be eligible for awards of reparations which the ICC may make.[8] It must be pointed out that not all victims of crimes are able to participate in proceedings and benefit from the ICC reparations regime. However, the Trust Fund for Victims[9] created under the ICC regime has in its earliest years addressed the plight of some victims in Uganda, providing psychosocial and medical treatment to help with injuries sustained from the LRA conflict.

> In light of the varied issues such as stigma, loss of sense of identity and lack of access to land bedeviling victims of wartime sexual violence and the children born of such relationships, the ICC offers hope for these victims and children. (Bunting and Ikhimiukor 2018, 351)

In this paper, I will explore what the prosecution of the crime of 'forced marriage' in war provokes and reveals in terms of the geopolitics and gender politics of international criminal law in Uganda and the region.[10] A critical analysis of the international and regional politics surrounding the ICC in Uganda would gesture toward more local, non-juridical solutions for social reparations in post-conflict Uganda; on the other hand, the gender politics that lead to a systemic lack of accountability for gender crimes in conflict situations gesture toward calls for criminal responsibility. In Uganda, as elsewhere, there is a robust discussion about the utility of international criminal law in post-conflict reconstruction. This paper presents the views of a number of former LRA abductees, along with academic commentary, on the gender politics of the Ongwen trial. I argue that, as with most complex problems, the answers should be grounded in multiple strategies that are reflexive and resist simplistic solutions. We ought to avoid the tendency to think of trials as solutions in themselves. Legal accountability, including the current trials before the ICC and International Crimes Division of the High Court of Uganda (Seelinger 2017), ought to be seen as opportunities for creating space for documenting survivors' narratives and needs in and outside the official proceedings (Bunting 2017) as well as laying the foundations for holistic socio-economic programming for reparations (Atim et al. 2017; Atim, Mazurana, and Marshak 2018).

Methods and context

The background empirical and archival research for this paper was conducted by an interdisciplinary team of researchers and includes over 250 interviews in five countries (Democratic Republic of Congo, Liberia, Rwanda, Sierra Leone and Uganda) with women who had experienced abduction and enslavement for forced marriage in war.[11] This data informs the general analysis in this essay. Using a standard interview question guide (developed collaboratively with the country team leads) and working with local community-based partners, researchers in Liberia interviewed 78 women in six communities in three districts in Nimba County, Liberia. Similarly, researchers in Uganda collected 48 interviews in Lango and Acholi sub-regions in northern Uganda (Atim et al. 2017). These interviews were translated, transcribed and analyzed. The interviews were conducted by our partners in teams of three in the local language and then translated in to French (in the case of the Congolese and Rwandan interviews) or English (for the remaining countries). The teams were very careful to work in private and secure locations, often in their offices or the participants' homes. In addition to these interviews, Ugandan journalist Gladys Oroma conducted four in-depth interviews in 2017 with LRA returnees (two men and two women), and I conducted supplementary interviews with civil society organization staff in February 2017 and May 2017.

The demographics of women and girls abducted by rebels varies a great deal across the five countries in our study: the average age of abduction of interviewees in Uganda was 13 years (Atim et al. 2017); in Rwanda the average age was 23; while in Liberia women were anywhere between 13 and 40 when they were abducted (CSiW interview statistics). The length of time spent in captivity also varied for the participants: in Rwanda the time in captivity was anywhere from 7 days to 15 years and in Sierra Leone it was from 2 days to 11 years while in Uganda the average time was 3.5 years. Finally, while I will focus on their experiences as 'spouses' in this paper, our results show that women, like men in rebel forces, had many roles including spies, fighters, porters and cooks. In Uganda, all the women interviewed reported that they were first trained to use a gun and fight. Many women were active combatants and many men were victims of sexual- and gender-based violence (Dolan 2018).[12] Abduction for the purposes of forced sexual and domestic labor was neither a uniform practice across these different countries nor *within* the LRA in Uganda.

The case of the LRA in Uganda, for example, stands out as a highly organized and particular rebel insurgent group. Women individually and collectively negotiated the constraints on their agency and consent in the context of captivity over many years (Amony 2015; Baines 2016; Kiconco 2018). The factors that were most important in their understanding of forced relations and capacity to resist included age (virginity and menstruation), familial and community participation, nature of violence, sexual exclusivity, the context of war, and lack of alternatives or imagined futures (Atim et al. 2017). This analysis makes clear that there is both a complex myriad of gendered experiences and agency to challenge their position in these coercive relationships.

Gender politics of international law

As earlier stated, the recognition of gender crimes has come a long way in international criminal law. Since the silences of early laws of war, testimony from victim survivors and advocacy by feminists have helped to draw attention to sexual violence and gender-based crimes and led to their subsequent prosecution. The first international criminal tribunal to find rape as a tool of genocide was the Rwanda Tribunal in the *Akayesu* decision of 1998.[13] The initial indictments against Akayesu did not include charges of rape. After witnesses testified about sexual- and gender-based violence during the genocide, and an amicus brief was filed calling for an amendment to the indictment, the Prosecutor did so in June 1997.[14] Binaifer Nowrojee had investigated and written the Human Rights Watch report 'Shattered Lives' (1996) that exposed the widespread sexual violence during the 1994 Rwandan genocide. She was called as an expert witness by the Prosecutor in the Akayesu case and testified at the ICTR.

In 2005, Binaifer Nowrojee reflected on her work with Rwandan genocide survivors. Returning to women who had provided evidence to ICTR investigators and witnesses who testified in Arusha, she asked them about their motives and reflections on the ICTR proceedings. She writes,

> when asked what they want from the international tribunal [ICTR], Rwandan women above all mention the law: they say they are looking for public acknowledgement of the crimes committed against them. They want the record to show that they were subjected to horrific sexual violence at the hands of those who instigated and carried out genocide.
>
> [...] Rwandan women express deep concern that the ICTR is not fully and properly prosecuting the crimes that occurred against them; that the court is not acknowledging their pain, *not telling their story*, not enshrining their experience of the genocide. Astonishingly, punishment and vengeance were the least articulated reasons for why Rwandan women wanted and valued the ICTR prosecution of rape. (Nowrojee 2005, 4)

This is an important echo of Holly Porter's (2016) discussion of social harmony versus punishment, and a reminder that calls for prosecution do not necessarily equate with calls for punishment – in the case of the Rwandan genocide, from Nowrojee's findings, women were calling for a more complete historical record of the genocide. As Porter (2016) argues, in Acholi culture the focus is on 'restoration of social harmony' not punishment:

> the need for social harmony is not exclusive of, but typically trumps, the desire for punishment. Further, I suggest that the determination of whether or not punishment poses a challenge to social harmony is also related to the position and moral jurisdiction of those who mete out the punishment as well as the wrongdoer'. (14)

While international law scholars have celebrated the recognition of gender crimes in international law, others have developed important critiques. There are many exclusions and silences. As will be discussed below, some dimensions of sexual violence remain unspeakable or very difficult to speak. Think of that which cannot be said. Thus, we have a call to end impunity for gender-based violence in conflict situations and a critique of the justice systems put in place to end impunity. Engaging with both of these lines of inquiry is important for those seeking to promote gender justice.

In so far as international courts and tribunals are seen to document and acknowledge the scope of harms suffered by victims of mass human rights violations and war, victim survivors rightly expect some reflection of their experiences. The trials before the International Criminal Tribunal for Rwanda and the ICC remind us that international criminal law is meant to challenge cultures of impunity and hold accountable those most responsible for crimes of genocide, crimes against humanity and war crimes. Justice should be seen to be done in the eyes of the communities affected. But for there to be accountability, practices must be considered a war crime or a crime against humanity. With gender violence, many harms women and men experienced in conflict situations were not considered crimes of international law until recently. This recognition is reflected in several charges of gender-based crimes contained in indictments before the

ICC. More particularly, the Ongwen trial is a product of that evolution; the prosecutor of the ICC, in an amended charge, included several counts of gender-based crimes.

We see this dynamic playing out in Uganda for both the harms of enslavement for forced marriage as well as sexual- and gender-based violence against men (Dolan 2018). Even after all the 'lessons' that investigators and prosecutors were to have learned by the mid-2000s from the earlier trials of sexual violence charges before the International Criminal Tribunal for Rwanda and the Special Court for Sierra Leone, indictments for sexual- and gender-based violence that occurred in the Uganda conflict came late in the Ongwen case. Indeed, it was only after pressure from civil society organizations that indictments for gender violence, including forced marriage, were added to the list of charges against Dominic Ongwen. No such indictments were added to address sexual violence against men and boys (*International Justice Monitor*, 24 April 2018). In the face of such exclusion and silence, survivors' groups call for the documentation of and accountability for sexual- and gender-based violence at all levels of justice. Chris Dolan spoke to this silence:

> The request to reconsider the scope of the charges to include sexual violence against men and boys within the LRA gave the judges of the ICC a golden opportunity to further demonstrate the progressive and inclusive potential of the Rome Statute's provisions on Sexual Violence, and an opportunity, through the testimonies, to create a more truthful and accurate account of sexual violence that occurred within the LRA. Instead, they chose to pass up that opportunity. Their decision to exclude these particular late disclosures suggests a lack of understanding of how the process of disclosure works when it comes to highly stigmatizing issues of this kind; by further entrenching the disincentives to disclosure by male victims, the judges' decision also entrenches impunity for crimes of sexual violence committed against men and thus undermines the very purpose of the ICC, namely the ending of impunity. (Quoted in *International Justice Monitor*, 24 April 2018)[15]

Let us now return to the lives of Ugandan survivors of conflict violence and the gendered forms of harm they experienced in the conflict between the LRA and the Government of Uganda. Beatrice Ocwee was abducted at age 15 in 1995 in northern Uganda. She returned in 2002. In the following excerpt from her interview, she describes how she was assigned to a high-ranking commander of the LRA:

> During the day there was nothing which happened but in the evening after we had moved from that and it was at night, it was at around 6 pm when we started to cook and after we have eaten at around 8 pm, then Odhiambo sent his escort to come and take me to him, then the escort came and took me to him, he started asking me if I had known what took me there, I told him I did not know, and he told me that starting from that day to date I would be his wife, he asked me if I had understood, but I kept quiet. But he reiterated that even if I kept quiet I was his wife. For me, I did not know what it meant to be a wife because when was abducted I had not started seeing my menstrual period. (Interview with Gladys Oroma, Uganda, September 2017)

The man who took Beatrice Ocwee as his captive 'wife' was Okot Odhiambo, one of the five LRA Commanders indicted by the ICC in 2005. (He has since died.) She was the second 'wife' in Odhiambo's compound, she said, where there were eventually seven women. She was not treated well by Odhiambo since she refused his sexual advances; she was also not treated well by the senior 'wife', Margaret, in the household. Trained to use a gun, Beatrice says Odhiambo sent her on four occasions to fight in active battle as punishment for 'being so rebellious throughout my life there with him over the issue of sex. He always forced me into sleeping with him' (Interview with Gladys

Oroma, Uganda September 2017). For Beatrice, she said it was important that LRA commanders face justice. But she also insists that the Ugandan government be held accountable and compensate those abducted:

> I think government is shielding themselves. It was the negligence of government that led to my abduction because they never protected me.
> Their negligence led to my abduction and which made to be raped, and government is running away from this by taking these fighters to ICC. (Interview with Gladys Oroma, Uganda, September 2017)

The trials of Dominic Ongwen at the ICC and Thomas Kwoyelo before the International Crimes Division of the High Court of Uganda, as one staff from the Refugee Law Project states, have opened up space for debates about marriage, violence and the nature of gender relations in the war (Fred Ngomokwer, Interview with Bunting, Uganda, May 2017). Importantly, Refugee Law Project has been engaged in documenting the violations committed against men, including their experiences of sexual violence, witnessing gender violence against women, being forced into relations with women, torture and other deprivations. In a recent Summer Institute CSiW co-hosted with Refugee Law Project in Kampala, men and women exchanged information about the range of relationships and violence that occurred over years in captivity with the LRA. This work both challenges the simplistic gender assumptions in this area and supports the survivors in their own advocacy for reparations. Nonetheless, the official legal narrative in the Ongwen trial did not include testimony from male victims.

The narratives of victims-survivors often reflected their aspirations and expectations from government. For example, Beatrice Ocwee, an LRA returnee, sums up in her own words her expectations from the Ugandan government below.

> How do you think you can get justice from what happened to you?:
> I think my future was ruined, for me to get justice, my ruined future must be compensated.
> How do you want it to be compensated?:
> I should be paid a big amount, on a month basis for ten years, so this will rehabilitate my life and restore hope in me, this is similar to healing a sickness, so that the anger, how struggle to pay children to school, getting food stuff and clothing and renting.
> If I had stayed home, and now my friends we were together in school are now working, I would have been like them, I would not be suffering like this, I would pull money and pay my children at school, I will take my children to good hospital, I would buy food for my children, I would dress my children well and I would be having my piece of land because my friends who were at home, have now set up their buildings and are not renting, but for me every morning I wake up I will be thinking where to begin from and what to eat, for example, last week we ate twice in the whole week with my children, this one hurts the wounds that have started healing and I think this should be done to heal the wounds we got during the war. (Interview with Gladys Oroma, Uganda, September 2017)

Geopolitics of international criminal law in Uganda

When 'crafting' Dominic Ongwen as a perpetrator of crimes against humanity, the ICC lands squarely on the issues of child soldiering, forced conjugal association, command responsibility, and the role of criminal prosecutions in bringing about lasting peace. The trial also comes at a moment of heightened controversy about the legitimacy of the ICC on the African continent (Mills and Bloomfield 2017; Olugbo 2014; Ssenyonjo 2013;

Eberechi 2011). The Office of the Prosecutor has been criticized for its almost singular focus on African perpetrators and some governments have responded with threats to withdraw their membership or cooperation with the ICC (*BBC News* 1 February 2017; Ssenyonjo 2018, 2017; Du Plessis and Mettraux 2017). While these debates/contestations surrounding the ICC and its engagement in Africa have been explored extensively by others (Clarke, Knottnerous, and de Volder 2016), they are the important backdrop against which the Ongwen trial unfolds (http://iccforum.com/africa). As Kamari Clarke argues,

> Two hundred years after the British abolished their slave trade (1807), it is now the language of 'humanitarianism' that embodies the international discourses around human entitlements to life… This new internationalized form of governance is subtler than earlier colonial forms yet represents a more tragic set of realities. International institutions work through the law to craft 'victims' and 'perpetrators' (or, indeed 'victim-perpetrators') within the parameters of legal science … to perform them, yielding new subjects through which humanitarianism is further legitimized. (2009, 110)

As many people in Uganda note – and as revealed in our research and in the public debates – Dominic Ongwen was abducted by the LRA as a child, reportedly at the age of 10. He rose through the ranks quickly and ultimately became one of the top Commanders in the LRA under the leadership of Joseph Kony. While Ongwen is not charged for acts committed when he was under the age of 18 or before the establishment of the ICC, his initial abduction remains an important fact in the politics of his trial. Ongwen is alleged to have taken four women as wives and fathered 11 children (*International Justice Monitor*, 13 December 2017). Ongwen spent a dozen years in the LRA (1990–2013) and did not surrender after the failed Juba peace talks in 2008. Rather, Ongwen was captured/surrendered in the Central African Republic in 2013. He was then handed over to American forces and transferred in January 2015 to The Hague.[16]

When asked by journalist Gladys Oroma (2017) 'What is your take on the indictment of some top LRA commanders by the International Criminal Court, ICC?', Akena Samuel, who was abducted by the LRA at the age of 11, replied:

> I do think for example on Dominic Ongwen who is now before ICC, it was not his making or bad things which he has done, and I find it useless to take him before ICC, he would have benefited from Amnesty as it was given to us, he was abducted when he was still young and he was still in primary school and the bad things he did was the LRA policy, and this will discourage so many rebels to return. (Interview, Uganda, October 2017)

Another LRA abductee, Patrick Lumumba, disagrees:

> In Uganda, a child is person below the age of 17, if he did something while you are above 18 years, and that is a crime, he should be punished that what I can say, people who commit crimes should be punished to make them change not only but to make people not to do such thing, if you are not punished, people would continue commit crimes with impunity, that why we have prison cells, like in Gulu, we have government prison, if you commit a crime they take you there for two, three months, you are not sent there to be killed but to make you learn and should not do similar crime again. (Interview with Gladys Oroma, Uganda, October 2017)

Dominic Ongwen is himself charged with the conscription and use of children under the age of 15 in active hostilities in the Sinai Brigade of the LRA against civilian populations and the Ugandan Peoples Defence Force (UPDF). Nonetheless, rather than a two-dimensional portrait of a perpetrator, Ongwen presents the complexities of victim/perpetrators who could be extended the same amnesty from government, the same forgiveness from community members, as other returning LRA insurgents. Who then ought to be held accountable for the violence of the LRA, others might ask? Joseph Kony alone?

Ten years after the collapse of the Juba peace talks, the role of the ICC in social reconstruction in Uganda remains controversial. LRA returnee, Patrick Lumumba, articulates this sense of frustration and argues that the ICC Prosecutor acted 'prematurely':

> Dominic Ongwen is now under ICC, if he is found guilty he should be sentenced accordingly and if he is found not guilty, should come home and stay with the community that what I can say about ICC, I know the issue of ICC would proceed like that, and I *see the ICC did their thing prematurely, they would have delayed the process so that other top LRA commanders return because this will make them not come even if they want to come back home,* it will bring question mark they still have alternative idea to do something differently. (Interview with Gladys Oroma, Uganda, 2017)

Patrick Lumumba nonetheless also stakes out a place in between punishment and social restoration (Porter 2016). Beatrice Ocwee too thinks that Ongwen should be tried for the crimes he committed: 'They should face the law, if they not be found guilty then they would be lucky, there I would have nothing to say about them' (Interview with Gladys Oroma, Uganda, September 2017). While there has been ample time for the Office of the Prosecutor to work with affected communities and for victim communities to participate in the process (since the ICC intervention from 2005), the 'moral jurisdiction' of the Office of the Prosecutor and the ICC is fraught and many within northern Uganda remain skeptical about punishment as a means to justice. This leads logically to the question of what is justice/gender justice or how do victims conceptualize justice and how does this conceptualization fit within the ICC strategy and prosecution of crimes generally.

A very similar debate played out almost a decade earlier in Sierra Leone when the hybrid court, the Special Court for Sierra Leone (SCSL), indicted Issa Sesay of the Revolutionary United Front (RUF) for crimes against humanity including the crime of forced marriage as an 'other inhumane act'. In his interview for the 2010 documentary *War Don Don,*[17] Sesay says he understands that someone has to be held responsible and he understands the international criminal law process. He goes on the ask, however, why he should be that person in the docket? He negotiated the laying down of arms and delivered his troops to civilian life. He, too, was abducted and groomed as a child. Why should he now be charged, he asks, with crimes against humanity and sentenced to life in prison? Sesay, like Ongwen, poses one of the key dilemmas of criminal law: how is a system premised on individual accountability to respond to violence that was structurally and historically produced? How and why are individuals to be held responsible for the past and the future of such wide-scale violence? These questions when placed in context of the ICC and its prosecution strategy illuminate the discussion. Many of these conflicts have given rise to wide-scale atrocities and different perpetrators with varying degrees of culpability. The ICC however seeks to punish those with the greatest responsibility.

Finally, we ought to ask whether international criminal law, as currently pursued in the Ongwen trial in The Hague, can bring about or contribute to meaningful justice in contemporary Uganda. This question is apt in light of the allegations of bias and selective prosecutions directed at the ICC's focus and prosecution of LRA crimes in

Uganda while ignoring the crimes committed by members of the UPDF. Allegations of victors' justice directed at the ICC are one that has been made out against international criminal tribunals since the World War II. While more than one militia or rebel group was indicted by the SCSL in Sierra Leone, the Ugandan government forces have not been indicted by the ICC for any war crimes and crimes against humanity for their part in the conflict. Further, the Ugandan government has not been held responsible for failing to protect their citizens nor for the conditions and violence in the internally displaced persons camps (Dolan 2009). Lily Aromo, who spent 10 years in LRA captivity, articulated this well in her response to a question about the amnesty certificates:

> They told us that they took our photo to show that they have forgiven us because of the war that we fought from the bush. *Then one day we sat down and asked our self; how do they say they have forgiven us yet we are the one to forgive the government for not taking care of us from captivity? We were debating because the government should be the one to come to us and apologize to us they did not take good care of you people that is why they abducted you.* So how can we be forgiven? But they are saying they have forgiven us; to that is not right; we also complains to the government it is the government to come and apologize to us. They are the one take care of us so that we are not being abducted. Like me they have spoilt my education and my future as a result of being in captivity in the bush for. I would be a minister. But now where do I start from. You have stayed in the bush for over 10 years, you have even produced children. All these are government mistake of not take care of her citizens. (Emphasis added) (Interview with Gladys Oroma, Uganda, 2017)[18]

A number of people interviewed mentioned that there was extensive violence by Ugandan government forces that has not been acknowledged. This includes sexual violence. Women noted that one of their fears in escaping was that they would be raped by government military soldiers. Beatrice Ocwee corroborates these stories:

> Yes, it happened on those who were escaping. When we came back home, we found it happened to people who escaped before us, like it happened to one of the ladies we come from the same place and who escaped in 1998, it was government forces who received her, she was raped and infected with disease, but she was not killed, she said every soldier she got there slept with her. (Interview with Gladys Oroma, Uganda, September 2017)

Beini Ye, an international criminal lawyer formerly with REDRESS (an organization based in the United Kingdom which works with victims of torture and other serious crimes) also noted that without some accountability for the violations perpetrated by the Ugandan military, many victims of conflict-related violence in Uganda will not have any access to reparations. She noted,

> We have to bear in mind that both trials, at the national (Kweyelo) and international level (Ongwen) … only talk about the crimes of the LRA. Therefore, only the victims of the LRA will only have a chance to speak, and to participate, and to seek reparations. There are many victims who have experienced rape and other forms of sexual violence at the hands of the government army, military … Those, at this point, are fully excluded from this justice process. And I think this deserves more attention. (Interview with Bunting, Skype, October 2017)

It is not only the economics of reparations for victims that deserves attention, Dubravka Zarkov argues (2018). Zarkov calls for analytical attention to the:

> global neoliberal economy and its nexus with militarism and their gendered effects at home and abroad [...] there is still no substantial feminist scholarship of war economies, the way it exists in critical mainstream war studies. (2018, 29)

Akena Samuel also expresses trepidation and confusion about the amnesty certificates issued to LRA returnees in light of the ongoing trials of Dominic Ongwen and Thomas Kwoyelo. Thomas Kwoyelo rose to the rank of colonel in the LRA and is on trial for crimes against humanity in the International Crimes Division of the High Court of Uganda after being charged with 93 counts under the Uganda Penal Code in 2009. Kwoyelo applied for amnesty in 2010: 'After a long and controversial procedural background in which the Supreme Court of Uganda ultimately denied his eligibility for amnesty' in 2015, his trial started in the International Crimes Division in 2017 (Seelinger 2017, 21). Some are concerned that they too may be put on trial for crimes committed during the conflict:

> Q: What should be done to allay such fear, do you think that Amnesty certificates should be returned or government should come out to tell people what amnesty is all about?:
> A: I think the certificate should not be returned and government should come out openly to tell us that people who were abducted and have got amnesty were due to their negligence to protect those were abducted and they should come out to tell us that those who have got amnesty certificates shall not crucified because we have seen Dominic Ongwen, the top LRA commanders are being tried, so the junior staff like us are fearing that it will come down to them, so it needs government to come out clearly for instance like support which world vision or Amnesty where from different organizations but government on their own never came out with a program for us who are the victims of the war; it was, World Vision, GUSCO, etc. who were giving us support. (Akena Samuel, Interview with Gladys Oroma, Uganda, 2017)

This section has argued that four issues are important to consider in the geopolitics of the Dominic Ongwen case in Uganda and internationally: the politics of responsibility for accused who were abducted as children; the impact of criminal prosecutions on peace negotiations during ongoing conflict; local cultural expectations of justice and reparations; and finally, selective prosecutions that exclude indictments for UPDF and government actions. I chose to highlight these dimensions of the politics of the Dominic Ongwen trial, but they take place in the context of broader debates about the ICC in Africa, feminist critiques of international criminal law and critical scholarship that questions a 'geopolitically informed worldview that represents the Western model of capitalist, neoliberal economy as a "peace economy", disconnected from "war economies" elsewhere' (Zarkov 2018, 29).

Conclusions

In this article I have discussed the case of Dominic Ongwen currently before the ICC as the central story around which I explore issues of post-conflict rebuilding, accountability, historical record/memorialization and personal relationships. I argued that while, at first glance, the geopolitics and gender politics may pull in different directions – suggesting different approaches to international justice and local reparations – on closer examination Ongwen demonstrates that calls for criminal accountability are usually paired with nuanced calls for justice beyond punishment. Or put another way, legal solutions are rarely proposed in isolation of more complex understandings of the geopolitics and gender politics in which the cases take place.

This paper presented the perceptions of victim survivors and community members in northern Uganda about the utility and efficacy of the international criminal proceedings to redress conflict-related harms, including sexual violence and gender-based crimes. I tack back and forth between the global politics and controversies related to the ICC and the micro-level politics of rebuilding a life in post-conflict Uganda. Gender figures prominently in both the geopolitics and the local controversies of international criminal law. In some ways the geopolitics and gender politics pull in different directions, or put another way as Doris Buss argues, the

> criminal law has always been a contradictory site for feminist activism. […] The international order performed through criminal law may do little to address the predicates of mass atrocity and the systemic forms of inequality and violence that motivate, at least in part, feminist engagement with international criminal law. (Buss 2011, 415, 423)

Given the long history of silence surrounding male victims of sexual and gender violence in war, for example, legal proceedings can be one venue to gather and validate the experience of male victims. Thus, I argue that so long as we do not expect too much from law, or imagine law too narrowly, then we may see the potential in a holistic approach where law forms one part of post-conflict rebuilding. Let us conclude with Patrick Lumumba who says 'forgiveness is the best justice':

> I think these people should be forgiven, because forgiveness brings happiness and hope, for instance there are some people who we know they are the one who killed your sisters, mother when you were being abducted but you met them at World Vision, and they told us to forgive them because if not because of the people would have fought at World Vision which would have been so bad. *Forgiveness is the best justice to your friends, not only about the war, if anybody does something wrong to you, you must think twice and you could forgive such a person so that lives should continue* because that is not the beginning or the end, the end is when you die, if you have been living good lives, when you die, you either go to heaven or hell. (Interview with Gladys Oroma, Uganda, 2017)

Notes

1. Interview by Gladys Oroma, Gulu Uganda. For Oroma's four-part series 'Uganda' see Life of the Law podcast January and February 2018 www.lifeofthelaw.org.
2. ICC, Press Release: President of Uganda refers situation concerning the Lord's Resistance Army (LRA) to the ICC ICC-20041029-44.
3. *Joseph Kony*, ICC-02/04-01/05, 8 July 2005; *Vincent Otti*, ICC-02-04, 8 July 2005; *Okot Odhiambo*, ICC-02-04, 8 July 2005; *Dominic Ongwen*, ICC-02-04, 8 July 2005 and *Raskia Lukwiya* ICC-02/04-01/05, 8 July 2005.
4. ICC, *The Prosecutor v. Dominic Ongwen* ICC-02/04-01/15.
5. The 2014 abduction of over 200 girls from their school in Chibok in northern Nigeria by Boko Haram also included reports that they were forced to be 'wives' to the insurgents bringing substantial popular attention to the phenomenon. There are ongoing trials against Boko Haram insurgents ongoing in Nigeria.
6. *Prosecutor* v. *Brima, Kamara & Kanu*, (*AFRC* Trial Judgment), 20 June 2007, Trial Judgment, Case No. SCSL-04–16-T; *Prosecutor* v. *Brima, Kamara* & *Kanu*, (*AFRC* Appeal Judgment), 22 February 2008, Appeals Judgment, Case No. SCSL-04–16-A.

7. Rome Statute of the International Criminal Court, July 17 1998, 2187 UNTS, 90, Articles 7(1), 8(2)(b)(xxii)) and 8(2)(e)(vi).
8. Rome Statute of the International Criminal Court, July 17 1998, 2187 UNTS, 90, Articles 68 and 75.
9. Rome Statute of the International Criminal Court, July 17 1998, 2187 UNTS, 90, Article 79.
10. For a discussion of the legal contours and expressive function of the crimes against humanity of enslavement, sexual slavery, conjugal slavery and the other inhumane act of forced marriage see: Bunting and Ikhimuikor (2018).
11. In 2017, our partner in Nigeria (dRPC) conducted over 100 interviews with young women and community members affected by the Boko Haram insurgency in northeast Nigeria. These interviews are in the process of being analyzed by the Nigerian team.
12. The interviews with women were conducted as part of the previous SSHRC-funded project. The SSHRC Partnership project includes as one of its research themes the experiences of men and boys who were subjected to gender violence, including sexual violence. The range of harms, but also range of relations in coercive settings, are now being documented. See: Csiw-ectg.org.
13. *The Prosecutor v Jean-Paul Akayesu*, 2 September 1998, Trial Judgment, Case No. ICTR-96-4-T.
14. For a documentary film on the witnesses at the ICTR, the amicus brief, and advocacy of Rwandan women, see, 'The Uncondemned' (2016), by Michelle Mitchell and Nick Louvel.
15. Lino Owor Ogora, 'Sexual Violence against Men and Boys and its Relevance to the Trial of Dominic Ongwen', International Justice Monitor, 24 April 2018. Accessed: https://www.ijmonitor.org/2018/04/sexual-violence-against-men-and-boys-and-its-relevance-to-the-trial-of-dominic-ongwen/.
16. For details of the ICC trial see https://www.icc-cpi.int/uganda/ongwen.
17. 'War Don Don: The war is over, a trial begins' DVD 2010 (See clip at 3:45). By Rebecca Richman Cohen, distributed in Canada by Mongrel Media (Toronto). *Prosecutor* v. *Sesay, Kallon & Gbao*, (*RUF* Trial Judgment), 2 March 2009, Trial Judgment, Case No. SCSL-04–15-T, Judgment; *Prosecutor* v. *Sesay, Kallon & Gbao*, (*RUF* Appeal Judgment), 26 October 2009, Appeals Judgment, Case No. SCSL-04-15-A.
18. Alim Santa, whose three children were abducted and never returned, agrees: 'we need some help like I said before that each household should be compensated. That will go a long way in relieving our sorrows because the dead can't come back even those still in captivity it is not easy for them to return even if they are still alive and there is no way the president can bring them back and I know that if they have land there they will end up there. I just want the president to help us' (September 2017, Gulu Uganda).

Acknowledgments

Generous funding support from SSHRC Partnership grant (895-2015-1006) and Drake University. Fabulous editors Renee Cramer and Debra L. DeLaet. Special thanks to our CSiW Postdoctoral Fellow Izevbuwa Ikhimiukor for helping me bring this piece to the finish line. Thanks to Teddy Atim, Rosaline Mcarthy, Godelième Mukasarasi, and Julienne Lusenge, *Conjugal Slavery in War Partnership*; and Emily Lockhart, Katrin Roots and Heather Tasker, *Graduate Program in Socio-Legal Studies*.

Disclosure statement

No potential conflict of interest was reported by the author.

Funding

This study was supported by SSHRC Partnership grant (895-2015-1006).

References

Amony, E. 2015. *I Am Evelyn Amony: Life in and after the LRA*. Madison, WI: University of Wisconsin Press.

Aoláin, F. N. 2014. "Gendered Harms and Their Interface with International Criminal Law." *International Feminist Journal of Politics* 16 (4): 622–646. doi:10.1080/14616742.2014.952126.

Askin, K. 2003. "Prosecuting Wartime Rape and Other Gender-Related Crimes under International Law: Extraordinary Advances, Enduring Obstacles." *Berkeley Journal of International Law* 21: 288.

Askin, K. 2004. "A Decade of the Development of Gender Crimes in International Courts and Tribunals: 1993 to 2003." *Human Rights Brief* 11: 3.

Atim, T., D. Mazurana, and Marshak. 2018. "Women Survivors and Their Children Born of Wartime Sexual Violence in Northern Uganda." *Disasters* 42 (S1): S61S78. doi:10.1111/disa.12275.

Atim, T., G. Acan, J. Etap, and A. Bunting. 2017. *Uganda Country Report on Forced Marriage Inside the LRA*. Toronto: Conjugal Slavery in War Partnership. Available http://csiw-ectg.org/wp-content/uploads/2018/04/CSIW-UgandaCountryreport.pdf

Baines, E. 2016. *Buried in the Heart: Women, Complex Victimhood and the War in Northern Uganda*. Cambridge: Cambridge University Press.

Baldez, L. 2018. "What's at Stake in the Treaty Reporting Process? Cuba and the United Nations' Convention on Women's Rights." *Global Discourse*. doi:10.1080/23269995.2018.1520009

Bunting, A. 2017. "Narrating Wartime Enslavement, Forced Marriage and Modern Slavery." In *Contemporary Slavery: Popular Rhetoric and Political Practice*, edited by A. Bunting and J. Quirk, 129–157. Vancouver: University of British Columbia Press, Law & Society Series, 2017.

Bunting, A., and I. Ikhimiukor. 2018. "The Expressive Nature of Law: What We Learn from Conjugal Slavery to Forced Marriage in International Criminal Law." *International Criminal Law Review* 18: 331–353. doi:10.1163/15718123-01802004.

Buss, D. 2011. "Performing Legal Order: Some Feminist Thoughts on International Criminal Law." *International Criminal Law Review* 11: 409–423. doi:10.1163/157181211X576339.

Campanaro, J. 2001. "Women, War, and International Law: The Historical Treatment of Gender-Based War Crimes." *Georgia Law Journal* 89: 2557.

Clarke, K.M. 2009. *Fictions of Justice: The International Criminal Court and the Challenge of Legal Pluralism in Sub-Saharan Africa*. New York: Cambridge University Press.

Clarke, K. M., A. Knottnerous, and E. de Volder, eds. 2016. *Africa and the ICC: Perceptions of Justice*. Cambridge: Cambridge University Press.

DeLaet, D. 2018. "Lost in Legation: The Gap between Rhetoric and Reality in International Human Rights Law Governing Women's Rights." *Global Discourse*. doi:10.1080/23269995.2018.1520006

Dolan, C. 2009. *Social Torture: The Case of Northern Uganda 1986-2006*. New York/Oxford: Berghahn Books.

Dolan, C. 2018. "Victims Who are Men." In *The Oxford Handbook of Gender and Conflict*, edited by N. Aoláin, N. C. Fionnuala, D. F. Haynes, and N. Valji, 86–102. New York: Oxford University Press.

Du Plessis, M., and G. Mettraux. 2017. "South Africa's Failed Withdrawal from the Rome Statute Politics, Law, and Judicial Accountability." *Journal of International Criminal Justice* 15: 361–370. doi:10.1093/jicj/mqx015.

Eberechi, I. 2011. "'Rounding up the Usual Suspects': Exclusion, Selectivity, and Impunity in the Enforcement of International Criminal Justice and the African Union's Emerging Resistance." *African Journal of Legal Studies* 4: 51–84. doi:10.1163/170873811X567970.

Engle, K. 2005. "Feminism and Its (Dis)Contents: Criminalizing Wartime Rape in Bosnia and Herzegovina." *The American Journal of International Law* 99 (4): 778–816. doi:10.2307/3396669.

Engle, K. 2018. "A Genealogy of the Centrality of Sexual Violence to Gender and Conflict." In *The Oxford Handbook of Gender and Conflict*, edited by N. Aoláin, N. C. Fionnuala, D. F. Haynes, and N. Valji, 132–144. New York: Oxford University Press.

Halley, J. 2008. "Rape at Rome: Feminist Interventions in the Criminalization of Sex-Related Violence in Positive International Criminal Law." *Michigan Journal of International Law* 30: 1.

Kapur, A. 2016. "The Value of International-National Interactions and Norm Interpretations in Catalysing National Prosecutions of Sexual Violence." *Oñati Socio-Legal Series [Online]* 6 (1): 62–90.

Kiconco, A. 2018. “Marriage for the ‘New Woman’ from the Lord’s Resistance Army: Experiences of Female Ex-Abductees in Acholi Regions of Uganda”. 68 Women’s Studies International Forum. 65–74. doi:10.1016/j.wsif.2018.02.008.

Mills, K., and A. Bloomfield. 2017. “African Resistance to the International Criminal Court: Halting the Advance of the Anti-Impunity Norm.” *Review of International Studies* 44 (1): 101–127. doi:10.1017/S0260210517000407.

Mouthaan, S. 2011. “The Prosecution of Gender-Based Crimes at the ICC: Challenges and Opportunities.” *International Criminal Law Review* 11: 775–802. doi:10.1163/157181211X587184.

Nowrojee, B. 2005. *“Your Justice Is Too Slow”: Will the ICTR Fail Rwanda’s Rape Victims? Gender Equality: Striving for Justice in an Unequal World*. United Nation Research Institute for Social Development

Olugbo, B. 2014. “The African Union, the United Nations Security Council, and the Politicisation of International Criminal Justice in Africa.” *African Journal of Legal Studies* 7 (3): 351–379. doi:10.1163/17087384-12342051.

Porter, H. 2016. *After Rape: Violence, Justice and Social Harmony in Uganda*. Cambridge: Cambridge University Press.

Press Release President of Uganda refers situation concerning the Lord’s Resistance Army (LRA) to the ICC ICC-20041029-44

Prosecutor v. *Brima, Kamara & Kanu*, (*AFRC* Trial Judgment), 20 June 2007, Trial Judgment, Case No. SCSL-04-16-T; *Prosecutor* v. *Brima, Kamara & Kanu*, (*AFRC* Appeal Judgment), 22 February 2008, Appeals Judgment, Case No. SCSL-04-16-A

Rome Statute of the International Criminal Court, July 17 1998, 2187 UNTS, 90, Articles 7 (1),8 (2)(b)(xxii)),8 (2)(e)(vi);68, 75 and 79.

Sankey, D. 2016. “Recognition of Gendered Experiences of Harm at the Extraordinary Chambers in the Courts of Cambodia: The Promise and the Pitfalls.” *Feminist Legal Studies* 24: 7–27. doi:10.1007/s10691-016-9309-9.

Seelinger, K. T. 2017. “Uganda’s Case of Thomas Kwoyelo: Customary International Law on Trial.” *California Law Review* 8: 19–39.

Ssenyonjo, M. 2013. “The Rise of the African Union Opposition to the International Criminal Court’s Investigations and Prosecutions of African Leaders.” *International Criminal Law Review* 13: 385–428. doi:10.1163/15718123-01302002.

Ssenyonjo, M. 2017. “African States Failed Withdrawal from the Rome Statute of the International Criminal Court: From Withdrawal Notifications to Constructive Engagement.” *International Criminal Law Review* 17: 749–802. doi:10.1163/15718123-01705003.

Ssenyonjo, M. 2018. “State Withdrawal Notifications from the Rome Statute of the International Criminal Court: South Africa, Burundi and the Gambia.” *Criminal Law Forum* 29: 63–119. doi:10.1007/s10609-017-9321-z.

The Prosecutor v Jean-Paul Akayesu, 2 September 1998, Trial Judgment, Case No. ICTR-96-4-T.

The Prosecutor v. Dominic Ongwen ICC-02/04-01/15.

Zarkov, D. 2018. “From Women and War to Gender and Conflict? Feminist Trajectories.” In *The Oxford Handbook of Gender and Conflict*, edited by N. Aoláin, N. C. Fionnuala, D. F. Haynes, and N. Valji, 17–34. New York: Oxford University Press.

Spaces of international gender justice: a reply to Baldez and DeLaet

Annie Bunting

ABSTRACT

In assessing the effectiveness of international human rights law to achieve meaningful gender equality, Lisa Baldez and Debra DeLaet offer two complementary yet different case studies. De Laet argues that despite the rhetoric and promise of international women's rights law, such codification has yet to achieve 'systemic progress' to address gender inequality. DeLaet concludes that progress is most often attributable to national law reform and enforcement rather than global legalism. Picking up on the importance of national context, Baldez comes to a different conclusion in examining the case of Cuba's submissions to Convention on the Elimination of All Forms of Discrimination Against Women. Both papers point not only to the limitations and potential of international law but also to the limitations of feminist strategies that emphasize law reform at the exclusion of other non-juridical strategies for social change. As I read the papers together, I am reminded of the need to see global legal strategies as embedded in and alongside other strategies for social change. I argue that, despite its frailties, international law remains a useful resource for national or grass-roots feminist strategies for positive social change.

This is a reply to:

Baldez, L. 2018. "What's at Stake in the Treaty Reporting Process? Cuba and the United Nations' Convention on Women's Rights." *Global Discourse*. DOI: 10.1080/23269995.2018.1520009

and

DeLaet, D. 2018. "Lost in Legation: The Gap Between Rhetoric and Reality in International Human Rights Law Governing Women's Rights." *Global Discourse. DOI*: 10.1080/23269995.2018.1520006

The articles in the Gender, Women's Rights and International Law cluster reflect the healthy feminist debates about the utility of international law, and indeed the efficacy of law in general, to redress gender inequality and gender violence. Much of the debate rests not only on where the strategic emphasis is placed – on legal strategies or extra-legal ones, at the local, national or international scale – but also on how we define international law and human rights in the first place. When we see women's human rights as discourse (Goodale 2009) rather than as narrowly legal in form, we can also see its potential as a strategy for social change – and this helps address the narrowness of global legalism critiqued by DeLaet (2018a). Thus, the three authors in this cluster (Debra DeLaet, Lisa Baldez and myself), agree that [codified] global legalism alone is inadequate for substantive gender equality. Where we diverge is 'how much' law should be relied on and, perhaps, what we mean by law.

Seen expansively and creatively, international law can be one strategy for activists, so long as it is not relied upon naively or narrowly (as DeLaet cautions us) nor seen in ahistorical or universal terms (as Baldez [2018] reminds us). As DeLaet (2018b) writes in her reply to our thematic cluster, she is not arguing international law ought to be abandoned altogether; rather, 'I am arguing that, in the context of scarce global resources, prioritizing local initiatives may be more impactful than extensive efforts to refine or expand existing global norms governing women's rights.' While I agree with this assessment of international law and global legalism, I do not see the local and the global as separate spaces. Local activists mobilize the language of international law in their grass-roots strategies just as international activists mobilize local understandings of justice and the needs for local reparations in their global strategies.

My contribution to the cluster in many ways confirms DeLaet's arguments: despite recognition and prosecution of sexual and gender-based violence (including the recent recognition of forced marriage) as crimes against humanity and war crimes, this violence continues in armed conflict; further, such recognition of gender violence has not undermined stereotypical gender roles for men and women and, arguably, has reinforced certain simplistic and racist views of women as victims and men as violent perpetrators. DeLaet rightly notes that 'international or national laws criminalizing violence against women will not necessarily overcome the toxic masculinity that drives men to commit violence or the gender biases that hinder women from reporting sexual assault' (DeLaet 2018a, this issue). As I argue in my piece (2018), more complex and nuanced understandings of violence, victimhood and gender have not been included in the record of the international criminal courts and tribunals. Nonetheless, DeLaet and I both come to the conclusion that international law can be 'one tool' of symbolic and discursive importance in the movement for gender justice.

Similarly, Lisa Baldez and I agree on key arguments about politics, international law and gender violence. As she argues, the geopolitics of the Cuba–United States relationship determines the rhetoric about domestic violence from the Cuban government. The potential for international women's rights and the constructive dialogue between the Cuban delegation and Committee monitoring the implementation of the Convention on the Elimination of All Forms of Discrimination Against Women, Baldez (2018) demonstrates, is shaped by the national socio-historical context and the US embargo. In the case of the International Criminal Court in Uganda, I argue that broader politics about the ICC in Africa as well as the local cultural understanding of justice and reparations impact the potential of the Ongwen trial to bring about meaningful gender justice.

This brings me to my final point in conversation with my colleagues: how do we measure gender justice and success? This is another key dilemma for critical feminist scholars. On the one hand, we know all too well the problems with quantification and indicators (Merry 2016) and the challenges of working without adequate disaggregated gender data from government sources (Bunting 2015); on the other hand, we need to convince policy-makers, funders and the general public that there is a problem. How do activists convince the Cuban government that domestic violence exists without data? How do victim survivors make claims for reparations from government commissions without testimonials? The papers in this cluster ask us to critically assess the measures of success and failure and indeed the relationship between legal and political reform and social behaviour. While some observers are true believers that social change is linked to either global legalism or national legal enforcement, others will remain sceptical. The factors at play are often too complicated and intertwined to determine conclusively how social change comes about.

The papers in this cluster and across the special issue of *Global Discourse* demonstrate the richness of interdisciplinary exchange and collaboration. Both trained in political science, Baldez and DeLaet are attentive to questions of state power and the institutional dimensions of international human rights law. Trained in law, ironically I see law's potential in its non-state or discursive form – mobilizing the language and symbolism of law, along with the space created by trials, to try to effect positive social change.

Disclosure statement

No potential conflict of interest was reported by the author.

References

Baldez, L. 2018. "What's at Stake in the Treaty Reporting Process? Cuba and the United Nations' Convention on Women's Rights." *Global Discourse*. doi:10.1080/23269995.2018.1520009.

Bunting, A. 2015. "Monitoring Gender Equality and Violence in Conditions of Structural Inequality and Violence." In *Disability, Rights Monitoring and Social Change: Building Power Out of Evidence*, edited by M. H. Rioux, P. C. Pinto, and G. Parekh, 67–79. Toronto: Canadian Scholars' Press.

Bunting, A. 2018. "Gender Politics and Geopolitics of International Criminal Law in Uganda." *Global Discourse*. doi:10.1080/23269995.2018.1520010.

DeLaet, D. 2018a. "Lost in Legation: The Gap between Rhetoric and Reality in International Human Rights Law Governing Women's Rights." *Global Discourse*. doi:10.1080/23269995.2018.1520006.

DeLaet, D. 2018b. "What's law got to do with it?: A reply to Baldez and Bunting." *Global Discourse*. doi:10.1080/23269995.2018.1520014.

Goodale, M. Ed. 2009. *Human Rights: An Anthropological Reader*. West Sussex, UK: Wiley-Blackwell.

Merry, S. E. 2016. *The Seductions of Quantification: Measuring Human Rights, Gender Violence and Human Trafficking*. Chicago: Chicago University Press.

Tacking between the global and the local: a reply to DeLaet and Bunting

Lisa Baldez

ABSTRACT

In these two pieces, DeLaet and Bunting express reservations about the potential for international law to have positive effects on the de facto status of the world's citizens—but point to activism on the local level as the most viable way to strengthen the human rights regime. In her thorough overview of the literature on the impact of international law, DeLaet focuses on the ability of local activists to domestic international treaties by mobilizing at the grassroots level to enact the provisions of international law. Bunting's analysis of the offers a different solution, one that involves tacking back and forth between the precepts of international law and the lived experiences of victims of human rights violations.

This is a reply to:

DeLaet, D. 2018. 'Lost in Legation: The Gap Between Rhetoric and Reality in International Human Rights Law Governing Women's Rights.' *Global Discourse*. doi: 10.1080/23269995.2018.1520006.

and

Bunting, A. 2018. 'Gender Politics and Geopolitics of International Criminal Law in Uganda.' *Global Discourse*. doi: 10.1080/23269995.2018.1520010.

Under what conditions will international law have positive effects on the de facto and de jure status of rights for the world's citizens? DeLaet (2018) and Bunting (2018) contribute new perspectives to this body of research, Bunting drawing from the perspective of victims of conjugal slavery in Uganda, and DeLaet on the basis of a birds' eye view of the field as a whole. The two pieces converge in their support for local-level activism as a 'corrective' to the gulf between international norms and the reality of implementation on the ground.

DeLaet's piece begins by acknowledging the positive impact of international human rights law. She focuses on the Convention on the Elimination of All Forms of Discrimination Against Women (CEDAW) and maintains that human rights treaties raise the profile of women's rights and provide a focal point for actors in civil society, facilitating advocacy. Signing on to human rights treaties increases the reputational costs that governments face in failing to comply with international norms. Finally, ratification of human rights treaties can improve the de facto status of women across a range of important indicators.

Change is not guaranteed, however, due to a range of factors that can be grouped into three categories: the nature of the treaty and treaty regime, the characteristics of States parties and the ways in which States parties interact with treaties. In DeLaet's analysis, the text of the convention is vague, has weak enforcement mechanisms and reflects a 'statist' bias in which non-state actors have little involvement. While other treaties, such as the International Covenant on Civil and Political Rights, address women's rights, imbedding women in a more general framework dilutes the focus on women. Finally, the international human rights regime is more effective at perpetuating itself than on addressing the problems of people whose rights have been violated.

I disagree with some of the specific points that DeLaet makes. While her piece maintains that CEDAW focuses more on public rather than private discrimination, for example, I maintain that CEDAW's embrace of women's right to be free from private violations makes it a more effective guarantor of women's rights than the US Constitution (Baldez 2014).

Different perspectives lie in our conceptions of the ability of the state to act on women's behalf. DeLaet's piece suggests that the state is inherently problematic in that it inevitably 'reinforces existing discourses and structures of power' and is thus antithetical to feminism. While I see the state as a more motile arena of contestation, I share DeLaet's concern about what to prioritize under conditions of resource scarcity – the permanent conditions under which we live. This is particularly relevant with regard to the question of whether the United States should ratify CEDAW: given that women's rights advocates would have to allocate significant resources to the ratification, does it make sense to focus on that, or to work more directly on pressing domestic issues? Ultimately, I agree with DeLaet that the 'fix' for CEDAW's limited power lies in the ability of grass-roots activists to serve as 'norm entrepreneurs', taking the lead in domesticating international norms at the local level.

Bunting's research focuses precisely on the local level. She too views ordinary people at the local level as the corrective to limitations in international law, but in a different way. While DeLaet advocates for local activists to make international norms relevant at home, Bunting suggests that the experiences of victims need to be incorporated into international law in order to make it more relevant and more effective as a means of achieving justice. Her article examines the views of victims of forced marriage toward the case against Dominic Ongwen, one of the leaders of the Lords' Resistance Army in Uganda, brought before the International Criminal Court (ICC). She addresses many important questions: Is the ICC an institution in which the language of humanitarianism is actually a new form of colonialism, used to punish African leaders in situations where they were victims as well as perpetrators? Did indictments of LRA leaders hinder peace talks? Should people be punished for being part of a system in which they are also victims?

Bunting's analysis 'tacks back and forth' between discussion of the geopolitics behind the trial and the way that victims make sense of what happened and start to rebuilt their lives. But her analysis also suggests that tacking back and forth between global norms and the perspectives of victims can improve international law. When we focus on what victims are saying about the Ongwen trial, for example, we see that they support punishing perpetrators, but also seek reparations and espouse a broader vision of justice that holds the Ugandan government responsible for not protecting them in the first place. Despite significant changes in the legal recognition of rape as a war crime, the ICC still has failed to address sexual violence against men and boys. Bunting's research urges that international law include a fuller account of gender-based violence in war.

The stories that victims tell do not suggest easy answers. Some victims view the ICC case as a waste of time and money that will not improve the lives or bring back the dead, while others maintain that "people who commit crimes should be punished to make them change. Still others seek 'more local, non-juridical solutions to social reparations' and some people espouse all of these views simultaneously. Regardless, however, the prosecution does not adequately convey these 'varied experiences' of victims and thus cannot adequately address victims' needs. For Bunting, the solution lies with the victims. If we conceive of human rights trials as 'opportunities for creating space for documenting survivors' narratives and needs', we potentially generate a form of justice that is more appropriate to their experiences. In the case of victims of in Uganda, 'calls for criminal accountability are usually paired with nuanced calls for justice beyond punishment'.

Together, these two pieces offer fresh perspectives on the 'tacking back and forth' between international law and grass-roots action. Local activists can use international law to make change, in ways that go beyond merely holding governments accountable to their promises. International human rights law can be a powerful tool for activists at the local level even when states have not ratified international human rights treaties – by mobilizing the moral authority that lies at their core. Citizens at the state and local levels can invoke international law as a tool in their efforts to pressure politicians to act and to adopt legislation at the local level. Local activists can also transform international law by insisting that international legal institutions take their experiences into account. Doing so can facilitate continuous efforts to refine the content of various articles to articulate clearer and more precise understandings of the ways that discrimination and violations of human rights manifest themselves in particular political situations.

Disclosure statement

No potential conflict of interest was reported by the author.

References

Baldez, L. 2014. *Defying Convention: U.S. Resistance to the U.N. Treaty on Women's Rights*. New York: Cambridge University Press.

Bunting, A. 2018. "Gender Politics and Geopolitics of International Criminal Law in Uganda." *Global Discourse*. doi:10.1080/23269995.2018.1520010.

DeLaet, D. 2018. "Lost in Legation: the Gap Between Rhetoric and Reality in International Human Rights Law Governing Women's Rights." *Global Discourse*. doi:10.1080/23269995.2018.1520006.

What's law got to do with it?: A reply to Baldez and Bunting

Debra L. DeLaet

ABSTRACT

This reply explores points of agreement, tensions, and lingering questions related to a scholarly conversation among the pieces by DeLaet, Baldez, and Bunting on the potential and limits of international human rights law as a tool for promoting women's rights and equality as part of this special edition of *Global Discourse* on Gender, Sexuality, and the Law. DeLaet's piece takes a macro view of this question and points to the failure of international human rights law to generate systemic change globally. In her examination of Cuba's participation in the Convention on the Elimination of Discrimination against Women, Baldez offers a relatively more positive assessment of the potential for international human rights law to transform human rights outcomes when states participate in treaty reporting processes. Focusing specifically on international criminal law, Bunting's exploration of Ugandan victim survivors' views on the prosecution of crimes against humanity at the International Criminal Court offers a mixed perspective, whereby international criminal trials may provide political space for meaning-making and historical documentation even if they do not provide for restorative justice, healing, or gender equality. Each of these pieces indicates that law in and of itself is insufficient to generate transformative change in support of women's rights and equality. They differ in the extent to which they view law as a primary tool for mobilizing change.

This is a reply to:

Baldez, L. 2018. "What's at Stake in the Treaty Reporting Process? Cuba and the United Nations' Convention on Women's Rights." *Global Discourse*. http://dx.doi.org/10.1080/23269995.2018.1520009

and

Bunting, A. 2018. "Gender Politics and Geopolitics of International Criminal Law in Uganda." *Global Discourse*. http://dx.doi.org/10.1080/23269995.2018.1520010

The articles in the research cluster on Gender, Women's Rights and International Law for the special edition of *Global Discourse* on Gender, Sexuality and the Law each explore the potential and limits of international human rights law as a tool for promoting women's rights and equality. Each author in this research cluster acknowledges the evidence that participation in international human rights treaty regimes correlates with improved outcomes regarding the status of women. At the same time, each author recognizes that the available evidence offers a mixed assessment regarding the capacity of formal law to directly produce change and how much the advancement of women's rights can be attributed to international human rights regimes. Despite these fundamental points of agreement, the authors in this research cluster offer divergent perspectives on how to interpret the mixed record of international law and, thus, on the extent to which scholars and activists should prioritize legal mechanisms for pursuing change in support of women's equality and rights.

My own contribution to this research cluster expresses reservations about over-reliance on international law as the primary mechanism for advancing women's rights and equality in the international system (DeLaet 2018, this issue). I acknowledge that international human rights law has been associated with positive outcomes related to the status of women and that proponents of global rights for women can mobilize human rights norms to seek further change. Despite my recognition that international human rights law has contributed to improvements in the status of women, I argue that formal law remains limited as a mechanism for transformative change. Thus, advocates for women's rights and equality cannot rely primarily or exclusively on the international human rights regime. Instead, feminist scholars and activists need to prioritize socio-cultural change in particular local contexts to challenge deeply embedded gender biases that hinder the realization of women's rights and equality. Law, national or international, is just one tool that proponents of women's rights may rely on in their advocacy. One size does not fit all contexts, and over-reliance on formal law will not provide the flexibility for responding to unique political and social circumstances on the ground. It also may produce unintended and counter-productive dynamics that generate cultural resistance to global norms.

In her case study of Cuba's engagement with the reporting process for the Convention on the Elimination of All Forms of Discrimination Against Women (CEDAW), Baldez also offers a mixed assessment of the potential for international law to mobilize changes within countries in support of women's rights (Baldez 2018, this issue). On the one hand, Cuba's reporting engagement with the CEDAW Committee has led to changed governmental discourse in policy areas connected to women's rights, and there is evidence that the government has taken steps to comply with Committee recommendations. On the other hand, Cuba has vigorously resisted the guidance and recommendations in other areas and vehemently refuted the Committee's assessment of its record on human rights. Nonetheless, Baldez ultimately emphasizes the potential value of international human rights law in supporting the advancement of human rights in general and women's rights specifically. Given that the development of international human rights laws governing women's rights are associated with positive outcomes, she takes the reasonable position that legal tools should be an important part of the toolkit in global advocacy for women's rights and equality.

Bunting's case study of the current prosecution of Dominic Ongwen at the International Criminal Court (ICC) for crimes against humanity also demonstrates the complexity of discerning the potential of international law to advance rights (Bunting 2018, this issue). Bunting emphasizes the limitations of international criminal law in providing criminal accountability. Yet, she shows that legal solutions are normally connected to non-legal initiatives that may advance broader and more complicated notions of justice. International criminal law and legal prosecution may create spaces of justice that foster public discourse, national memorialization, gender debates, and claims for reparations and social repair that go beyond law narrowly defined. As her case indicates, legal tools alone are insufficient for mobilizing human rights change. Yet, they can play an integral role in redressing sexual violence, gender-based crimes, and other conflict-related harms advancing when connected to micro-level politics and local post-conflict justice initiatives.

As these brief summaries indicate, the articles in this research cluster all agree that law may be associated with positive outcomes and, as such, may be a valuable tool for mobilizing change. Nevertheless, they disagree on *how much* law should be relied upon in advocacy for women's rights and equality and in regards to how heavily to weigh the potential costs or downsides of legal mechanisms for pursuing socio-cultural change.

In her reply to our research cluster, Baldez accurately notes that I favor local politics and activism as a way to strengthen the existing international human rights regime rather than further expansion and development of international law. To be clear, my position is *not* that international human rights law has not had positive effects, that it should be circumvented altogether, or that the development of international law and local initiatives are necessarily mutually exclusive. However, I am arguing that, in the context of scarce global resources, prioritizing local initiatives may be more impactful than extensive efforts to refine or expand existing global norms governing women's rights. As both the pieces by Baldez and Bunting show, global norms shape outcomes in particular cases via unique and particular political processes. Human rights norms take root in particular societies when local actors mobilize these norms and leverage them through localized political processes and initiatives.

Human rights treaties are not implemented via strong enforcement by international institutions operating in countries that have ratified them. A system of voluntarist participation by states in treaty regimes necessarily means that global norms will be filtered through the particular political contexts within countries, and the interest of these states inevitably shape outcomes. This reality suggests that efforts to refine or expand existing international law by global institutions may not produce significant gains. An expanded list of codified rights for women in the human rights regime will face the same set of constraints that limits the implementation of existing norms. Efforts to refine the meaning of codified rights or to clarify state obligations will not override state reluctance to relinquish sovereignty or to accept more robust enforcement measures. Building on Bunting's conclusions, my fundamental argument is that advocates for women's rights and equality should use existing law governing women's rights to create space for localized initiatives with the goal of mobilizing change. Leveraging international human rights law in this way does not require more or better law; it requires flexible and sophisticated efforts to use the law as one tool of many in pursuit of transformational change.

The argument that states should leverage the symbolic power of existing human rights norms in local contexts rather than trying to bolster the substantive provisions and legal machinery of human rights treaties also helps to mitigate some of the downside risks of relying on formal international law in pursuit of change in diverse countries and societies. An over-emphasis on the legalization and institutionalization of human rights may ultimately undermine their emancipatory purpose. Proponents of global legalism risk treating law as an end in itself. When law is seen as its own end, one of its primary functions may be to legitimate states whether or not their participation in treaty regimes produces actual policy change (Hopgood 2013). When conceived in this narrow way, international human rights treaties may serve to regulate society and to legitimate state power more than to liberate individuals (Wong 2006). At the same time, efforts to continue to expand and institutionalize international human rights law has the potential to generate backlash by states reluctant to give up sovereignty (Helfer 2002).

Like all forms of law, international human rights law is infused with politics. The law neither transcends nor subsumes politics. An eternal quest to perfect the law – to diminish the ambivalence of its language, to close loopholes in ways that will constrain self-interested states, to strengthen enforcement in order to force change – will be elusive. International human rights law has helped to move the needle in improving the status of women across the globe, and scholars and activists should continue to utilize it in the pursuit of equality and rights for women. Yet, it remains one tool among many, and its limitations need to be recognized and considered in developing global initiatives related to women's rights and equality.

Disclosure statement

No potential conflict of interest was reported by the author.

References

Baldez, L. 2018. "What's at Stake in the Treaty Reporting Process? Cuba and the United Nations' Convention on Women's Rights." *Global Discourse*. doi:10.1080/23269995.2018.1520009.

Bunting, A. 2018. "Gender Politics and Geopolitics of International Criminal Law in Uganda." *Global Discourse*. doi:10.1080/23269995.2018.1520010.

DeLaet, D. 2018. "Lost in Legation: The Gap between Rhetoric and Reality in International Human Rights Law Governing Women's Rights." *Global Discourse*. doi:10.1080/23269995.2018.1520006.

Helfer, L. R. 2002. "Overlegalizing Human Rights: International Relations Theory and the Commonwealth Caribbean Backlash against Human Rights Regimes." *Columbia Law Review* 102 (7): 1832–1911. doi:10.2307/1123662.

Hopgood, S. 2013. *The Endtimes of Human Rights*. Ithaca, NY: Cornell University Press.

Wong, C. 2006. "Taking Back Our Language: The Consequences of Legalizing Human Rights." *Interdisciplinary Journal of Human Rights Law* 1 (1): 43–67.

Attempting international normative change in gender and the law: a reply to DeLaet, Baldez and Bunting

Darby Matt

ABSTRACT

This reply responds to contributions by DeLaet, Baldez and Bunting to the issue's sub-theme on 'The Role of International and Domestic Law in Attaining Gender and Sexual Equality'. While each paper allocates different degrees of importance to the role of international actors in international normative change, all agree that domestic attempts are more important to sustainable change than international attempts. This reply attempts to determine the reasons for divergence on the attribution of importance to international actors, while examining means by which these international actors can better service domestic actors rather than merely replicating neo-colonialist policies.

This is a reply to:

Baldez, Lisa (2018) "What's at Stake in the Treaty Reporting Process? Cuba and the United Nations Treaty on Women's Rights". *Global Discourse*. doi: 10.1080/23269995.2018.1520009.

and

Bunting, Annie (2018) "Gender Politics and Geopolitics of International Criminal Law in Uganda". *Global Discourse*. doi: 10.1080/23269995.2018.1520010.

and

DeLaet, Debra L. (2018) "Lost in Legation: the Gap Between Rhetoric and Reality in International Human Rights Law Governing Women's Rights". *Global Discourse*. doi: 10.1080/23269995.2018.1520006.

Papers in this research cluster of the special edition of *Global Discourse* on Gender, Sexuality and the Law examine the role of international and domestic law in attaining gender and sexual equality. All three articles point to the limitations of statist policies within international law and identify cultural factors as major challenges to normative change.

DeLaet's (2018) piece, 'Lost in Legation: The Gap Between Rhetoric and Reality in International Human Rights Law Governing Women's Rights', analyzes international human rights law as a limited tool for promoting human rights. DeLaet suggests that a reliance on formal law as a means of normative change is limiting, in part because formal law often utilizes traditional language that serves to reinforce conservative gender norms and replicates unfounded assumptions about women's inherent need for special protections. She underscores tensions that exist within many legal documents, between 'western' and more local cultures, and indicates that a further limitation of international law is its difficulty in taking cultural differences into consideration. In these ways, statist bias and local political interests influence how individuals conceive of and access rights.

Baldez's (2018) piece, 'What's at Stake in the Treaty Reporting Process? Cuba and the United Nations Treaty on Women's Rights', looks at Cuba's support of the Convention on the Elimination of All Forms of Discrimination Against Women (CEDAW). Baldez identifies political reasons behind Cuba's support of the Treaty and questions whether Cuba has deeply instituted CEDAW policies. She identifies the statist bias that is often associated with the United Nations and its related documents in her consideration of the way the UN monitors and evaluates CEDAW's implementation. Cuba presents itself as a model CEDAW ratifier yet continues to resist some recommendations and requests made by the United Nations, primarily, Baldez argues, because Cuban policies understand women's rights and roles differently than UN policy imagines them. Bunting's (2018) piece, 'Geopolitics and Gender Politics of International Criminal Law in Uganda', analyzes interviews from women who experienced violence in Uganda. Bunting argues that international law and international norms often fail to serve in these post-conflict societies because of their focus on punitive justice. International criminal law often mobilizes seeks, while many in Ugandan society seeks restorative justice because it can better reintegrate victims and perpetrators into society. Bunting argues that victims, and societies, are better served by international law that is flexible, attentive to individual experiences and created around differing understandings of victimhood.

The authors all acknowledge the effectiveness of human rights treaties that target gender equality. Baldez cites research on CEDAW that shows ratification increases the likelihood of countries identifying progressive women's rights policies (2018). DeLaet also cites research establishing positive correlations between the ratification of women's rights treaties and improvements in the status of women (2018). Bunting argues that more treaties may be necessary to address gaps in the law (Bunting 2018). But, still, a major theme that connects these articles is the concept of statist bias. Both Baldez and DeLaet directly refer to this bias and identify it as a major obstacle to achieving women's rights by way of the politicization of human rights. Statist bias in the UN gives precedence to states over associations of people or organizations, and particularly gives greater credence to stronger states. DeLaet points out that because states create, interpret and execute laws, their own political interests influence these laws (2018). At the same time, states will not comply with treaty obligations unless they align with the state's political interests (DeLaet 2018). Additionally, the power behind evaluation and monitoring lies with the states, not the United Nations, which is a further indication of the power of normative change as it occurs within states, not international bodies (Baldez 2018). While United Nations' treaties are binding documents, the treaty-monitoring bodies established by the United Nations for compliance can only provide nonbinding recommendations, meaning it is up to the state to create normative change (DeLaet 2018). Baldez explains that Cuba's motivations for supporting CEDAW may lie more with the government's political interests than its actual concern for women's rights. Supporting CEDAW gives Cuba more power in the United Nations and works to counter United States power and influence (Baldez 2018). CEDAW support also serves to defend Cuba's human rights record and works to lessen the United States' control of the embargo (Baldez 2018). Cuba also claims that the United States' embargo is a direct source of violence against women and that therefore, until the embargo is completely removed, violence against women in Cuba can never be fully addressed (Baldez 2018).

Bunting argues that 'victor's justice', whereby some perpetrators of violence are protected from prosecution for their crimes because they were the 'winners' in the conflict, is at risk of occurring in sttes like Uganda. So, while forces in Uganda were punished, the governmental forces that were complicit were able to get away with their crimes (2018). Victor's justice is another way to mobilize and legitimate a statist bias, because whoever ends up on top in a conflict generally ends up making the new government. This potentially ignores victims' needs, and may perpetuate systematic fear and violence. In this scenario, governmental forces are legitimized even if they perpetrated similar war crimes that rebels perpetrated. Bunting argues that this 'system premised on individual accountability to respond to violence that was structurally and historically produced' (2018) serves to perpetuate violence and inequality by providing an easy scapegoat for state actors: individuals with (supposed) choice.

All three articles identify cultural difference as a major challenge to normative change. Bunting notes the difference between western and international legal norms, and local customs and needs. Tribunals forget about women and sexualized victims because conflict is assumed to involve men in 'typical' war violence (Bunting 2018). Western law fails to identify and satisfy the complexity that is embodied by a victim-perpetrator, like Dominic Ongwen (Bunting 2018). Western/international law is more punitive, whereas conflict-ridden countries like Uganda may seek rehabilitative or restorative justice because it better encourages the envelopment of rebels back into society and can better address and fix structural, systemic problems (Bunting 2018). DeLaet notes that while advancements come from countries that already have a basis of human rights, progress actually results from domestic legal and political processes, not international (2018). This is because of manifestations of 'western' ideals within international treaties may be at tension with local norms and so for substantial change to occur, focus must be given to local customs and legal systems (DeLaet 2018). Baldez notes that in recent years, Cuba's reporting to the CEDAW committee indicates differences in understandings of women's rights and human rights, something that is further indicated by the CEDAW committee's adamancy in recommendations and Cuba's habit of ignoring their recommendations (2018).

A tension between these three articles arises from their differing perceptions of the importance of the United Nations. Both Baldez and DeLaet cite research indicating that ratification of United Nations treaties increases the likelihood of better women's rights (Baldez 2018; DeLaet 2018). Baldez's article implies a greater importance for United Nations' participation because the UN offers developing countries like Cuba a means by which to gain strength through rights granting. DeLaet cautions that constitutive view of law and society is necessary to avoid policy that forgets differing cultural needs in an attempt to force western ideals on nonwestern societies. DeLaet also notes that there is not too much enforcement power behind the United Nations in terms of monitoring and evaluation. Bunting's article shows the importance of self-sustainability within nonwestern countries and indicates, while the United Nations is great for setting goals, it is not the means to executing said goals.

The challenge to increase gender equity throughout the world is identified throughout the articles written by Baldez, Bunting and DeLeat. While each article focuses on cases from different regions with distinct contexts, these authors produce an important discussion on international law pertaining to women's rights and gender equality. First, the United Nations and strong states need to consolidate their goals pertaining to gender and incorporate them into more binding documents while creating more tangible monitoring and evaluation techniques. Second, states must be encouraged to both sign and ratify these treaties because of the positive correlation it has with increasing rights. Third, state bias must be recognized to remove as much political influence from rights discussion as possible, because human rights should not be political. Finally, recognition of cultural difference is an important first step to creating the normative change women's rights treaties are attempting to do.

Disclosure statement

No potential conflict of interest was reported by the author.

References

Baldez, L. 2018. "What's at Stake in the Treaty Reporting Process? Cuba and the United Nations Treaty on Women's Rights." *Global Discourse*. doi:10.1080/23269995.2018.1520009.

Bunting, A. 2018. "Gender Politics and Geopolitics of International Criminal Law in Uganda." *Global Discourse*. doi:10.1080/23269995.2018.1520010.

DeLaet, D. L. 2018. "Lost in Legation: The Gap between Rhetoric and Reality in International Human Rights Law Governing Women's Rights." *Global Discourse*. doi:10.1080/23269995.2018.1520006.

'The stigma of Western words': asylum law, transgender identity and sexual orientation in South Africa

B Camminga

ABSTRACT

'Gays Engage' was the headline of Malawi's Nation newspaper on 28 December 2009. A colour photograph dominated the front page showing Steven Monjeza and what the paper described as 'his bride', Tiwonge Chimbalanga. Arrested soon after and charged with 'unnatural offences' under the Malawi Penal Code, the couple made international headlines. Yet the situation was far more complex than the news media or transnational NGOs intimated. While the case was being touted as 'a test case for gay rights' the court documents noted that Tiwonge, assigned male, identified as a woman. Rights groups called for South Africa – the only country on the African continent that constitutionally protects Lesbian, Gay, Bisexual and Transgender (LGBT) individuals – to not only advocate for the couple's release but to offer them asylum. In 2010, after receiving a presidential pardon, Chimbalanga was sent to South Africa where she was granted refugee status. Offering a post-colonial reading of transgender, this paper asks what it would mean for a person to be seen as transgender, to be presumed to be transgender, but to never take on that term for themselves – to refuse that subjectivity – while seeking asylum.

One of the critical elements of the negotiations to end Apartheid in South Africa was the creation of a new Constitution for the country. Arguably one of the more controversial introductions of the Interim Constitution of 1993, which garnered widespread international coverage, was its Bill of Rights and in particular the Equality Clause (*Interim Constitution of the Republic of South Africa*, Act no. 200 of 1993). It was during this time that a burgeoning 'gay rights' movement – lead by the National Coalition for Lesbian and Gay Equality (NCGLE) – also began to show political promise. The inclusion of protection from discrimination on the grounds of sexual orientation, sex and gender within the proposed Equality Clause was particularly controversial. Several countries responded to South Africa's legislative inclusion of sexual orientation, sex and gender[1] as an opportunity to establish their sovereignty, independence and critically their moral superiority (Phillips 2000). This controversy over what was widely touted as the inclusion of 'gay rights' in the South African Constitution became one of the most effective means of publicising these new rights beyond the country's borders. Within the international arena, the shift towards framing gay and lesbian rights – or LGBT rights[2] – as human rights was gaining traction, and the

Clause, given its uniqueness, held particular importance in this regard. Aside from gay and lesbian rights, these developments heralded in remarkable new possibilities for South Africa, not least of which, I argue, was the evolution of transgender politics within the country along with a distinctive asylum regime.

Part of the aim of this paper is to understand the meaning-making of the term 'transgender' in relation to asylum in South Africa. David Valentine (2007) notes in considering transgender discourse and politics that 'while every word we speak is a category, some have more power to explain who we are, and thus to limit (as much as enable) the possibilities for our action in the world' (233). I argue that the term 'transgender' has come to hold a certain currency for transnational, regional and local South African organisations, most notably in relation to 'universalised' principles of LGBT human rights. Drawing on the story of Malawian Tiwonge Chimbalanga, a high-profile transgender refugee who moved to South Africa with the assistance of transnational organisations, after her widely publicised marriage to Steven Mojenza in 2009, I also explore the limits of transgender as an identity. Chimbalanga's story presents, I argue, a moment 'out of joint' (Chakrabarty 2000, 113). She brings us to the point within which Dipesh Chakrabarty would suggest we are required to acknowledge 'cracks in the structure of homogeneity' (2000, 90) to read transgender's finitude. Her story, I suggest, provides a moment in which it becomes possible to question the limits and utility of the growing universalisation of the term 'transgender' in relation to the specific lived experiences of refugees seeking asylum due to persecution based on gender expression in South Africa. In essence, I ask, what might it mean for a person to be seen as transgender, to be presumed to be transgender, but to never take on that term themselves, and what might this reveal about the theoretically radical potential of South Africa's legal-constitutional make up.

South Africa's constitutional development: sexual orientation and gender

Promulgated on 18 December 1996 as part of the Constitution of the Republic of South Africa, the Equality Clause states:

> 9. (1) Everyone is equal before the law and has the right to equal protection and benefit of the law.
> (2) Equality includes the full and equal enjoyment of all rights and freedoms. To promote the achievement of equality, legislative and other measures designed to protect or advance persons, or categories of persons, disadvantaged by unfair discrimination may be taken.
> (3) The state may not unfairly discriminate directly or indirectly against anyone on one or more grounds, including race, gender, sex, pregnancy, marital status, ethnic or social origin, colour, sexual orientation, age, disability, religion, conscience, belief, culture, language and birth.
> (4) No person may unfairly discriminate directly or indirectly against anyone on one or more grounds in terms of subsection (3). National legislation must be enacted to prevent or prohibit unfair discrimination.
> (5) Discrimination on one or more of the grounds listed in subsection (3) is unfair unless it is established that the discrimination is fair.

The Equality Clause's appearance in the interim Constitution and its eventual inclusion in the new Constitution were not only controversial but in many ways exceptional, given the wider lack of both favourable international precedent, and a visible, cohesive, lobbying force within South Africa, initially (Christiansen 2000). Neville Hoad (1999) suggests that this relational link between the international circulation of LGBT human rights at the time and South Africa's specific constitutional developments was in fact crucial to the Clause's development. He argues that in the drafting of the Constitution,

> A self-conscious attempt was made to learn from the failures of prior liberation movements across the globe. Given the illegitimacy of the old regime and the imperative to incorporate the most recent or 'advanced' form of human rights, the timing of the South African constitution in the history of postcolonialism facilitated the entrenchment of lesbian and gay human rights. (Hoad 1999, 576)

The provision prohibiting discrimination on the grounds of sexual orientation provided the basis for several important cases in the first years of democracy. Key amongst a series of rulings in the 1990s was *The National Coalition for Gay and Lesbian Equality vs Minister of Justice and Others* (1998), which declared the criminalisation of sodomy unconstitutional while also providing the grounds for recognising myriad other rights for 'sexual minorities' in South Africa (de Vos 2009). Edwin Cameron's (1993) article *Sexual orientation and the Constitution: a Test Case for Human Rights* was highly influential in both the majority and minority judgements of the case. In his paper, Cameron makes it clear that 'homosexual identity as a political fact is a recent phenomenon and one whose social roots are the subject of deep controversy' (452). People who have been attracted to the same sex have always existed, but those who would recognise themselves as 'gay' or 'lesbian' – an identity connected to this – are a far more recent event. He argues, though, that the law has been

> less concerned with homosexual identity than with homosexual conduct. But social discrimination at large occurs principally on the basis of what people perceive as categories of sexual orientation. In other words, men and women are discriminated against not only because they perform sexual acts with others of their own gender, or because they accept for themselves the labels 'gay' or 'lesbian', but because they are perceived as likely or disposed to perform homosexual acts – *even if in fact they never do*". [emphasis added] (Cameron 1993, 452)

Cameron acknowledged that discrimination, in a number of cases, is based on the perception of homosexuality, as opposed to the actual practice of homosexuality. Thus, he pointed out strongly that there was a need for general protection, as opposed to simple decriminalisation. In arguing that adequate protection for sexual orientation within the Constitution would entail the right to freedom of speech, association and conduct, he notes that this would also include the freedom to 'cross-dress (that is, appear in drag)' – a reflection on the case of *S v Kola* (Cameron 1993, 471). Following from this, the majority judgment of Justice Ackerman gave a broad reading of sexual orientation:

> The concept "sexual orientation" as used in Section 9(3) of the 1996 Constitution must be given a generous interpretation of which it is linguistically and textually fully capable of bearing. It applies equally to the orientation of persons who are bi-sexual, or transsexual, and it also applies to the orientation of persons who might on a single occasion only be erotically attracted to a member of their own sex. (*National Coalition for Gay and Lesbian Equality v The Minister of Justice* 1998, para 21)

This 'generous interpretation' meant that sexual orientation, as envisioned in the Bill of Rights, extended to prohibiting discrimination against transsexual people. The judgement did more than just recognise transsexuality; it provided a space for the varying ways that individuals come to identify themselves using a mixture of signifiers and language. It acknowledged that while the *language* is contingent, the experience the language attempts to name or describe is not (de Vos 2009), ostensibly providing for the future possibility of transgender. The concurring judgement by Justice Sachs stated:

> Only in the most technical sense is this a case about who may penetrate whom where. At a practical and symbolic level it is about status, moral citizenship and sense of self-worth of a significant section of the community. At a more general and conceptual level, it concerns the nature of the open, democratic and pluralistic society contemplated by the Constitution. (*National Coalition for Gay and Lesbian Equality v The Minister of Justice* 1998, para 107)

This is not to say that a reading of transgender, within the Constitution, outside the bounds of sexual orientation is not possible. Along with 'sexual orientation', the use of the words 'sex' and 'gender' within the Bill of Rights was very particular, as Janet Kentridge (1998) explains in *Constitutional Law of South Africa*. Based largely on an understanding drawn from feminist literature, sex refers to biological characteristics while gender refers to social characteristics – which often derive their meaning from being attributed to a particular biological sex. Gender, as utilised in the Bill then, is 'a psychological and cultural' notion: accordingly, 'we might say that a person is female or male according to her or his sex, but man or woman according to his or her gender' (Kentridge 1998, 14.26D). In arguing for the need to include both sex and gender in the new Constitution, Denise Meyerson states, 'The whole point of using the word "gender" is to express the belief that sex does not determine gender, and that point cannot be made unless different meanings attach to the words "sex" and "gender"' (Meyerson 1993, 295). Kentridge adds that both sex and gender were included in the Bill so as to ensure the greatest possible protection (Kentridge 1998, 14.26D). This understanding would suggest that a possible constitutional reading of transgender identity as a protected element of sex or gender within the Equality Clause is entirely possible, given the theoretical acknowledgment that sex and gender are separate and that the 'one does not determine the other' (Meyerson 1993, 295). Notably though, at the time of these discussions, 'transgender', as the 'T' of LGBT rights in Southern Africa, held limited political impetus, meaning or indeed visibility, even though it was in circulation to some degree in the Global North.

The South African Refugee Act: asylum seekers as 'members of a particular social group'

> Sunday night at the Summit Club in Hillbrow. Anita, a pint-sized Whitney Houston lookalike in white micro-mini and fuck-off platforms, is belting out a flawless lip-sync of Miss Whitney's classic, 'It's not right, but it's OK'. Anita's upturned almond eyes sparkle as the red stage light brushes her high, honeyed cheekbones. She gyrates, bends, touches her toes, and flashes that impossibly broad white smile. Her energy is total. The audience – mostly black, male and heterosexual – chug down their Black Labels and cheer raucously. Little do they realise the title of the song has a certain hidden poignancy. (Levin 2003)

As notions of enshrined LGBT rights and models for organisational political, legal and social engagement circulated outwards from South Africa, asylum seekers began to trickle towards the country.[3] For many, their move was a direct result of what they had heard about the possibilities of protection and prosperity in South Africa. Considered one of the first known asylum seekers to claim refugee status due to persecution based on sexual orientation, Anita – or as she was known offstage, Azu Udogu, a former winner of both the Miss Nigeria and Miss Lagos drag competitions – arrived in South Africa in December 1998 (Levin 2003). Crucially though, something often overlooked within the archive in relation to Udogo's life is her[4] gender identity

> I'm a transgender and I'm a transvestite because I do cabaret shows for transvestites … everyday of my life I live like a woman … and I would like to be related to like a woman … I'm on hormones … I don't want to be related to as a gay man because I'm a transgender I want to be treated I'm just like a woman. (Udogu 2003)

It was after experiencing multiple arrests, public harassment and beatings for being – perceived to be – gay, that Udogu fled Nigeria: for the country that, as local news media had reported, had enshrined the rights of sexual minorities (Levin 2003). Critically reflecting the paradoxical nature of both the proclamation and denigration of LGBT human rights across the continent during the 1990s, Udogu notes that her attackers would beat her saying, 'let them just like what Mugabe said that they are worse than dogs anyway' (Udogu 2003).

The NCGLE suggested that by the mid-1990s, there were probably, among the estimated 6–8 million 'aliens' living in South Africa, 'many thousands of gay and lesbian people displaced because of their sexual orientation' (Wakeford 1996, 2). Many of these 'aliens' arrived in the country only to experience a system of profound contradiction. While the Constitution explicitly forbade discrimination on the basis of gender, sex or sexual orientation, some of the provisions of the Aliens Control Act (ACA) – a document largely based on the deeply racist, homophobic and xenophobic Aliens Act of 1937 and the 1913 Immigration Act – directly contravened this (Dodson 2001). The incongruence between South Africa's Constitution, notions of the Rainbow Nation and the country's non-existent asylum regime was further exacerbated when, in 1995, South Africa became party to the *1951 UN Convention on the Status of Refugees* and the *Protocol to the UN Convention on the Status of Refugees* – both of which are central to the international refugee protection regime today. Article 1A (2) of the UN Convention provides a singular, universally applicable definition of a refugee providing five grounds[5] on which a person may claim asylum. Within these five grounds, 'membership of a particular social group' is broadly understood to include those fleeing persecution on the basis of sexual orientation and/or gender identity.

The lack of legislation implementing post-Apartheid South Africa's obligations under both the UN and the African Union Conventions[6] meant that much of what was meant by 'refugee', 'asylum seeker' and 'refugee rights', let alone the 'particularly contentious' (Wakeford 1996, 2) issue of discrimination 'based on sexual orientation', were open to interpretation by the Department of Home Affairs. Udogu, perhaps unsurprisingly then, first applied for asylum on the basis of 'political opinions' (Udogu 2003). The NCGLE played an undeniably critical role in challenging the constitutionality of the ACA, in some ways expediting the evident need for refugee-specific legislation. It must be noted, though, that at the time their focus was the gaining of immigration rights for same-sex couples. Refugee issues were a secondary concern. In the wake of the constitutional challenge and the clear lack of adequate legislation in South Africa, the UNHCR's regional office developed a draft Refugee Bill for the country incorporating the central tenets of the UN Convention. It is arguable that, at this point, the idea of transgender-specific asylum seekers would have been almost entirely inconceivable to the NCGLE. Prior to making a submission to Home Affairs in 1997, regarding immigration and asylum, a memo of the proposed document was circulated within the NCGLE with a request for clarity over whether 'sexual orientation included transgender people?' (Wakeford 1996, 1). In the final submission sent to Home Affairs, the NCGLE noted that South Africa had signed the UN Convention and that internationally, those fleeing persecution due to sexual orientation and/or gender identity had increasingly been able to claim asylum on the grounds of 'membership of a particular social group'. Moreover, the NCGLE argued, reading the UN Convention alongside the Constitution allowed for a uniquely inclusive approach which they commended, and urged the DHA to retain in the final Act (Wakeford 1996, 8). Conspicuously, all references by the NCGLE to transgender people were removed from the submission.

Following Udugo's case, and the work of the UNHCR and the NCGLE, the final Act was legislated in 1998. South African Refugees Act, no. 130 of 1998[7] aligned refugee protection with the Constitution, giving asylum seekers fleeing a broad scope of persecutions an explicit legal claim to protection (Handmaker 2011, 73). The combination of the UN Convention along with subsequent UN guidelines and the South African Constitution ostensibly ensure the rights and recognitions of transgender individuals fleeing persecution in their countries of origin. Seen as members of a particular social group transgender people would theoretically be able to attain refugee status in South Africa due to persecution based on gender identity or expression. Yet, after the establishment of the Refugee Act, Udogu, with the assistances of the Equality Project (formerly the NCGLE) changed her application to one of sexual orientation. To date, not a single known applicant has ever requested or gained asylum on the basis of gender identity in South Africa. While transgender identity and politics was certainly a contentious political topic internationally in the 1990s – influencing both the language of human rights work and the focus of transnational organisations – Udogo provides some insight into its presence and perception in relation to South Africa:

> I would like to have sponsors of gay rights to know that what they don't know is that there are other homosexuals like transgender and transvestites. Not just gay men ... This [being transgender] is not allowed in my country but it is allowed in this country. (Udogu 2003)

It would take Udogu five years after the passing of the Act to be awarded refugee status.

Regionality: the emergence of a politics of transgender in South Africa

Within these intra-African circulations of rights and language transgender, as a politics, remained vacant until the establishment, in 2005, of Cape Town-based NGO Gender DynamiX (GDX), describing themselves as the 'first African based [*sic*] organisation solely focused on the transgender community' (Gender DynamiX (GDX) 2012). The organisation marks a key shift in the development and circulation of transgender discourse not simply as a term functioning within a wider LGBT human rights mandate, but as a stand-alone politics within South Africa and across the continent. What is critical to note here is that GDX emerged as a direct result of the lack of support and information available to transgender and transsexual people in South Africa (Klein 2009). This is in stark contrast to most LGBT organisations, which emerge, as for instance the NCGLE did, to agitate for rights. In some ways, given the pre-exiting circulation of 'LGBT', the organisation stepped into a ready-made category, but not without difficulty, particularly as the constituency they hoped to serve was considered invisible or lacking 'the terminology to identify their gender identity' (Valenza 2011). In light of this, the terminology of 'transgender' was something the organisation has often had to introduce – in some cases to replace existing language – something they have had to 'stimulate' (Klein 2009, 19). As founder Liesl Theron explains,

> I visited ... a support group ... in Mamelodi ... When I introduced myself and Gender DynamiX and the work we do, I kept on saying I work with transgendered people and I kept on seeing these blank stares ... I said to the people 'so, do you all know what transgender is?' And then again blank stares ... So I say to them, I work with people who are known as sex changes. 'Oh yes! We all know' ... so then the whole conversation lit up ... I realised that in many black communities ... here in the 80's ... it was known to speak of a transgender person as 'a sex changes' ... So it is a clear thing for me that on the one hand you want to educate people, to use better terminology that is more acceptable ... on the one hand we want to keep up, in speed and terminology and things internationally, to be in the same league, but on the other hand we ... don't want to enforce terminology on people. (Klein 2009, 19)

As a South African-based organisation, GDX is peculiar in relation to what has historically been the standard trajectory or model for LGBT human rights groupings. From the outset, unlike its predecessors, the organisation situated itself as 'African based', de-emphasising notions of South African exceptionalism (Mamdani 1996; Lazarus 2004). In both rhetoric and practice, their approach has been distinctly transnational, situating themselves as a key player within the wider global trans movement. In essence then, the organisation has not only been taking 'better terminology' to South Africans, but also actively cultivating it regionally, simultaneously engaging in transnational structures which espouse a specific language. For Theron, the need for regional work was clear:

> South Africa is not an island and what we are doing as South Africans has an impact on the rest of the continent and what happens in the rest of the continent again comes to us ... If we then try to be an organisation that's proactive try to seek one, two or three other countries where there is [sic] a number of transgender people who need medical help and we can try start working there, they don't have to come here, we can equip and help them in the country where they are. (Theron 2012)

As the term 'transgender' reached a wider audience in South Africa, the organisation registered a growing number of requests for support, advice and often tangible assistance both from within South Africa and regionally. Victor Mukasa, a trans-identified individual from Uganda, was thrust into the spotlight in 2005 when he took the Attorney General of Uganda to court for an illegal raid on his home (Staff Writer 2005). Although in numerous news articles the case was framed as a landmark judgement affecting gay and lesbian people in Uganda, in reality the situation was far more nuanced. Due to the nature of the investigation and the threat it posed to Victor's life, he became one of the first visible transgender nationals from another country to seek refuge in South Africa. In 2006, Mukasa spoke at the UN about the hardships of being transgender in Africa. Referencing the emergent politics of transgender, he heralded the establishment of GDX and their work as a victory: 'We are now claiming language and claiming spaces. Sometimes it is even difficult for us to understand ourselves because the world has been constructed to make us completely invisible. But now we are finding words to use for ourselves' (Mukasa 2006).

GDX has described itself as being instrumental in the growth and the spread of 'better terminology' beyond South Africa's border. Regardless of their own eschewing of South African exceptionalism, the organisation, in the same manner as the NCGLE/Equality Project, has been upheld as a model for transgender political organising across Africa, playing 'a mentorship role in the Eastern and Southern African emerging trans movement' (Theron 2013). The organisation's *Founders' Statement* makes clear that this regional focus in particular has been financially beneficial.[8] This positive funding situation has come with certain requirements that cannot be overlooked in accounting for this politics of transgender, its emergence and its deployment. Sibusiso Kheswa, former director of GDX explains:

> You know, because there are people who are just living their lives … but we … say no, we see that life, That is trans. But the people don't own the word, don't identify, they don't even know the meaning of the word. In many instances people will still call themselves gay or lesbian while they live the lives they live, you know? … Like everything else, the donors have a lot of power and they decide what language and what activities or what work should be done … they have so much influence … And organisations then buy into it and we pass it on to the constituencies. That's how it works … because if there are people who would live the lives that they live and they don't call themselves trans and we do work with them, I'm sure the donor would say, 'but those are not trans people' … so we are also in this space where there is power dynamics amongst the stakeholders and the one with money has the most say. (Kheswa 2012)

What is critical here is that prior to GDX, there was very little political substance to transgender discourse in South Africa. However it certainly was a term, as the words and presence of Udogu suggest, that was already in circulation beyond South Africa's borders. As noted this travel was part of the initial circulation of the wider rhetoric of LGBT human rights and so linked to a notion of both rights and South Africa. These power dynamics and this regional flow of transgender, as a politics, not only accounts for how people come into contact with transgender as a term but also how they might end up in South Africa, applying for asylum. Reflecting on Mukasa's UN speech the emergence of transgender as a politics directly linked to South Africa arguably facilitated the political possibility of visibility and a claiming of space. Returning to the introductory words of Valentine, transgender as a politics for people like Mukasa then became a site of 'power to explain who we are', and enabled possibilities for 'action in the world' (Valentine 2007, 233). Yet, as Valentine suggests and perhaps Kheswa reflects, transgender as term with political power also contains the ability to 'limit' possibilities. It is to these limits and their relationship to the constitutional-legal make up of asylum in South Africa that I now turn.

'The Stigma of Western Words'[9]

In December 2009, Malawian Tiwonge Chimbalanga was arrested and charged with 'unnatural offences' and 'indecent practices between males' after her engagement ceremony to Steven Monjeza was made public (International Gay and Lesbian Human Rights Commission 2010).

> Journalists came to my wedding with Steven Monjeza. One of the journalists questioned Steven Monjeza, "Steven are you gay?" and he said "yes" because he does not go to school [he was not well educated] … So another question come, Auntie Tiwonge are you gay or

> straight? I didn't answer because this was a nonsense question. So they wrote the story about the wedding and Monday 12 o'clock the police came to Mankhoma Lodge and arrested me and Mr Monjeza. On our way to the police station people were dancing, some saying 'kill Tiwonge', people was talk, talk, talk, talk saying lots of things but it's a part of life. (Pereira 2012)

The jailed 'gay lovebirds' made headlines worldwide (Gevisser 2014). International donors and human rights groups condemned the Malawian State for what they called the abuse of 'gay human rights' (Reuters 2010) and called for the South African government not only to advocate for the couple's release but to offer the two asylum (NPR Staff and Wires 2010). The case itself was far more complex, politically and socially, than was intimated by the news media or the transnational NGOs – who became immediately involved in advocating for the release of the two. While the case was being touted as 'a test case for gay rights' and the vast majority of news headlines suggested that the pair were the 'first "gay" couple to attempt marriage in Malawi' (Smith 2010), Chimbalanga identified as a woman (Price 2010). Indeed, Chimbalanga, assigned male at birth, had been raised by her uncle – the village chief – and accepted as female since she was a child:

> My uncle and family accepted me as a girl. ... When people insulted me, my family made a complaint, and the culprits were taken to traditional court and fined some chickens. (Gevisser 2013)

Prior to the engagement, Chimbalanga had been living as a woman and Monjeza had presented her to his family as such. She performed several duties set aside for women within her community and was an active member of her local church's Women's League. Members of her community, including her employer – interviewed in the aftermath of the arrest – expressed surprise at the idea that she was anything other than female (Price 2010, 528).

It is notable that until the day of their engagement ceremony or chinkhoswe, there is no evidence to suggest that either of the words 'gay' or 'transgender' were used either in relation to the couple or by the couple themselves. Arguably, the local news media – recognising the possible traction of a report on gay marriage, a controversial topic internationally at the time, and in an African country, no less – took a seemingly unknown couple, removed from the politics of LGBT/gay rights, and propelled them into the international spotlight. As Theron explains, 'with the whole stigma of these western words ... it immediately became quite well known that this [the engagement/marriage] is wrong, this is not the right thing, so now they were in trouble' (Theron 2012). As noted by Chimbalanga, the question of whether she was 'gay' was a 'nonsense question' because as a woman this simply did not make sense for her: 'I have been like this since I was a child. I will never change. I am a woman forever. Even if they keep arresting me or kill me, they won't change my mind' (Blecher 2012).

Chimbalanga explains that it was not until her arrest that she had even heard the term gay, let alone transgender: 'They told me that I was paid to do my chinkhoswe by the LGBTs from overseas. But the first time I heard the word "gay" was when I saw it next to my photograph in the newspaper' (Gevisser 2013). As it became apparent that Chimbalanga actually identified as a woman, transgender organisations around the world voiced frustration at the seemingly dominant framing of the case as a gay rights issue. As one transgender blogger stated,

> This is a multilayered issue: clearly, trans and gay rights activists within Africa are identifying Tiwonge as a trans woman and see her conviction as transphobic state violence and injustice. However, mainstream international press and gay rights groups are co-opting the story to fit into their concept of the fight for marriage equality. The resulting coverage both silences trans women and ignores the voices and identities of Africans. (Ray 2010)

As the leading voice of transgender advocacy on the continent, GDX weighed in on the issue, elucidating that to their knowledge Chimbalanga identified and expressed herself as a woman. In light of this, they argued, 'If she knew the word transgender she would come home to a world of understanding of herself' (Hamblin 2010). Yet, she never used the word transgender. Even while in prison, when asked – as it seems she was – by representatives from transnational organisations and media houses, she continued to identify simply as a woman. UK rights campaigner Peter Tatchell stated, regarding whether Chimbalanga identified as transgender: 'I have arranged Malawian prison visitors for the last four months. I have got them to ask Tiwonge about his/her gender identity but the answers are unclear. I will get them to keep asking' (Staff 2010). For Chimbalanga, the matter regarding who she was and whether she had broken the law was simple: 'Which laws? I am a woman, I can do what a woman can do' (Tenthani and Low 2010).

Due to international pressure, the two, after being sentenced to 14 years' hard labour, were pardoned by the President 'on humanitarian grounds' (Gevisser 2010). A far more plausible explanation, for one of the continent's most aid-dependent countries, seems to lie with the clear threat of withdrawal of Malawi's foreign aid and donor support, pending the continued imprisonment of the couple (Blecher 2012). Monjenza almost immediately established himself with a new cisgendered female partner – many believe this was in order to avoid further public persecution (Simon 2010). Due to the seeming level of notoriety Chimbalanga had gained in Malawi, the situation was somewhat different from that of Monjeza. As Chimbalanga explains: 'After I was released from prison I experienced a lot of challenges in my country. People were calling me names and it was a very difficult time for me, so I decided to run away to South Africa' (Chimbalanga 2016). To assist in the process, Amnesty International contacted GDX. As Theron recalls:

> We were very cautious to not call her transgender because that wasn't the word or the language she was using, but she was definitely saying she is a woman … it seemed strange at the time to have like this court case where they are arguing gay/sexual orientation … and them accepted by the community and afterwards, Amnesty is like, okay trans organisation, now you can have her. (Theron 2012)

In October 2011, she arrived in South Africa and was eventually settled in Cape Town. Within a month of being in the country, due to a combination of international pressure and notoriety/celebrity, Chimbalanga was awarded full refugee status on the grounds of *sexual orientation* (Theron 2012).

To be simply a 'woman' and the finitude of transgender identity

Chimbalanga, assigned male, identifies as a woman. This understanding of herself is not dependent on a greater discourse or politics or anyone believing in it for it to be real. Her subject position resonates with transgender and yet she does not inhabit its discourse or politics. Two readings are possible here. The first might position Chimbalanga as transgender, as part of the universal, regardless of her own subject position. Indeed, in this reading Chimbalanga would simply become part of current contested universalist perceptions of transgender (Chakrabarty 2000, 108). The second reading would be to understand Chimbalanga as an individual 'illuminating life possibility for the present' in connection to how the relationship between gender, sex and sexuality might be framed (Chakrabarty 2000, 108).

In the latter reading, she would be troubling the very nature of the category of transgender as a universal. This would be would mean reading Chimbalanga's experiences as illustrative of 'times that produce cracks in the structure of homogeneity' (Chakrabarty 2000, 90). Chakrabarty, in offering a post-colonial critique, suggests that the reading need not be 'either-or' but rather that, 'taken together, the two gestures put us in touch with the plural ways of being that make up our own present … bring[ing] to view the disjointed nature of any particular "now" one may inhabit' (Chakrabarty 2000, 108).

As has been argued, the legislative process in South Africa, at least on paper, seemingly does not necessarily require a person to define themselves with terms like transsexual or transgender. Alongside this *the Sex Description and Sex Status Act 49 of 2003*, which facilitates the adjustment of sex on legal documents in South Africa, unlike other countries,[10] requires limited medical intervention. It also allows for the opportunity to seek assistance from a traditional healthcare practitioner as opposed to simply a medical doctor. This limited intervention coupled with the ability to seek assistance from a traditional healthcare practitioner suggests that the Act might not actually suppress local notions of, or possibilities for the expressions, of sex/gender/sexuality as has been argued by critics like Klein (2012). Rather, when a person desires to have their sex registered as something other than that designated at birth, the possibility to have been assigned male and present as a woman, without necessarily taking on the term transgender, is theoretically a liveable and protected expression of life in South Africa. Surprisingly then, it is the imposition of language from NGOs that creates the disjuncture here, and the law that theoretically outlines possibility.

This possibility for Chimbalanga ostensibly works in terms of legal grounding but there may be wider social and cultural issues – particularly as terms like 'transgender' become increasingly pervasive as a way of naming within society.[11] Here we find the line between the statements of Mukasa and Kheswa. Mukasa speaks a transnational language of human rights, proposing a particular visibility, while suggesting universality and, by extension, naturality (Kollman and Waites 2009, 13). Kheswa notes that people at a local level 'live the lives they live'. It is donors/funders who require organisations to pass 'better terminology' on to constituencies, in order to make them identifiable and, by extension, part of the modern universal. For Chakrabarty, Chimbalanga may be a moment where the 'limits of a discourse of history' – in this instance that of transgender – come to into view: the 'signposts of … [a] … border'. He suggests that modern public life requires a principle of narration that can be considered rational. He adds, 'that this requirement for a rational principle, in turn, marks the deep connections that exist between modern constructions of public life and projects of social justice' (Chakrabarty 2000, 110). In this case, transgender is a rational way to frame Chimbalanaga's sex/gender within the pervasive ideological construction of the gender binary. Transgender is a way to frame her corporeal sense of self. Transgender represents here the rational and universal – the T in the circulation of LGBT human rights.

The question becomes: why should Chimbalanga say she is transgender? What if bodies outside the Global North did not readily accept these terms, these rational principles linking public life and projects of social justice, instead maintaining alternate language, simply refusing or feeling that being assigned male and identifying as a woman, makes one a woman? Arguably, as is the case for most people assigned female who identify as women. Why is it that Chimbalanga should, in this instance, have to frame her gender identity or have her gender identity framed as transgender, and assigned female people who identify as women, simply have a gender? I'd like to return here to the fact that no known asylum seeker in South Africa identifying as transgender – or who expresses gender in a way that organisations would call transgender – has ever received or applied for asylum other than on the grounds of sexual orientation. There are two possible readings of this. The first is that in providing asylum on the grounds of sexual orientation – perceiving it here as synonymous with sexuality and same-sex identities such as gay and lesbian – the gender identity of applicants is overlooked, suppressed or lost. I would like to offer an alternate reading. In relation to sexual orientation, Sara Ahmed asks:

> What does it mean to be oriented? … What difference does it make what or who we are oriented toward in the very direction of our desire? If orientation is a matter of how we reside in space, then sexual orientation might also be a matter of residence, of how we inhabit spaces, and who or what we inhabit spaces with. (Ahmed 2006, 543)

In the *The First National Coalition Case* (1998), both Sacks and Ackerman clarified that sexual orientation was not meant to be read as a limiting category within the Constitution, but rather as a radical and destabilising envisioning of human difference. The meaning here arguably for Sachs/Ackerman seems to be not so much about sexuality or specific sexual identities but the orientation, the directionality, of one sex towards others.[12] In essence, within the borders of South Africa, the Constitution does not deal with discrimination based on sexual orientation 'as a matter of discrimination against a fixed, essentialised group named "homosexuals", but … rather focus[es] on the social and sexual practices which might mark individuals as "other" because of their practices and because of their shared experience of oppression and exclusion' (de Vos 2009, 13). This particular 'queer' reading separates South African constitutional notions of sexual orientation from the 'trajectory of its European colonial antecedents' (de Vos 2009, 13). Justice Sachs, in the concurring judgement for the case, makes this understanding most explicit:

> What the constitution requires is that the law and public institutions acknowledge the variability of human beings and affirm the equal respect and concern that should be shown to all as they are. At the very least, what is statistically normal ceases to be the basis for establishing what is legally normative. More broadly speaking, the scope of what is constitutionally normal is expanded to include the widest range of perspectives and to acknowledge, accommodate and accept the largest spread of difference. What becomes normal in an open society, then, is not an imposed and standardised form of behaviour that refuses to acknowledge difference, but the acceptance of the principle of difference itself, which accepts the variability of human behaviour. (*National Coalition for Gay and Lesbian Equality v The Minister of* Justice 1998 (12) BCLR 1517 (CC) at para 134)

This, as with the notions underpinning Act 49, again reiterate an understanding regarding the historically contingent nature of discourse, language and identities. This reading makes room for Chimbalanga, along with Udogu, and many others, in that while noting that transgender as a politics or identity may exist or be mergent, being/claiming/identifying as transgender is not necessary in relation to asylum. Rather it is the perception of a person's orientation, both at the level of their own sex and towards other sexes, in combination with their gender and the assumptions made in relation to this, that presumably have led to their persecution and subsequent claim. It is an acknowledgement that people may engage in same-sex activities but may not utilise a particular given language to identify themselves in relation to this. As Ahmed notes, 'The sex of one's object choice is not simply about the objective when "desire" is directed toward that object: it affects what we can do, where we can go, how we are perceived and so on' (Ahmed 2006, 563). Indeed, after five years of being in South Africa, after having come into contact with 'transgender', Chimbalanga has continued to state 'I am a woman' (Gevisser 2013).

Conclusion

In comparison to the development of a transgender politics in the Global North, which initially took place within LGB organisations, the route taken by the transgender movement in South Africa and to some extent Africa has been somewhat different. It would take almost 10 years from the emergence of a democratic South Africa for a movement to emerge, and when it did it was independent of any LGB organisation. Due to the 'T' in 'LGBT', organisations like GDX stepped into an already-established, though politically vacant, category. In fact, their emergence was in some ways facilitated by South Africa's constitutional-legal make up. Although mainstream gay organisations within South Africa carried the LGBT acronym – arguably following funder mandates which were couched in that language – work done to address trans issues or needs was slim to non-existent. South African transgender NGOs,[13] since their emergence, have strategically taken on a mantel of regionalism, working hand in hand with larger 'transnational' organisations to precipitate the development of transgender beyond the country's borders. As Udogu's case illustrates, the pathways created initially by LGBT activism, along with the denigration of 'gay rights' by religious and political leaders and the publication of this by international news media, have combined to create the perception that South Africa is a safe haven for individuals experiencing persecution. It is this network that proliferates around the politics of transgender in relation to gender identity and expression as human rights that has allowed transnational NGOs to assist gender refugees in coming to South Africa.

'Transgender' as term, politics and discourse has certainly travelled: along the way it has gathered bodies, organisations, attendant terms, laws, repudiations, accusations and questions. It has inhabited and been inhabited, deployed and been treated with a certain amount of deference due to its Global Northern origin. Chimbalanga represents a 'scandal' within this travel, within the possible discourse of transgender. For all intents and purposes, transnational organisations and donors spoke *for* Chimbalanga – ensuring her asylum in South Africa, but also defining her identity in ways that they considered the most politically useful to the wider transnational LGBT human rights regime. Since arriving in South Africa, now well-aware of the language of trans, Chimbalanga has continued to simply state that she is a woman (Takati 2012). Charlie Takati, the Outreach Officer at GDX, notes that he respects her for this and says that many people respect her 'as a woman and not as trans'.

It is clear that transgender has come to hold some political function at the level of organisations regionally, and that in using the requisite language of transgender they are able to communicate more clearly on a transnational level. It is also clear that, as yet, the spread of this 'better terminology' may not be taken on in the ways expected, if at all, and that this language is not a necessity for gaining refugee status. Returning to Ahmed: South Africa represents a space wherein the tending towards certain objects is admissible, protected and possible. A space which suggests that one's orientation in terms of desire and the shape of one's body might be supported without necessarily having to use a specific discourse. Clearly, what Udogu may have imagined, and what certainly created the room for someone like Chimbalanga to come to South Africa, is the Constitution. It is this very imagining of *the variability of human behaviour* that provides the possibility to embrace the Chimbalanaga's of the world, and many others we may not even be able to imagine yet.[14]

Notes

1. A 2010 decision in the South African labour court regarding the unfair dismissal of a trans person further suggests a possible reading of gender to include gender identity/expression. Source: *Ehlers v Bohler Uddeholm Africa (Pty) Ltd* 2010 (JS296/09) [2010] ZALC 117; (2010) 31 ILJ 2383 (LC) (13 August 2010).
2. In principle LGBT rights do not only refer to lesbian and gay rights but in practice there has been an ongoing tension regarding who has come to be represented by the LGBT acronym and who has come to access rights and protections under it.
3. The first reports of asylum seekers requesting protection due to their sexual orientation or gender identity started to appear in the late 1990s. Although no longer in existence, the Equality Project assisted some of the first gays and lesbians seeking asylum. See: Isaack (2009).
4. In almost all news articles published on Udogu, she has been referred to as 'he'; however, I take guidance from her words regarding her preferred pronoun:

   > I've always told myself that I'm transgender, I thought and lived like a woman and I think that is comfortable with me. I always like it when somebody calls me she, when they call me he I ask them 'which one is he?', I'm a girl.

5. Owing to well-founded fear of being persecuted for reasons of race, religion, nationality, membership of a particular social group or political opinion, is outside the country of his nationality and is unable to, or owing to such fear, is unwilling to avail himself of the protection of that county. Source: Art 1A(2) of the 1951 Convention Relating to the Status of Refugees.
6. The 1969 African Union Convention created to address the protection of refugees across Africa. It remains the only treaty to include an elaboration of the definition of refugee found the 1951 convention. The extended definition is considered by the UNHCR as 'complimentary protection', created to address the region's specific refugee generating issues which include 'external aggression, occupation, foreign domination or events seriously disturbing public order'. Its necessity is rooted in the perception that the UN Convention is unable to address two key issues for the African continent in particular: 'the struggle against colonialism and apartheid, as well as relations between African states including the control of subversive activities'. Source: UN High Commissioner for Refugees (UNHCR). (2005, June). Protection Mechanisms Outside of the 1951 Convention

('Complementary Protection'). Retrieved 13 July 2014, from http://www.refworld.org/docid/435e198d4.html p. 13.

7. The Act established a single asylum procedure, based on an approach of local integration, allowing refugees to integrate into society and access constitutional rights and freedoms. This differed from the general African approach, as seen in countries like Kenya, of accommodating refugees in large camps. Asylum seekers and refugees now had a legal right to registration and documentation and – importantly for gender refugees – access to services such as healthcare, including the ability to access gender-affirming healthcare.
8. Our work in the region did not only advance GDX in the current financial situation, but due to our relationships with activists and organisations in other countries over a period of a few years, we managed to build a reputable name for us – Theron (2013).
9. Camminga, B. (6 November 2012). Interview with Liesl Theron – Director. *Gender Dynamix*. Cape Town.
10. Several European countries still require extensive and evasive medical intervention including forced sterilisation in order to have the sex on legal document adjusted. See: Transgender Europe (TGEU). (10 May 2016). Trans Rights Europe Map & Index 2016. Retrieved 11 October 2017, from https://tgeu.org/trans-rights_europe_map_2016/.
11. The backlash to this visibility is evident in the number of reports by NGOs remarking on the extent of violence against lesbian and transgender people in particular. As an example: Human Rights Watch (2011).
12. Defined by reference to erotic attraction: in the case of heterosexuals, to members of the opposite sex; in the case of gays and lesbians, to members of the same sex. Potentially a homosexual or gay or lesbian person can therefore be anyone who is erotically attracted to members of his or her own sex – *National Coalition for Gay and Lesbian Equality v The Minister of Justice* 1998 (12) BCLR 1517 (CC) at para 20.
13. The list includes several other regionally focused organisations including The Social, Health and Empowerment Feminist Collective of Transgender Women in Africa (SHE) and Transgender and Intersex Africa (TIA).
14. It is arguable that the Constitution is in fact compatible with a far more pluralistic and radical/fluid notion of gender and sex than is currently envisioned by legislation such as Act 49. The Constitution is, after all, a living document. At the time of its creation, notions of sex and gender as existing in a far more fluid manner may not have been at the forefront of its creators' minds if indeed these understandings existed at all. It is clear that Act 49 functions on the assumption that gender is unambiguous. Moreover that sex and gender exist in binary and in a correlating relationship to one another. As understandings about sex and gender evolve, the possibility remains for diversity to be read into the Constitution. A recent briefing paper presented to Home Affairs by GDX and the Legal Resources Centre (LRC) has noted along these lines

> that in the context of the constitutional democracy in South Africa, limiting access to rights and services to only those who have gender identity that is "acceptable" undermines the spirit and purport of the Constitution, which requires that the State must take steps to protect, promote and fulfill everyone's rights, which includes transgender persons. (p. 5)

In light of this, they stress that the law has lagged in relation to medical and social developments regarding 'thinking about gender and sex beyond the male-female/man-woman binary' (Legal Resources Center, Gender DynamiX (GDX) 2015, 21).

Disclosure statement

No potential conflict of interest was reported by the author.

References

Ahmed, S. 2006. "Orientations: Toward a Queer Phenomenology." *GLQ: A Journal of Lesbian and Gay Studies* 12 (4): 543–574. doi:10.1215/10642684-2006-002.

Blecher, S. 2012. *Two Men and a Wedding*. Johannesburg: CINGA Productions.

Cameron, E. 1993. "Sexual Orientation and the Constitution: A Test Case for Human Rights." *South African Law Journal* 110 (January): 450–472.

Chakrabarty, D. 2000. *Provincializing Europe: Postcolonial Thought and Historical Difference*. Princeton: Princeton University.

Chimbalanga, T. 2016. 'Tiwonge's Story – Where Love Is Illegal'. *Whereloveisillegal.Com*. Accessed 1 January. http://whereloveisillegal.com/tiwonges-story/.

Christiansen, E. 2000. "Ending the Apartheid of the Closet: Sexual Orientation in the South African Constitutional Process." *New York University Journal of International Law and Politics* 32 (4): 997–1058.

de Vos, P. 2009. "From Heteronormativity to Full Sexual Citizenship? Equality and Sexual Freedom in Laurie Ackermann's Constitutional Jurisprudence." In *Dignity, Freedom and the Post-Apartheid Legal Order: The Critical Jurisprudence of Laurie Ackerman*, edited by J. Barnard, D. Cornell, and F. du Bois, 254–273. Cape Town: Juta.

Dodson, B. 2001. "Discrimination by Default? Gender Concerns in South African Migration Policy." *Africa Today* 48 (3): 73–89. doi:10.1353/at.2001.0051.

Gender DynamiX (GDX). 2012. 'About Us'. *Gender Dynamix*. Accessed 2 August. http://www.genderdynamix.org.za/about/.

Gevisser, M. 2010. "Homosexuality and the Battle for Africa's Soul". *Mail and Guardian*. Accessed 1 June. http://mg.co.za/article/2010-06-04-homosexuality-and-the-battle-for-africas-soul/.

Gevisser, M. 2013. "Love in Exile". *The Guardian*. Accessed 1 January. http://www.theguardian.com/news/2014/nov/27/-sp-transgender-relationship-jail-exile-tiwonge-chimbalanga.

Gevisser, M. 2014. "No Respite for Africa's Transgender Poster Girl". *Mail and Guardian*. Accessed 1 January. http://mg.co.za/article/2014-12-05-no-respite-for-africas-transgender-poster-girl/.

Hamblin, R. 2010. "Press Release: Malawian Couple Sentenced to 14 Years Hard Labour – Transgender Activists Speak Out". Gender DynamiX. http://pinaytg.blogspot.com/2010/05/jailed-and-gay-ed.html.

Handmaker, J. 2011. "Public Interest Litigation for Refugees in South Africa and the Potential for Structural Change." *South African Journal on Human Rights* 27 (1): 65–81. doi:10.1080/19962126.2011.11865005.

Hoad, N. 1999 January . "Between the White Man's Burden and the White Man's Disease: Tracking Lesbian and Gay Human Rights in Southern Africa". *GLQ A Journal of Gay and Lesbian Studies* 559–584. doi:10.1215/10642684-5-4-559

Human Rights Watch. 2011. *We'll Show You That You're a Woman: Violence and Discrimination against Black Lesbians and Transgender Men in South Africa*. New York: Human Rights Watch.

International Gay and Lesbian Human Rights Commission. 2010. "IGLHRC and CEDEP Condemn Malawi Court's Conviction of Imprisoned Couple". *IGLHRC*. Accessed 18 May. http://iglhrc.org/content/iglhrc-and-cedep-condemn-malawi-courts-conviction-imprisoned-couple.

Isaack, W. 2009. *African Lesbian & Gay People – Final Destination South Africa?* Johannesburg: Legal Resource Centre. www.lrc.org.za/papers/939-african-lesbian-a-gap-people-final-destination-south-africa-by-wendy-isaack.

Kentridge, J. 1998. 'Equality'. In *Constitutional Law of South Africa*, edited by J. Kentridge, M. Chaskalson, S. Woolman, J. Klaaren, D. Spitz, and G. Marcus, Revisions Service 5:14.1-14.67. Johannesburg: Juta Legal and Academic Publishers.

Kheswa, S. 2012. Interview with Sibusiso Kheswa – Advocacy Coordinator Interview by B Camminga.

Klein, T. 2009. "Intersex and Transgender Activism in South Africa." *Liminalis* 3 (January): 15–41.

Klein, T. 2012. "Who Decides Whose Gender? Medico-legal Classifications of Sex and Gender and Their Impact on Transgendered South Africans' Family Rights." *Ethnoscripts* 14 (2): 12–34.

Kollman, K., and M. Waites. 2009. "The Global Politics of Lesbian, Gay, Bisexual and Transgender Human Rights: An Introduction." *Contemporary Politics* 15 (1): 1–17. doi:10.1080/13569770802674188.

Lazarus, N. 2004. 'The South African Ideology: The Myth of Exceptionalism, the Idea of Renaissance.' *The South Atlantic Quarterly* 103 (4): 607–28.

Legal Resources Center, and Gender DynamiX (GDX) 2015. Briefing Paper: Alteration of Sex Description and Sex Status Act, No 49 of 2003. Cape Town. https://genderdynamix.org.za/wp-content/uploads/LRC-act49-2015-web.pdf.

Levin, A. 2003. '"Pink Refugees" in South Africa Seek Refuge from Persecution at Home'. *Rainbow Network*. Accessed 7 May. http://www.rainbownetwork.com/content/Feature.asp?featid=13214.

Mamdani, M. 1996. *Citizen and Subject: Contemporary Africa and the Legacy of Late Colonialism*. Princeton: Princeton University Press.

Meyerson, D. 1993. "Sex and Gender in the South African Law Commissions Proposed Bill of Rights, the ANC's Draft Bill of Rights, and the Governments Proposal on a Charter of Fundamental Rights." *South African Journal on Human Rights* 9 (2): 291–297.

Mukasa, V. 2006. "On Transgender Human Rights Issues in Africa". *Pambazuka*. Accessed 7 December. http://pambazuka.org/en/category/comment/38727. *National Coalition for Gay and Lesbian Equality v The Minister of Justice* 1998 (12) BCLR 1517 (CC)

NPR Staff and Wire. 2010. "Gay Couple in Malawi Sentenced to 14 Years". *NPR.Org*. Accessed 20 May. https://www.npr.org/templates/story/story.php?storyId=127014509.

Pereira, J. 2012. "Tiwonge & Steve's Story". Iranti.org. https://www.youtube.com/watch?v=-ucE_3IT1iU.

Phillips, O. 2000. "Constituting the Global Gay: Issues of Individual Subjectivity and Sexuality in Southern Africa." In *Sexuality in the Legal Arena*, edited by D. Herman and C. Stychin, 17–34. London: Athlone Press.

Price, L. 2010. "The Treatment of Homosexuality in the Malawian Justice System: R V Steven Monjeza Soko and Tiwonge Chimbalanga Kachepa." *African Human Rights Law Journal* 10 (January): 524–533.

Ray, A. 2010. "In the Interest of "Equality," Malawian Woman's Identity is Erased – International Women's Health Coalition". *International Womens Health Coalition*. Accessed 21 May. http://iwhc.org/2010/05/in-the-interest-of-equality-malawian-womans-identity-is-erased/.

Reuters. 2010. "Malawi Gay Couple 'Has a Case'". *News24*. Accessed 22 March. www.news24.com/Africa/News/Malawi-gay-couple-has-a-case-20100322.

Simon, M. 2010. "'Same-Sex' Malawi Couple Splits". *Salon.Com*. Accessed 9 June. http://www.salon.com/2010/06/09/malawi_gay_couple/.

Smith, D. 2010. "Married Malawian Gay Couple Face Test to Prove They had Sexual Relations". *The Guardian*, Accessed 1 January. http://www.theguardian.com/world/2010/jan/01/malawi-gay-couple-married-test.

Staff. 2010. "Frustration at Coverage of Malawi Couple". *Gaynz.Com*. Accessed 31 May. http://www.gaynz.com/articles/publish/3/printer_8869.php.

Staff Writer. 2005. "Court Gives Christmas Present to Ugandan Gays". *Afrol.Com*. Accessed 25 December. http://www.afrol.com/articles/32072.

Takati, C. 2012. Interview with Charlie Takati – Outreach Officer Interview by B Camminga.

Tenthani, R., and V. Low. 2010. "We Have Been Beaten in Jail, Say First Openly Gay Couple in Malawi". *Times Online*. Accessed 4 January. http://www.timesonline.co.uk/tol/news/world/africa/article6974678.ece?print=yes&randnum=1262621202492.

Theron, L. 2012. *Interview with Liesl Theron – Director*. Gender Dynamix in Cape Town Interview by B Camminga.

Theron, L. 2013. "The Founder". *Gender Dynamix*. Accessed 1 July. http://www.genderdynamix.org.za/about/gdx-founder-liesl-theron/.

Udogu, A. 2003. Interview with Azu Udogu Interview by Anthony Manion. 'Archiving GALA collection' – AM3160. Gay and Lesbian Memory in Action Archive William Cullen Library, University of the Witwatersrand.

Valentine, D. 2007. *Imagining Transgender: An Ethnography of a Category*. London: Duke University Press.

Valenza, A. 2011. "South Africa: Lack of Bisexual, Transgender and Intersex People Causes an Imbalance in Representation – ILGA". *ILGA*. Accessed 2 March. http://ilga.code8.cz/south-africa-lack-of-bisexual-transgender-and-intersex-people-causes-an-imbalance-in-representation/.

Wakeford, C. E. 1996. *Lobbying and Advocacy Project Report*. Johannesburg: National Commission for Gay and Lesbian Equality.

Gender, sexuality and the right to a non-projected future: a reply to Camminga

Elizabeth Mills

ABSTRACT

This reply considers the movement of words as discussed in Camminga's article with reference to South Africa's Constitution and its Refugee Act. It explores the value and limitations of performing subjectivities like 'transgender' in contexts where these words have been introduced and, in some cases, imposed. This discussion considers the 'Stigma of Western Words', as articulated by Camminga, in light of the broader politics of international development and aid conditionality linked to LGBT rights. These politics are contrasted with some of the dynamics underpinning an international development programme that sought to advance LGBT rights and livelihoods, as discussed in the accompanying article on gender, sexuality and the limits of the law.

This is a reply to:

Camminga, B. 2018. "'The Stigma of Western Words': Asylum Law, Transgender Identity and Sexual Orientation in South Africa." *Global Discourse*. doi:10.1080/23269995.2018.1521045.

Gender, sexuality and the right to a non-projected future

In 1971, Albert Hirschman challenged social scientists to disrupt their assumptions about the world, to relinquish their attempts to fit complex social, economic and political transformation into paradigms that had become so familiar they stopped being analytically helpful. Instead, looking particularly to South American countries, he challenged us to engage the unexpected. The ethical implication of this challenge is captured by Joao Biehl's description of the right to a non-projected future, where thinking beyond what we perceive to be possible is not only intellectually important but ethically critical:

> At stake is helping to 'defend the right to a nonprojected future as one of the truly inalienable rights of every person and nation; and to set the state for conceptions of change to which the inventiveness of history and a 'passion for the possible' are admitted as vital actors'. (2007, 3)

In his reflections on Hirschman's (1971) call with respect to his ethnography of precarious life and access to AIDS medicines in Brazil, Biehl (2007) explains that engaging the unexpected is not simply an abstract academic principle, but that it is an ethical task.

Writing about the meaning-making of 'transgender' in relation to asylum in South Africa, Camminga traces the journey of this word as it accumulates weight and travels with Tiwonge Chimbalanga from Malawi to South Africa. In doing so, Camminga proposes that rather than limiting or constraining people's expression of their gender and sexuality to a series of fixed categories, legal interpretations of South Africa's Equality Act reflect a radical disruption to terms like 'lesbian', 'gay' and 'transgender' that have become reified by non-governmental organisations working in and beyond South Africa. Through a careful examination of Constitutional meanings of sexual orientation, sex and gender, the paper reveals the radical possibility of South Africa's refugee regime – a possibility that, I suggest, echoes Biehl's call for the right to a non-projected future and the imperative of thinking at or beyond the limits of categories as they function to constrain rather than liberate gender and sexual minorities.

Tiwonge Chimbalanga's marriage to Steven Monjeza was captured and projected into the world as one of Malawi's first 'gay marriages' in 2009. Monjeza and Chimbalanga, who were both assigned male at birth, were swiftly arrested and charged with 'unnatural offences'. However, as Camminga notes, Chimbalanga identified as a woman: at the time of their marriage, the term 'gay' did not resonate for the couple and the term 'transgender' held no meaning for Chimbalanga. It was also at this time that international development organisations started to direct foreign aid to advance the rights of gender and sexual minorities. In 2011, for example, the British Prime Minister, David Cameron was reported to said that 'British aid should have more strings attached'. At that time, and following the global outrage over Monjeza and Chimbalanga's treatment as a 'gay couple', the United Kingdom's Department for International Development (DfID) suspended £19 million of budget support to Malawi, due to infractions on progress on media freedoms, human rights and the government's approach to gay rights.[1]

David Cameron's 'aid conditionality' approach has been thoroughly eviscerated (Dunne 2012; Klapeer 2018; Lind 2018) with sexual and gender rights organisations arguing that this approach generated more harm than good for minority groups (Onapajo and Isike 2016; Tamale 2013). It was at this time, too, that the Sexuality, Poverty and Law Programme was funded by DfID to explore the impact of legal and policy discrimination on the lives and livelihoods of gender and sexual minorities. In their article, Camminga traces the movement of the word 'transgender' from the West into and across African countries. One of the key challenges of the SPLP centred on the limits of language, and the dangers of mobilising terms like 'lesbian', 'gay' or 'transgender' in countries where these terms did not previously exist.

Through their research in Nepal, Coyle and Boyce (2015) challenge the imposition of the term 'transgender' onto the lives of people who did not identify with this word but who sorely needed international resources to enable them to manage the challenges they faced as a marginalised group. In other countries, like India, researchers found that the crystallisation of terms like 'transgender' resulted in an increased visibility of people who were then assigned this subjectivity without discussion or consent, and who were consequently subjected to discrimination by their employers, colleagues and families because of the stigma that these 'western' terms carried (Dhall and Boyce, 2015; c.f. Waites 2009).

Camminga's discussion of the movement of the term 'transgender' into Malawi, and into Chimbalanga's life, articulates some of the difficulties facing those who are living at the margins and who require resources – to travel to South Africa to claim asylum, in Chimbalanga's case – but who need to perform a particular subjectivity in order to access those resources. I would be interested to understand how Chimbalanga experienced this process, and the requirement to perform this subjectivity in order to access asylum. Further, I imagine that Amnesty and Gender DynamiX – the organisations assisting Chimbalanga in her application for asylum – are well aware of the 'stigma of Western Words' (as quoted by the Director of Gender DynamiX) and I am curious to understand how these organisations view their own politics as they walk a tightrope to access funding while recognising the limits of international development and global LGBT rights discourse.

The 'Stigma of Western Words' engages the unexpected: it offers a novel conclusion on the emancipatory potential of the law – as read by judges like Edwin Cameron, for example – for opening up rather than closing down the range of ways people can inhabit their bodies and make claims on the state through their bodies. Indeed, it is the non-governmental organisations involved in interpreting and utilising South Africa's Refugee Act that run the risk of closing down the possibility of imagining 'the variability of human behaviour' (Camminga 2018, 14). The right to a nonprojected future, in the context of my own and Camminga's articles, therefore circles back around to the value of thinking of and beyond the margins of the words we use in order to extend the horizon of the worlds we inhabit.

Note

1. BBC, 2011. "Cameron threat to dock some UK aid to anti-gay nations." https://www.bbc.co.uk/news/uk-15511081. Accessed July 2018.

Disclosure statement

No potential conflict of interest was reported by the author.

ORCID

Elizabeth Mills http://orcid.org/0000-0002-0388-9437

References

Biehl, J. 2007. *Will to Live: AIDS Therapies and the Politics of Survival*. Princeton: Princeton University Press.

Camminga, B. 2018. "'The Stigma of Western Words': Asylum Law, Transgender Identity and Sexual Orientation in South Africa." *Global Discourse*. doi: 10.1080/23269995.2018.1521045

Coyle, D., and P. Boyce. 2015. "Same-Sex Sexualities, Gender Variance, Economy and Livelihood in Nepal: Exclusions, Subjectivity and Development." *IDS Evidence Report 109*. Brighton: Institute of Development Studies.

Dhall, P., and P. Boyce. 2015. "Livelihood, Exclusion and Opportunity: Socioeconomic Welfare among Gender and Sexuality Non-Normative People in India." *IDS Evidence Report 106*. Brighton: Institute of Development Studies.

Dunne, P. 2012. "LGBTI Rights and the Wrong Way to Give Aid." *Kennedy School Review* 12: 66.

Hirschman, A. O. 1971. *A Bias for Hope*. New Haven: Yale university press.

Klapeer, C. M. 2018. "Dangerous liaisons?: (Homo) Developmentalism, Sexual Modernization and LGBTIQ Rights in Europe." In *Routledge Handbook of Queer Development Studies*, edited by C. Mason. Abingdon: Routledge.

Lind, A. 2018. "Heteronormative Legacies, Queer Turns." In *Routledge Handbook of Queer Development Studies*, edited by C. Mason. Abingdon: Routledge.

Onapajo, H., and C. Isike. 2016. "The Global Politics of Gay Rights: The Straining Relations between the West and Africa." *Journal of Global Analysis* 6 (1): 21–45.

Tamale, S. 2013. "Confronting the Politics of Nonconforming Sexualities in Africa." *African Studies Review* 56 (2): 31–45. doi:10.1017/asr.2013.40.

Waites, M. 2009. "Critique of 'Sexual Orientation' and 'Gender Identity' in Human Rights Discourse: Global Queer Politics beyond the Yogyakarta Principles." *Contemporary Politics* 15 (1): 137–156. doi:10.1080/13569770802709604.

Gender, sexuality and the limits of the law

Elizabeth Mills

ABSTRACT

This article reflects on a programme of research conducted by gender and sexuality activists, academics and legal practitioners in Latin America, Africa, the Middle East, South Asia and South East Asia. Running over 4 years, the Sexuality, Poverty and Law Programme (SPLP) aimed to generate new evidence-based knowledge and policy options to support efforts that would strengthen, through legal reform, the rights of lesbian, gay, bisexual and transgender (LGBT) people and others marginalised because of their sexuality. The SPLP also aimed to demonstrate the impact of legal and policy marginalisation on the livelihoods of LGBT across the world. Instead of claiming answers or offering conclusions based on this body of work, the article draws on Sara Ahmed's writing and raises questions based on the SPLP around what it means to encounter 'brick walls' – specifically the materiality of juridical and productive power – through one's body. The article explores how international discourses and institutions are implicated in the shape of domestic legal frameworks that centre on gender and sexuality, and it explores how these frameworks shape which bodies are made visible, effaced or entirely ignored. Given the politics of international development and global LGBT rights discourse, this article concludes that laws are never quite sovereign and it makes a case for understanding the implications of this 'legal porosity' on people's embodied experiences of inequality as they fall under (beside or outside) the law.

(En)Countering walls

> I watched from the other side of a stone wall, a wall that was part self-preservation, part bones and blood of aloneness, part the impossible assumptions I could not shape my body around. (Clare 2015 [1999], 144)

> Walls are how some bodies are not encountered in the first place. Walls are how some bodies are stopped by an encounter. (Ahmed 2017, 145)

In her account of coming up against institutional walls as a diversity worker, Sara Ahmed describes how material histories become inscribed in institutional structures, affecting which bodies can or cannot access institutional spaces. Reflecting on her work to address sexual harassment in universities, for instance, Ahmed articulates this diversity work as entailing 'the work we do when we aim to transform the norms of an institution, and the work we do when we do not quite inhabit those norms. These two senses often meet in a body: those who do not quite inhabit the norms of the institution are often those given the task of transforming these norms' (2017, 89). In this paper, I use Ahmed's notion of 'brick walls' to denote the materiality of juridical and productive power and I do so in order to explore the edges, or the limits, of the law. Put differently, I explore how the law – that endlessly shape-shifting 'thing', in Appadurai's (2006) terms – is encountered and embodied, as bodies are stopped, or welcomed, or not encountered at all.

Genderqueer poet and activist, Eli Clare, echoes Ahmed's (2017) reflections on how some bodies are recognized and welcomed when others face a choice of risking the violence that comes from making one's body visible and therefore risking a brutal encounter with the hardness of a wall in the shape of a discriminatory law, for example. Clare suggests that certain forms of analysis of inequality that fail to recognize the diversity of bodies run the risk of closing down rather than opening out transformative engagement. There is a risk that in discussing people's embodied experiences of inequality, academic discussions of intersectionality – for example – may perpetuate a dangerous academic voyeurism; in this hypothetical world, embodied inequalities become a source of debate, extracted from lived reality and abstracted for the sake of theory. This is strikingly evident, for example, in the context of the United Kingdom's current (2018) open consultation on the Gender Recognition Act (GRA) 2004. The extent of 'debate' on the GRA has revealed deep cracks in the façade of a universal feminism, with some feminists challenging the rights of trans and non-binary people to choose how they wish to identify and the spaces they may inhabit. These debates often utilise intersectional theory alongside antiquated thinking about sex to make dangerous claims, and powerfully illustrate the danger of invoking theory to build new (legal) walls and impossible definitions, with reference to Clare's quote (2015 [1999], 144), that people cannot (and should not be asked to) shape their bodies around.

This article draws on research that sought to understand the relationship between the law and people's embodied experiences of inequality related to their gender and their sexuality. Instead of claiming answers or offering conclusions based on this body of work, the article raises questions around what it means to encounter walls – to encounter, and counter, the materiality of juridical and productive power through our bodies. Specifically, it asks how international discourses and institutions are implicated in the shape of domestic legal frameworks that centre around gender and sexuality, and it explores how these frameworks shape which bodies are made visible, or effaced, or entirely ignored. Throughout the paper, I explore the extent to which laws are never quite sovereign, and I consider the implications of this 'legal porosity' on people's embodied experiences of inequality as they fall under (beside or outside) the law.

In this article, I focus primarily on Domestic Law and distinguish between public law (including constitutional, criminal and administrative law) and private law (including property, contract, commercial and tort law). As a social anthropologist, I recognise that I am not a legal expert. Instead, my focus will be on factors that shape the law and, conversely, factors that shape people's embodied experience of the law. This approach reflects Van Hoecke and Warrington's (1998) call to situate the law in people's lives. They write that, 'Describing the law entails more than just reporting the legal rules, and certainly more than simply quoting the wording of legislative texts' (523). Specifically, this article pays attention to the lived experiences of marginalization that are created through failing legal systems, or – conversely – through the effective implementation of discriminatory laws.

Research background

This paper reflects on research generated through the *Sexuality, Poverty and Law Programme* (SPLP).[1] Funded by the Department for International Development in the United Kingdom, and running from 2012 to 2016, the SPLP connected activists, academics and legal practitioners working in over 30 countries. These legal practitioners, activists and academics generated a series of policy and legal case studies on the relationship between poverty and legal discrimination in Latin America, Africa, the Middle East, South Asia and South East Asia. Resulting in 25e research papers, these studies were conducted alongside a series of workshops, interactive and online toolkits for activists, lawyers and academics working in the field of sexuality and social justice,[2] and international and national legal and policy engagements. Running over 4 years, the programme aimed to generate new evidence-based knowledge and policy options to support efforts that would strengthen, through legal reform, the rights of lesbian, gay, bisexual and transgender (LGBT) people and others marginalised because of their sexuality. Funded and run through the Institute of Development Studies in the UK, the SPLP also aimed to demonstrate the impact of legal and policy marginalisation on the livelihoods of LGBT across the world.

Following the principles of Grounded Theory (Corbin and Strauss 1990), I worked with a team of researchers to develop a set of qualitative codes through a narrative analysis of each of the empirical studies. Two overarching findings emerged from this cross-cutting analysis, and they are discussed in turn in the sections below. First, we found that national legal frameworks are not sovereign; they are malleable instruments of international aid, foreign policies and global discourses that shape which bodies are stopped, welcomed or not encountered at all. Second, we found that these legal frameworks have a material impact on people's lives as they encountered the 'brick walls' of linked legal and social discrimination. The ontological manifestations of these encounters are explored in the second section, through Butler's concept of precarity (2009) and in relation to Ahmed's (2017) reflections on the importance of bringing the politics of bodies into focus.

A note on terminology: in this article, I draw on Corrêa and Muntarbhorn's (2007) definition of gender identity and sexual orientation.

> Sexual Orientation is understood to refer to each person's capacity for profound emotional, affectional and sexual attraction to, and intimate and sexual relations with, individuals of a different gender or the same gender or more than one gender.
>
> Gender identity is understood to refer to each person's deeply felt internal and individual experience of gender, which may or may not correspond with the sex assigned at birth, including the personal sense of the body (which may involve, if freely chosen, modification of bodily appearance or function by medical, surgical or other means) and other expressions of gender, including dress, speech and mannerisms. (Corrêa and Muntarbhorn 2007, 6)

Sexual orientation and gender identity (or SOGI) are themselves terms that represent power, as they are used in powerful international institutions like the United Nations, for example; I define SOGI here, as I turn to discuss international discourse and actors in the section below. However, as many studies on the SPLP reflect, SOGI is a political term and one that did not resonate with the people and communities that engaged in this research. The authors of these studies use terms that are appropriate and relevant for the people with whom they worked, and wherever possible I use these terms when discussing these studies.

The 'brick walls' of the law and its embodied implications

The selective utilization of human rights discourse by western states to constitute new national identities is a well-established critique. Described by Jasbir Puar as 'homonationalism', the 'acceptance' or 'tolerance' for lesbian and gay citizens in some countries 'have become a barometer by which the right to and capacity for national sovereignty is evaluated' (Puar and Rai 2007, 4). Through a careful examination of LGBT activist responses to the 2003 United States (U.S.) Supreme Court ruling in *U.S. v. Lawrence* (which decriminalized anal sex between consenting adults), Puar revealed how the celebration of the queer subject runs alongside an acceptance of 'a regime of racialized surveillance, detention and deportation' (Puar 2017, 336).

Just as historic and contemporary critics of international development shun the application of a simplistic model of economic development that advances neoliberalism as the moniker of progress (Kothari 2005; Radcliffe 2012), international development actors have been cautioned against measuring a country's commitment to human rights by the presence of 'LGBT-friendly' laws and policies (Alqaisiya 2018; Harcourt 2016). This cautious approach has a long history, stemming back to scholars like Jacqui Alexander and Oliver Phillips in the 1990s. These authors echo the findings discussed in sections below, as they warned that post-colonial nationalisms may be crystallised in opposition to the economic necolonialisms and nationalisms of former colonial states (Alexander 1994; Phillips 1997).[3]

(International) bodies and the law

In their research in Nepal for the SPLP, Paul Boyce and Danny Coyle (2013) trace the significant changes that have taken place over the past 15 years in terms of legal recognition of sexual rights. They suggest that Nepal's adoption of laws that advance the rights of sexual and gender minorities functions primarily as a signal to international actors that the country is 'modern'. They write that:

> While the new legislative context for same-sex sexualities in Nepal can be interpreted in terms of Nepali-specific social change, it can also be seen within a larger context of shifts in international politics concerning same-sex sexualities. 'Modern states', are increasingly prevailed upon to 'recognize a sexual minority within the national body and grant that minority rights-based protections', as a symbolic marker of a democratic, neoliberal polity (Franke 2012: 19). Through such policies states can signal that they are aspiring to take their place within a progressive international community, which can accrue benefits from trade and development aid. (Franke 2012; Boyce and Coyle 2013, 13)

The pace of Nepal's legal change is contrasted with the resurgence of government-level prejudices. The rates of arbitrary arrests of transgender women and gender-nonconforming men have escalated on the grounds of 'public indecency', major political parties revoked the candidacies of sexual and gender minority parliamentary candidates and recently a new draft of the criminal code included provision for the criminalization of 'unnatural' sex with incarceration (Boyce and Coyle 2013).

In contrast with findings from Nepal, SPLSP research in Rwanda indicates that government officials are aware of the danger of international intervention in laws that concern gender and sexuality. Rwanda holds a neutral legal position on homosexuality, and Haste and Gatete suggest that:

> [T]he constitutionally enshrined discourse of tolerance and non-discrimination was ... a useful entry point for addressing social stigma and discrimination on the basis of sexual orientation and gender identity...... Because of this, sensitisation of local officials to the law, and to their responsibility to uphold the law without exception, was seen as a top priority. (2015, 24-25)

A member of Rwanda's parliament told the researchers that the country's history of brutal genocide meant that law-makers 'knew better' than to criminalise people because they were 'different'. While Rwanda does not have the kind of progressive laws and policies that we see in Nepal, human rights principles appeared to reside in the discourse of government officials. During their research, Haste and Gatete (2015) heard the importance of keeping international NGOs, donors and the diplomatic community away from the complex processes through which laws and policies were established at a national level. The Member of Parliament, whom we met earlier, emphasized the need to find 'Rwandan solutions to Rwandan problems' (Haste and Gatete 2015, 35). The authors of the study suggest then, that:

> The international community should therefore avoid conspicuous public recognition of, or congratulatory comments on, Rwanda's legal and policy framework in relation to LGBT rights, and avoid any approach that could be perceived as positioning LGBT rights as a 'special', or particularly Western, concern'. (Haste and Gatete 2015, 35)

The studies discussed above suggest that progressive laws fail when they are used to signal 'modernity' to international actors at the expense of generating meaningful societal transformation to advance the rights of all people, regardless of gender or sexuality. The disjuncture between *de jure* and *de facto* laws can only widen when international actors place pressure on national governments to 'conform' to human rights provisions. We see, in the case of Nepal, that access to international trade agreements or donor funding run alongside the risk of a resurgence in political and socio-economic discrimination as an assertion of nationalism. Further, the case of Rwanda suggests some value in a non-interventionist approach. Significantly, this case calls for a recognition of national and local approaches to securing the everyday wellbeing of LGBT people beyond the reach of the law or of formal rights-based programmes that are internationally funded.

In both Nepal and Rwanda, international actors run the risk of creating the kinds of walls that Ahmed (2017) refers to, in which bodies are encountered – or made especially visible. In Nepal, for instance, the increasing rates of arbitrary arrests – brutal attacks on people's bodies – run alongside the expansion of laws that claim to protect LGBT rights. Boyce and Coyle (2013) suggest that these laws are not necessarily protecting LGBT people: they are, in fact, working to signal 'modernity' in order to encourage greater investment in by international actors in the country. In doing so, these laws may be contributing to the greater visibility of particular sexual subjectivities (the language of LGBT, for instance, is not one that many people recognized in the study conducted in Nepal) and in turn, to greater levels of embodied vulnerability.

(National) bodies and the law

In the Philippines, GALANG – a lesbian-initiated, lesbian-run feminist human rights organization – described their decade long struggle to compel the government to introduce the country's first anti-discrimination bill (ADB). Working with a network of human rights advocates including feminists, disability rights activists and reproductive rights activists, GALANG has campaigned to introduce the ADB by invoking the country's Bill of Rights, and specifically its equal protection clause (GALANG 2013). They suggest that religion is one of the main barriers to the ADB:

> With the vast store of resources available to it, the Roman Catholic hierarchy has been able to not only stall the enactment of the RH [Reproductive Health] Law but also block the decade-old anti-discrimination bill that would protect LGBTs from discrimination in schools, workplaces and public institutions. (GALANG 2013, 6)

The relationship between religious discourse and discriminatory laws and practices was emerged across the majority of the research studies on the SPLP. Brazil, like Nepal, has a number of progressive laws in place to protect the rights of gender and sexual minority groups. These laws translate into policies, for example, that ostensibly seek to challenge homophobia and transphobia in primary and secondary schools. In practice, however, religious actors have lobbied government officials to retract these laws and policies, and discriminatory attitudes within schools, among teachers and students, have escalated to eclipse the last vestiges of laws protecting the rights of sexual and gender minorities. In the excerpt below, Mountian describes the role of religious actors in shaping policy at the national level, as well as social attitudes within school in Brazil:

> In May 2011, the Evangelical group in Congress, in alliance with other conservative actors, directly pressured the Ministry of Education and the Presidential Cabinet itself to suspend the planned distribution in schools of educational material (6,000 copies of videos) produced under the sponsorship of the Minister of Education as part of the sexual diversity promotion programmes'. (2014, 14)

> Interviewees 4 (teacher) and 6 (academic, activist) mentioned that religious pressures are also strongly at work at school level where intimidation and harmful actions against teachers who deal with the theme of sexual diversity as part of their educational plan have also been reported. (2014, 15)

Many of sexual minorities, with whom Mountian conducted the research, who did manage to enrol into learning institutions or gain some form of employment had to abandon their education or profession in order to escape stigma, discrimination and even violence. All SPLP studies found that all people who are discriminated against, legally and/or socially, on the basis of their gender or sexuality are less likely to complete their formal education. This in turn hampers their subsequent ability to access employment and other livelihood strategies.

> Research has shown that many LGBT people stopped attending their school after suffering violence there. As a result, access to employment for LGBT people with low levels of schooling is severely limited… This negative impact translates into barriers to employment and therefore correlates with low socioeconomic indicators that link poverty with poor levels of education. This research has shown that after suffering violence in schools, many LGBT people stop attending schools. Work for this group is then limited to the informal sector with its attendant precariousness. (Mountian 2014, 10, 15)

Like Brazil, South Africa has a raft of progressive laws in place to recognise the rights of lesbian, gay, intersex and transgender people. In practice, however, these rights are rarely realized for most, particularly given the nature of intersectional forms of inequality in South Africa – and in Brazil. Tanya Charles followed the development of South Africa's White Paper on Families. Her research documents the consultations held with civil society representatives, government representatives and the general public, and it highlights the power dynamics among these actors that lead to the inclusion and exclusion of discourses around the nature of 'the family' in the White Paper. Specially, Charles notes the participation of religious actors who sought to narrow the definition of the family to strictly heteoronormative family configuration. In doing so, these actors managed to generate a White Paper that excludes all non-heterosexual family types who may require state support – but who would not be able to access this support because their family is not recognized as 'legitimate':

> By involving religious groups like the Family Policy Institute… it becomes apparent that there is an attempt to discourage the formation of same-sex families in South Africa. In what they term 'biblical advocacy' the Family Policy Institute states that they have actively become engaged in policymaking processes in South Africa as a result of government pushing through legal recognition of same-sex marriage in 2007. This Institute is '… committed to restoring and upholding marriage as a one-man, one-woman institution, defending the sanctity of human life, protecting religious liberty, fighting for family tax relief, and combating judicial activism that leads to court rulings that harm the family'. (www.familypolicyinstitute.com/fpi/about-us/purpose) (as cited in Charles 2013, 15-16)

The recent ground-breaking lawsuit against Scott Lively, filed by the Centre for Constitutional Rights (CCR) on behalf of Sexual Minorities Uganda (SMUG), also highlights the harmful nature of religious discourse on the lives of gender and sexual minorities. Adrian Jjuuko and Francis Tumwesige analysed the implications of Uganda's Anti-Homosexuality Bill (AHB) on the country's legal system, and they highlight the divisive nature of international religious actors – like Scott Lively – and religious groups. In their study, Jjuuko and Tumwesige (2013) trace the intricate threads linking local faith groups to international ministries; these threads move out to draw in discourses that cast homosexuality as a 'unAfrican' and a 'western import'. Like members of South Africa's Family Policy Unit, these transnational religious networks coalesced around a concern for the 'preservation of traditional family'.

> Evangelical pastors led by Martin Ssempa of Makerere Community Church, Stephen Langa of Family Life Network and supported by American evangelical groups led by Scott Lively, President of Abiding Truth Ministries launched a campaign to fight what they described as the western and unAfrican vice of homosexuality. They used the language of protection of children from homosexuality and preservation of the traditional family. This language later found its way into the bill. (Jjuuko and Tumwesige 2013, 7)

The quote above captures a range of actors and discourses that, together, shaped some of the language in the AHB. The fact that the Ugandan penal code, criminalizing same-sex relations, was itself a colonial import seemed to evade the 'anti-western' logic proposed by these actors. The next section turns to consider some of the embodied implications of domestic law as it continues to be shaped by national and international actors.

Embodied precarity

> My body its memory: to share a memory is to put a body into words. What do we do when these kinds of things happen? Who do we become?... You begin to feel a pressure, this relentless assault on the senses; a body in touch with a world can become a body that fears the touch of a world. The world is experienced as sensory intrusion. It is too much. Not to be assaulted: maybe you might try to close yourself off, to withdraw from proximity, from proximity to a potential...
>
> The violence does things. You begin to expect it. You learn to inhabit your body differently through this expectation. When you sense the world out there as a danger, it is your relation to your own body that changes: you become more cautious, timid; you might withdraw in anticipation that what happened before will happen again. (Ahmed 2017, 21)

The studies discussed above suggest that when laws are in place, in Nepal, Brazil and South Africa, for example, everyday embodied experiences of discrimination continue and in some cases, escalate, as a result of attempts to establish human rights within domestic law. They Also detail some of the embodied ramifications for encountering the 'brick wall' of the law, in the places it exists and in the spaces where its absence is felt more than its presence – or where failure to protect citizens from discrimination amounts to standing silent in the face of violence. This section traces some of these embodied encounters, and it draws on Butler's notion of precarity, described as:

> that politically induced condition in which certain populations suffer from failing social and economic networks of support and become differentially exposed to injury, violence, and death. Such populations are at heightened risk of disease, poverty, starvation, displacement, and of exposure to violence without protection. Precarity also characterizes that politically induced condition of maximized vulnerability and exposure for populations exposed to arbitrary state violence and to other forms of aggression that are not enacted by states and against which states do not offer adequate protection. (Butler 2009, 2)

Stigma from government officials – and government programmes – emerged as of the main ways that people were rendered invisible in their encounters with the state and its laws. In their research in Odisha and Manipur in India, for example, Dhall and Boyce (2015) found that frontline government officials wielded enormous social power at the ground level. The study respondents in Odisha and Manipur said that until these government officials had "undergone an attitudinal change that would stop them from turning away people who don't fit the norm 'visually', they would continue to turn people away from crucial state resources". For example, the authors write that,

> Meera Kinner, a long-time hijra community leader in Odisha, feels that stigma and the inhibition created by it is the reason why to date hardly any trans women living with HIV have been able to access the 'Madhu Babu Pension'. (Dhall and Boyce 2015, 21)

The authors describe the impact of the government's 'incomplete acknowledge of nuances around diverse sexualities', thus rendering some people more visible than others – enabling the former, and not the latter, to access critical resources, like housing:

> [T]he Mo Kudia housing scheme requires a beneficiary to own their own plot of land to be eligible. But this completely ignores the reality that many trans women are evicted from their home and denied property rights. Such a prerequisite, therefore, acts as a barrier to social welfare access for the very groups of people who need it the most. (Dhall and Boyce 2015, 21)

The absence of any legal protections for gender and sexual minorities, in countries like Ethiopia, results in naked exposure to the materiality of the 'brick wall' – in this case, the 'wall' is the absence of juridical protections and it becomes embodied through the presence of state-sanctioned discrimination by police and prison officers. The respondents in the SPLP study conducted in Ethiopia recalled their experiences of discrimination because they were identified or 'outed' as gay (Overs 2015). They were dismissed from work, expelled from their schools and from their houses, and they found it enormously difficult to access health resources, as Overs describes in the quote below:

> The illegality of homosexuality was cited by staff members of more than one health agency as justification for inaction within their own programmes – including one that supports programmes for female sex workers whose activities are also illegal. Four agency staff said that as a statement of fact, homophobic attitudes made any kind of service provision to known gay men impossible but did not specify if they were a part of that consensus; on further questioning one said no, one said yes and two refused to answer. (2015, 16–17)

The absolute refusal – by the Ethiopian state – to acknowledge the lives of sexual and gender minorities meant that there were 'no programmes or policies to protect same-sex attracted people from economic hardship, crime, disease or human rights violations' (Overs 2015, 4).

If laws and policies provide one of the main areas through which citizens encounter the 'brick walls' created by the state, then by rendering gender and sexual minorities invisible, the state and its legal instruments are not held accountable to individuals or to groups for their embodied experiences of precarity. We hear about Maria, for example, from Nirantar (an education non-governmental organization in India) who is unemployed and believes this is largely a result of discrimination because she is transgender (Nirantar 2013). In Brazil, Mountian (2014) similarly found that many *travesti* experienced brutal violence in their schools and were compelled to leave their school early: 'Work for this group is then limited to the informal sector with its attendant precariousness' (15).

While the SPLP studies found that there was a range of social and economic ramifications of failing or discriminatory legal structures, there were numerous accounts of people and organisations that had resorted to forming their own social and economic subcultures and community-based income generating projects. In Ethiopia, Cheryl Overs (2015) described networks of friends who would support people who had lost homes or livelihoods as a result of discrimination. She writes that, 'Such economic subcultures occur in rich and poor countries alike and while they include visible and stereotypical enterprises such as hairdressing, show business, fashion and sex work, they are not limited to those occupations (18–19).' Similarly, in Rwanda, Gatete and Haste suggest that a common feature of many organisations was 'their desire to provide economic opportunities for their members and the communities they served. In most cases this was for men who were isolated from their families and communities because of their sexual or gender non-conformity' (23). Therefore, while some people were exposed to the brutality of legal discrimination as a hard-edged 'brick wall', others found refuge and support through non-governmental organisations in contexts where the law either failed to protect gender and sexual minorities from discrimination, or where the law actively generated this form of precarity. As the SPLP ended in 2016, one of its main recommendations centred on the vital importance of global solidarity to advance rather than stipulate the agendas of local organisations that were working to dismantle the 'brick walls' of discriminatory legislation in the countries that formed part of the programme.[4]

Conclusion

Researchers and social justice advocates have historically approached gender and sexuality from a rights-based logic in which the rights of all people, irrespective of their gender, class, sexuality, race, are asserted (Alexander 1994; Lacey 1998; Narrain 2005). While this approach is supported by international treaties and conventions and, in some cases, national law, research conducted by through the SPLP demonstrates that the moral assertion of rights is not enough (c.f. Fellmeth 2008; Lennox and Waites 2013; Marzullo and Herdt 2011; Roseman and Miller 2011; Thoreson 2012). This article suggests that if embodied equality – in contrast to embodied precarity – is in part about enabling access to resources (social care, health care, education and employment) then there is still work to do to show how people encounter juridical 'brick walls' that stop certain bodies from accessing these resources.

Because social welfare programmes are – in theory – built around taking down 'brick walls' and enabling access to resources like health care, housing, employment in order to move towards addressing intersecting inequalities, we cannot dislocate sexuality from gender, class, caste, age and disability. This conclusion follows theorists who, like Butler (1993) before them, criticized a narrow approach to LGBT – or queer – issues without taking into account the broader socio-economic and political context in which rights-debates were raised at a national level (Eng, Halberstam, and Muñoz 2005; Hennessy 1995; Prosser 2006; Puar and Rai 2007). If we take an intersectional approach to gender and sexuality, then it is more possible to locate the social and economic factors shaping the lives of gender and sexuality minorities. Further, by shifting away from abstract theory towards understanding people's everyday lives, it may also become more possible to recognise a diversity of bodies and to identify and address the ways that some bodies are stopped by an encounter with the law as a 'brick wall' and how others are simply not encountered at all.

Notes

1. For more information, please see: http://www.spl.ids.ac.uk.
2. These toolkits include: The Sexuality and Social Justice Toolkit; the Sex Work Law Map; and the Faith, Gender and Sexuality Toolkit.

3. Mark Gevisser (2000), similarly, highlights the working of moral discourse to exclude certain same-sex sexualities and gender forms that had been defined as 'western'.
4. For more information, please see this Policy Brief entitled, Avenues for Donors to Promote Sexuality and Gender Justice: https://opendocs.ids.ac.uk/opendocs/handle/123456789/11640.

Acknowledgements

The author wishes to acknowledge the enormous work of all those who engaged in the SPLP over the course of its 4-year life. Thank you, too, to Aimen Majeedullah, Kimberly Wied and Ntokozo Yingwana for the careful coding and analytical work they did on all of the SPLP's research papers. The feedback from the peer-reviewer was enormously helpful - thank you.

Disclosure statement

No potential conflict of interest was reported by the author.

ORCID

Elizabeth Mills http://orcid.org/0000-0002-0388-9437

References

Ahmed, S. 2017. *Living a Feminist Life*. Durham: Duke University Press.

Alexander, M. J. 1994. "Not Just (Any) Body Can Be a Citizen: The Politics of Law, Sexuality and Postcoloniality in Trinidad and Tobago and the Bahamas." *Feminist Review* 48 (1): 5–23. doi:10.1057/fr.1994.39.

Alqaisiya, W. 2018. "Decolonial Queering: The Politics of Being Queer in Palestine." *Journal of Palestine Studies* 47 (3): 29–44. doi:10.1525/jps.2018.47.3.29.

Appadurai, A. 2006. "The Thing Itself." *Public Culture* 18 (1): 15–22. doi:10.1215/08992363-18-1-15.

Boyce, P., and D. Coyle. 2013. *Development, Discourse and Law: Transgender and same-sex sexualities in Nepal*. IDS Evidence Report. Institute of Development Studies.

Butler, J. 1993. "Critically Queer." *GLQ: A Journal of Lesbian and Gay Studies* 1 (1): 17–32.

Butler, J., 2009. Precarious life, grievable life. *Frames of War*, pp.1–32.

Charles, T. 2013. "'Marriage above All Else': The Push for Heterosexual, Nuclear Families in the Making of South Africa's White Paper on Families." IDS Evidence Report 41.

Clare, E. 2015[1999]. *Exile and Pride: Disability, Queerness and Liberation*. Durham, NC: Duke University Press.

Corbin, J., and A. Strauss. 1990. "Grounded Theory Research: Procedures, Canons, and Evaluative Criteria." *Qualitative Sociology* 13 (1): 3–21. doi:10.1007/BF00988593.

Corrêa, S., and V. Muntarbhorn. 2007. "The Yogyakarta Principles: Principles on the Application of International Human Rights Law in Relation to Sexual Orientation and Gender Identity." Manual/2007/070517_yogyakarta_principles_en.Pdf.

Dhall, P., and P. Boyce. 2015. "Livelihood, Exclusion and Opportunity: Socioeconomic Welfare among Gender and Sexuality Non-Normative People in India." IDS Evidence Report 106.

Eng, D. L., J. Halberstam, and J. E. Muñoz. 2005. *What's Queer about Queer Studies Now?* Durham: Duke University Press.

Fellmeth, A. X. 2008. "State Regulation of Sexuality in International Human Rights Law and Theory." *Wm & Mary L Reviews* 50: 797.

Franke, K. 2012. "Dating The State: The Moral Hazards Of Winning Gay Rights." *The Columbia Human Rights Law Review* 44: 1.

GALANG, 2013. *Policy audit: Social protection policies and urban poor LBTs in the Philippines.* No. Evidence Report; 21. Institute of Development Studies (IDS).

Gevisser, M. 2000. "Mandela's Stepchildren: Homosexual Identity in Post-Apartheid South Africa." In *Different Rainbows*, edited by P. Drucker, 111–136, Prowler Press.

Harcourt, W., ed. 2016. *Bodies in Resistance: Gender and Sexual Politics in the Age of Neoliberalism*. New York: Springer.

Haste, P., and T. K. Gatete 2015. "Sexuality, Poverty and Politics in Rwanda." IDS Evidence Report 131.

Hennessy, R. 1995. "Queer Visibility in Commodity Culture." *Social Postmodernism: Beyond Identity Politics* 29: 142–186.

Jjuuko, A., and F. Tumwesige. 2013. "The Implications of the Anti-Homosexuality Bill 2009 on Uganda's Legal System." IDS Evidence Report 44.

Kothari, U. 2005. "Authority and Expertise: The Professionalisation of International Development and the Ordering of Dissent." *Antipode* 37 (3): 425–446. doi:10.1111/anti.2005.37.issue-3.

Lacey, N. 1998. "Unspeakable Subjects, Impossible Rights: Sexuality, Integrity and Criminal Law." *Canadian Journal of Law and Jurisprudence* 11: 47. doi:10.1017/S0841820900001685.

Lennox, C., and M. Waites. 2013. "Human Rights, Sexual Orientation and Gender Identity in the Commonwealth: From History and Law to Developing Activism and Transnational Dialogues." In *Human Rights, Sexual Orientation and Gender Identity in the Commonwealth: Struggles for Decriminalisation and Change*, 1–59. London: Human Rights Consortium, Institute of Commonwealth Studies.

Lorde, A. 1984. *Zami: A New Spelling of My Name*. London: Sheba Feminist Publishers.

Marzullo, M. A., and G. Herdt. 2011. "Marriage Rights and LGBTQ Youth: The Present and Future Impact of Sexuality Policy Changes." *Ethos* 39 (4): 526–552. doi:10.1111/j.1548-1352.2011.01204.x.

Mountian, I. 2014. "A Critical Analysis of Public Policies on Education and LGBT Rights in Brazil." IDS Evidence Report 61.

Narrain, A. 2005. *Queer: Despised Sexuality, Law and Social Change*. Bangalore: Books for Change.

Nirantar. 2013. *Policy Audit: A Heteronormativity Audit of RMSA – A Higher Education Programme in Indian Schools*. IDS Evidence Report. Institute of Development Studies.

Overs, C. 2015. "BOOSHTEE! Survival and Resilience in Ethiopia." IDS Evidence Report; 129.

Phillips, O. 1997. "Zimbabwean Law and the Production of a White Man's Disease." *Social & Legal Studies* 6 (4): 471–491. doi:10.1177/096466399700600402.

Prosser, J. 2006. "Judith Butler: Queer Feminism, Transgender, and the Transubstantiation of Sex." In *The Transgender Studies Reader*, edited by S. Stryker and S. Whittle, 257–280. Abingdon: Routledge.

Puar, J. K., and A. S. Rai. 2007. "The Sexuality of Terrorism." In *Terrorist Assemblages: Homonationalism in Queer Times*, 37–78. Durham: Duke University Press.

Puar, J. K. 2017. *Terrorist Assemblages: Homonationalism in Queer Times*. Durham: Duke University Press.

Radcliffe, S. A. 2012. "Development for a Postneoliberal Era? Sumak Kawsay, Living Well and the Limits to Decolonisation in Ecuador." *Geoforum* 43 (2): 240–249. doi:10.1016/j.geoforum.2011.09.003.

Roseman, M. J., and A. M. Miller. 2011. "Normalizing Sex and Its Discontents: Establishing Sexual Rights in International Law." *Harvard Journal of Law & Gender* 34: 313–321.

Thoreson, R. R. 2012. "Realizing Rights in Manila. Brokers and the Mediation of Sexual Politics in the Philippines." *GLQ: A Journal of Lesbian and Gay Studies* 18 (4): 529–563. doi:10.1215/10642684-1600725.

Van Hoecke, M., and M. Warrington. 1998. "Legal Cultures, Legal Paradigms and Legal Doctrine: Towards a New Model for Comparative Law." *International & Comparative Law Quarterly* 47 (3): 495–536. doi:10.1017/S0020589300062163.

Wo/andering about walls: a reply to Elizabeth Mills

B Camminga

ABSTRACT

This paper is a response to Elizabeth Mills article 'Gender, Sexuality and the Limits of the Law'. Mills provides concise evidence based unpacking of how domestic law can inhibit or impact the lived realities of sexual and gender minorities in the Global South. Drawing on research carried out within the UK based Sexuality, Poverty and Law Programme (SPLP) Mills considers what (and who) shapes the law and what, in turn, shapes peoples experiences of the law. Mills is particularly concerned with issues of embodiment, materiality and precarity in the lives of those who often find themselves excluded from the law - either actively or through negation. As we see an increasing reliance on homonationalism as an indicator of modernity, linked to investment by the Global North in the Global South, the article raises several key questions that are pertinent to the current global moment.

This is a reply to:
Mills, E. 2018. "Gender, Sexuality and the Limits of the Law." *Global Discourse*. https://doi.org/10.1080/23269995.2018.1521099.

What is a wall? A brick and mortar construction made to keep specific versions of those, considered human, goods and benefits in and other versions out? A line which delineates the worthy from the unworthy? A marker of space and time? A political distraction? Can a wall be a web? A flow of power, perception and meaning defined against certain bodies in favour of others? Embedded, constructed and indicative of the material experience of bodies? Alternatively, can walls, as Sara Ahmed (2017) suggests, be metaphors, which affect the lives of some people and not others, those that are forced to reckon with them in their daily lives. The self-same people who are then forced to see walls, to know walls, to be walled off, in or out.

As walls, boundaries and borders, both physical and metaphorical, across the Global North have become seeming obsessions, Beth Mills (2018) article is a welcomed and timeous intervention. Situating the law in the lives of people, as an embodied experience, Mills offers a snapshot of what embodiment in relation to various legal settings, predominantly, in the Global South might mean. Raising more questions than answers, the article attends to the task of considering how particular gendered and sexed bodies experience the materiality of juridical power.

Drawing on data gathered from the UK-based Sexuality, Poverty and Law Programme (SPLP), Mills considers what (and who) shapes the law and what, in turn, shapes peoples experiences of the law. The article plots what this materiality might tell us about not only the limits of the law but critically who the law limits and how, asking distinct questions about the perceptions, imaginations and weaponisation of the law. Indeed, how the law might wall.

The article, written as it is from a project situated in the Global North, is in some senses embedded in institutions and vectors of power that may perpetuate certain kinds of structural exclusions. To this end, it pays acute attention to the issues of language or what Stella Nyanzi (2014) has referred to as 'languaging'. It is refreshing to see several broad examples of both gender identity and sexual orientation used side by side. Particularly, when so often sexual orientation and examples thereof are relied upon as the acceptable catchall category when referring to either SOGI issues or LGBT.

Mills links the ways in which laws are produced at a domestic level to the kinds of lives that people are subsequently able to live, or not live, as the case may be. The evidence she presents suggests that often, with issues of sexual orientation and gender identity, the development of laws or legal policy has not, as would be expected, been about the populations they are intended to serve. Rather laws protecting or acknowledging LGBT populations have increasingly become a condition of neoliberalism, a shallow investment, a tool used to signal modernity and by extension approval and indeed investment from the Global North, indicating state-based aspirations in the Global South to enter the international community. Indeed the article seems to point to the ongoing tensions between North and South over issues regarding gender identity and sexuality and the dangers of signalling modernity on terms dictated externally. That this focus on LGBT issues by donors and NGOs tends to exacerbate tensions rather than assist in the safe passage of laws and their general acceptance by a given populous is in no way new knowledge but rather a fact that bears repeating. Indeed, what the article does exceptionally well is provide some of the groundwork for thinking through the ongoing coloniality of law (Mignolo 2000; Lugones 2016).

What is clear is that the establishment of human rights in domestic law has not generally lead to what had perhaps been initially understood to be the possible outcome – substantive equality for sexual and gender minorities. The law then is perhaps not the site of social transformation it is often purported to be, indeed it is seemingly limited in this capacity. The law, as the article attests to, is often doing other work, walling work, in some sense, embedding the precarity that many bodies experience as a material reality. How then do we generate meaningful social transformation? This is the question that seems to haunt Mill's paper. Mills suggests that what may be needed is embodied equality a corollary to Butler's notion of embodied precarity. I wonder here if, within legal systems that lean so easily towards walls, boundaries, borders and webs, whether embodied equality is enough? Mill's Rwandan example seems to offer a glimmer of something else here. What that might be is not entirely clear. It would seem though that when difference is not the definition of exclusion from the law but rather something which reinforces the need for tolerance, as a human aspect of legislative systems, there is the possibility for the 'hardenings of history' to manifest not as 'barriers in the present: barriers that we experience as physical' but physical openings (Ahmed 2017, 135–136).

Disclosure statement

No potential conflict of interest was reported by the author.

References

Ahmed, S. 2017. *Living a Feminist Life*. Durahm and London: Duke University Press.

Lugones, M. 2016. "The Colonality of Gender." In *The Palgrave Handbook of Gender and Development: Critical Engagements in Feminist Theory and Practice*, edited by W. Harcourt, 13–33. London, UK: Palgrave Macmillan.

Mignolo, W. 2000. *Local Histories/Global Designs: Coloniality, Subaltern Knowledges, and Border Thinking*. Princeton, NJ: Princeton University Press.

Mills, E. 2018. "Gender, Sexuality and the Limits of the Law." *Global Discourse*. doi:10.1080/23269995.2018.1521099.

Nyanzi, S. 2014. "Queering Queer Africa." In *Reclaiming Afrikan: Queer Perspectives on Sexual and Gender Identities*, edited by Z. Matebeni, 65–69. Johannesburg: Modjaji Books.

The problem of visibility in LGBT human rights: a reply to Camminga and Mills

Phoebe Clark

ABSTRACT

This reply responds to contributions by Camminga and Mills to the issue's sub-theme of 'The Role of International and Domestic Law in Attaining Gender and Sexual Equality'.

This reply argues that the papers show how increased visibility exposes queer people to a greater risk of discrimination, which lawmakers must navigate when crafting policy. The reply also notes that a neo-colonial power dynamic exists between Global North and South policies which influences the creation of symbolic queer-specific human rights policy. This dynamic prompts the spread of Western language and conceptualizations of gender and sexual identity. Clark develops examples from Mills' and Camminga's articles to present a possible alternative way to create policy to protect LGBT human rights and rethink identity informed by experiences of discrimination.

This is a reply to:

Camminga, B. 2018. "The Stigma of Western Words: Asylum Law, Transgender Identity and Sexual Orientation in South Africa." *Global Discourse*. https://doi.org/10.1080/23269995.2018.1521045

and

Mills, E. 2018. "Gender, Sexuality and the Limits of Law." *Global Discourse*. https://doi.org/doi:10.1080/23269995.2018.1521099.

This response explores connections between B Camminga's (2018) article 'The Stigma of Western Words: Asylum Law, Transgender Identity and Sexual Orientation in South Africa' and Elizabeth Mills (2018) article 'Gender, Sexuality and the Limits of Law'. Camminga's piece explores the utility and limitations of transgender identity in the context of South African asylum cases. Mills' article reviews the body of research complied under the Sexuality, Poverty and Law Programme (SPLP) to develop theory on the relationship between 'shapeshifting' laws and which bodies are 'stopped, welcomed, or not encountered at all'. These articles demonstrate a need to re-evaluate the 'shape' of laws that aim to protect LGBT human rights and examine how they come to be. Assuring *access* to LGBT rights may instead require more than centring legal remedies on LGBT visibility and identity. Rather, policymakers should focus on crafting anti-discrimination laws that do not require identification with a particular marginal social group, coupled with a framework that prioritizes a strong commitment to human rights, broadly conceived.

Drawing on SPLP conclusions, Mills argues that legal frameworks are 'porous' and mutate subject to a variety of international and domestic pressures. In the first section of the article Mills focuses on the role of international actors in shaping domestic policy. In the second, Mills traces the embodied repercussions of these changing laws. Noting that laws are 'malleable instruments of international aid, foreign policies and global discourses' Mills adopts Scoone's framework of overlapping spheres – denoting politics, actors, and discourse – to shed light on the dynamics at play in shaping laws specifically related to gender and sexuality. Camminga's article aims to understand the meaning-making surrounding transgender identity in relation to asylum proceedings in South Africa. It does so through study of the development of relevant legal texts and politics while pondering the particular case of Tiwonge Chimbalanga in order to explore the implications of the dominant discourse of transgender identity. Chimbalanga faced arrest and further persecution in Malawi after local media announced her engagement to her husband as the first same sex couple to attempt marriage in the country in December 2009. Chimbalanga fled Malawi and eventually gained asylum in South Africa. Publicized as a 'test case for gay rights', court documents from the case noted that Chimabalanga was assigned male at birth, but identified as and participated in her community as a woman. Camminga's study of the case begins with the controversial Equality Clause of the South African constitution which protects South Africans from discrimination on the basis of sex, gender, and sexual orientation. Camminga shows that a broad judicial interpretation of 'sexual orientation' in an early gay rights case extended protection to all transgender people. They argue that this judicial interpretation acknowledges the contingency of language, allows for a diversity of transgender identity and expression, and provides for unknowable future possibilities of transgender identity and expression. The article continues by tracing a recent history of how LGBT and other queer people came to be seen as 'members of a particular social group' in the asylum regime and the emergence of a stand-alone 'politics of transgender' in South Africa. Camminga concludes that the South African legal regime supports a diversity of way of living for people without specific discourse to describe themselves because the constitution allows for the variability of human behaviour.

Both Camminga and Mills describe a neo-colonial power dynamic shaping discourse and policy in the Global South. Camminga describes this structure by tracing the spread of the term 'transgender' in South African and the rest of the African continent as well as narrating the development of a stand-alone 'politics of transgender' through profiling a South African organization called Gender DynamiX (GDX). Camminga argues the founding of GDX in 2005 marks a shift in transgender discourse from being 'a term functioning within the wider LGBT human rights mandate' to a 'stand-alone politics'. GDX faced difficulty due to the fact that the constituency it aimed to reached is largely invisible and lacks 'the terminology to identify their gender identity'. The term 'transgender' exists within international LGBT human rights discourse but was almost entirely unknown by GDX's target populations. GDX began to introduce 'transgender' into its discourse, in order to serve the population they intended to. Camminga, quoting a former GDX director at length, emphasizes how engaging in this discourse benefits GDX as well because of the influence international donors have over its work. This influence creates a certain power dynamic that Camminga argues accounts for how 'people come into contact with' the term 'transgender' and transgender politics in South Africa and other parts of the continent. That is to say, GDX used the term 'transgender' and spread it to their constituency because 'donors… decide what language and what activities and what work should be done' So while GDX '[doesn't] want to enforce terminology on people' GDX has to use the word 'transgender' to describe people who may or may not use it for themselves in order to make their work legible and attractive to donors. Mills notes that international pressures, and a desire to appear modern and progressive, often dictate policy priorities, and other state actions. Both Mills and Camminga argue that terms from international LGBT discourse – like the term 'transgender' – have a symbolic currency in the progressive international community and can accrue benefits to actors that use terms, and otherwise participate in LGBT discourse.

Mills notes a pattern of backlash against increased LGBT visibility and inclusion in law that tends to result in increased discrimination against the most marginalized in the queer community by local-level government actors, and agitation to retract laws protecting LGBT rights. This pattern holds in Camminga's case study of Malawian refugee to South Africa Tiwonge Chimbalanga who faced arrest and later harassment after being made visible as first 'gay' then 'transgender'. Here, the second salient thematic connection between Mills' and Camminga's articles, the politics of queer visibility, becomes the most apparent. Just like Chimbalanga faced violence for being thrust into the international spotlight, queer bodies faced violence and newly established queer rights came under attack in the countries Mills profiles. From these cases, and recent history of same-sex marriage in the United States one can conclude that where discriminatory attitudes and policies exist visibility is a risk factor queer bodies must navigate. In Nepal and the other states Mills studies, queerness was made 'visible' in domestic discourse through symbolic legal change. This visibility provoked a response from both international and domestic actors. The former channelled resources toward the country, while the latter reacted against the symbolic inclusion of queer subjects. What becomes apparent in paying attention to the power dynamics at play in international and domestic law is that the consequences and benefits of using identity terms accrue unevenly between individuals and state-level actors. That is to say, actors like GDX and Nepal stand only to gain from using identity terms to signal their values to the international community and individual queer bodies must bear the consequences – both positive and negative – of their doing so.

A representative of GDX argued that if Chimbalanga 'knew the word transgender she would come home to a world of understanding of herself'. This quote displays GDX's contention that the spread of transgender discourse and terminology can immensely benefit individuals. Victor Mukasa, a trans-identified Ugandan, echoed this sentiment when he connected learning terminology with visibility and greater self-understanding as he spoke to his experience front of the UN. In a progressive international paradigm, the term 'transgender' has a certain value to all actors because of its international origin. Camminga refers to this understanding of transgender identity as one which is universalized and Western. They read Chimbalanga's refusal to identify as a transgender woman as a 'moment out of joint' with this version of transgender identity. There is no evidence to indicate that Chimbalanga ever used the terms 'gay' or 'transgender' to describe herself prior to her arrest, nor has she used them while living in South Africa. Instead, she continues to refer to herself as a woman. Camminga argues Chimabalanga's use of language illuminates possibilities for more diversity in LGBT politics and ways of gender identification and expression than exist within politics and dominant discourses of transgender identify and illustrates the flexibility written into the Equality Clause in the South African Bill of Rights.

Early in their paper, Camminga draws attention to the way queer identity was 'created'. Drawing on Edwin Cameron's work, they note homosexual identity is a fairly recent phenomenon. Camminga, through Cameron, argues that homosexual conduct has been the object of criminal prohibition, but social and legal discrimination occurs when someone perceives that an individual engages such conduct. In this way, the notion of homosexual identity posits that the sex an individual is a defining characteristic and a way of forming groups of people – 'typical' and 'criminal' or 'normal' and 'deviant'. Because of this, assigning and accepting homosexual and other political identity labels is fraught with social and legal consequences for individuals. To illustrate this point I'll expand on Camminga's example, 'transgender' is a political word. It acknowledges and names the possibility of that movement. For this reason, the term transgender can open new ways of understanding the self as GDX claims it does. It also marks a subject who has moved or is moving across the 'field' of gender conceptualized as a social role. Referring to a person as 'transgender' continues to mark them as a traveller even after they have come to rest somewhere in that field. In this way, calling someone 'transgender' separates them from those who are proximate to them in the field on the basis of their travels just as the term 'homosexual' separates those who experience same-sex attraction from the 'normal' population. Not only may this separation be experienced as a subtle discrediting of their current position, it calls the attention of those who object to gender flexibility to the person being referred to as transgender. This attention can have violent consequences. At the same time, referring to someone as transgender attracts the attention of those who support gender flexibility as well as spread the term's powerful possibilities to others.

Applying international LGBT discourse directly to domestic law is a poor solution to the problem of LGBT human rights. Mills offers Rwanda as a counterpoint to the Nepal case study. Rwanda presents an alternate way to secure LGBT human rights in domestic policy, one that skirts around the risk of visibility. There are no Rwandan laws specifically prohibiting discrimination against sexual and gender minorities but SPLP researchers found a strong commitment to tolerance, non-discrimination, and the rule of law among government officials and in legal texts. These result in a legal framework in which queer subjects are absent, but the rights of queer persons are protected – without being differentiated from all others. In other words, LGBT rights are not made visible, that is explicit in legal text, but are made accessible under a broader valuation of tolerance of difference regardless of the form of that difference. Camminga's subject of interest – those perceived to be transgender who do not use that term to describe themselves – are included in the South African asylum regime in much the same way that LGBT rights are included in Rwandan law. That is, in these two frameworks it is not necessary for an individual to make themself visible as some particular identity in order to access their rights or claim discrimination. This allows the individual to maintain their privacy instead of exposing themself to further violence by 'coming out'. Regardless of whether Chimbalanga calls herself transgender, is 'properly' considered transgender, or is in fact transgender in the universal sense, the South African asylum regime recognizes the persecution she endured. Whether or not she is part of the 'particular social group(s)' her persecutors perceived her to be a part of is not relevant to her refugee status. The fact of her persecution renders her, in the eyes of the South African constitution, someone in need of the protection offered by asylum. The same is the case in Rwanda – the reason for discrimination and whether it was properly directed is not relevant to whether discrimination occurred.

The second benefit to the Rwandan and South African models of a diversity of experiences subsumed under a broader commitment to human rights, is that such models will continue to be applicable to the unpredictable identities and forms of discrimination that may emerge as time progresses. Missing from Mills work, and only touched upon in Camminga's is the notion that individual bodies too are 'porous', that is; they are shaped by the discourses and politics they exist in relation to. Mills' article frames the bodies that are becoming visible or invisible as static. Camminga as well, in their discussion of GDX's introduction of the term transgender, frames transgender people as a fixed population that can be taught the term and choose to accept or reject it as a descriptor. But, a re-reading of Victor Mukasa's and the GDX director's quote reveals that introduction to identity terminology changes how people understand themselves. 'Transgender', 'gay', 'lesbian' and other identity markers have existential power because they mark alternate ways of being. When an individual encounters a new term, they have the option of coming to embody that term by 'orienting' themself toward the identity category that term names. In this way, individuals exist in the same neo-colonial power dynamic states and international actors do. To preserve autonomy and prevent violence, individuals must be empowered explore the terrain in accordance with this 'orientation' on their own terms, and using which terms they choose. State-level actors constrain this choice, and possibly provoke direct physical violence when they write policy which requires queer people to claim an identity in order to claim discrimination and access rights.

Disclosure statement

No potential conflict of interest was reported by the author.

References

Camminga, B. 2018. "'The Stigma of Western Words': Asylum Law, Transgender Identity and Sexual Orientation in South Africa." *Global Discourse*. doi:10.1080/23269995.2018.1521045.

Mills, E. 2018. "Gender, Sexuality and the Limits of Law." *Global Discourse*. doi:10.1080/23269995.2018.1521099.

The limits of law in securing reproductive freedoms: midwife-assisted homebirth in the United States

Renée Ann Cramer

ABSTRACT
Recent years have seen increased activism on behalf of homebirth midwives, with grassroots movements in many states focused on gaining professional status for midwives, and legislation regulating and decriminalizing their practice. However, changing the legal status of homebirth midwifery in the United States may not be the most important issue in creating access for maternal services of this type; in fact, legal status is relatively unimportant to this issue. Participant-observation and interviews indicate that, regardless of legal status, homebirth midwives may be subject to prosecutorial discretion, onerous reporting and insurance requirements, and increased state reach via administrative agencies. These findings reaffirm other studies that have pointed to the limits of law; the gap between doctrine and legislation, and implementation; and the contingent and constitutive relationships between law and transformational change.

The legal status of certified professional midwives (CPMs) in the United States is not uniform, and access to midwifery services is not widespread for people in many states. In addition to formal legal barriers to finding midwives, those who seek to hire them also face informal legalistic barriers to engaging their services, including hegemonic norms and expectations that women will engage in hospital birth practices. While arguing that legalization and decriminalization are necessary, this article examines the limited impact of legalization of CPMs, and the way that both formal and informal legalities constrain their practices. In it, I argue that cultural change will be as important as legal change in pursuing formal and informal protection for midwives and laboring people who seek out-of-hospital birth.[1]

Since 2004, I have been engaged in ethnographic, participant-observation and interview research in three states with varying status for midwives, as well as within national organizations and professional associations supporting their practice (Cramer 2009). I focus here primarily on the experiences of midwives – who operate in states where their practice is legal, including Missouri (where legalization occurred rather recently) and California, which has a relatively long-standing pro-midwifery legislation and activism. In states with a well-established legal status for midwifery practice, we might reasonably expect that midwives feel secure and confident, and that parents are easily able to access homebirth midwifery care. Unfortunately, my findings and analysis may surprise and even dishearten activists attempting to decriminalize and regulate midwifery care:

> Certified Professional Midwives operating in states where their practice is perfectly legal and explicitly regulated continue to face state interference, detrimental regulatory governance, and social approbation, such that they define parts of their practice as illegal, and experience their practices as precarious.

Legal and cultural landscape for midwifery in the United States

Since the move towards 'scientific motherhood' facilitated by modern medical advances, as well as feminism, in the mid-1950s, women in the United States have, as a cultural position, accepted that birth is a medical event (Solinger 2007; Kitzinger 2005; Davis-Floyd 1993; Rothman 1982). Homebirth is simply not the norm. It accounts for fewer than 1% of births in the United States, and the practice is often met with suspicion.

Even so, a woman in the United States who chooses to give birth at home, unassisted by a doctor, nurse or midwife, is completely protected in her choice – in no state is unassisted birth illegal. A woman who chooses a midwife-assisted homebirth, however, may be hiring someone who is breaking any number of laws, depending on the jurisdiction in which she lives, and the status and training of the midwife she hires. It may, in fact, be impossible for her to hire a legal out-of-hospital birth attendant.

The legality of the birth attendant depends upon the state she lives in and the certification she holds. For instance, Certified Nurse Midwives (CNMs) are legal and regulated in every state; however, their scope of practice is often limited to hospital and birth center care, and in many states they are barred from attending homebirth. CPMs – midwives who do not have a nursing degree, but have trained in the profession through both didactic and practical coursework, and who have sat for a series of exams to certify their professional competence[2] – do not work in a hospital setting and seek to attend homebirth as their scope of practice. CPMs can legally attend homebirths in 32 states; their practice is illegal in 8 states. In the remaining 10 states, the status of midwifery is not recognized via statute or court decision; midwifery practice there remains unregulated, and licensure is not available.

Certainly, within the 'illegal states', midwives face the most overtly onerous bars to their practice – in fact, CPMs operating in illegal states do so under near constant threat of prosecution and understand themselves to be operating 'outside of the law', or, as one put it to me in an interview, 'off the grid'. Penalties for criminalized practice or aspects of practice range from jail time, to fines, to loss of eligibility for licensure. Prosecution, even absent conviction, carries reputational costs and does considerable economic and emotional damage to a midwife. Midwives do much to avoid prosecution, short of halting their practice. I have interviewed midwives who drive to 'safe houses' in neighboring (legal) states to assist couples from their illegal state in prenatal care and birth. I have interviewed a midwife who has been jailed twice for her practice; both prosecutions were for 'good outcome' births. Oftentimes, even in 'bad outcome' births (where the baby dies or is born with severe injuries or conditions), the prosecution takes place against the wishes of the child's parents, and at the hands of activist prosecutors. Again, even if they are exonerated, midwives who are prosecuted face enormous legal bills and damage to their reputation and practice.

In legal but unregulated states, midwives are subject to a confusing set of interpretations of regulatory law, and increasing state interest in and action against their practices. They report in interviews that they are often worried about what seems to be increasing prosecutorial discretion in pursuing wrongful death or medical malpractice cases. I live and research in a state that recently had such a prosecution – as a result, midwives who were previously willing to be interviewed for this project asked that we wait until the 'hoopla' died down. Yet midwives and their advocates in legal and illegal states continue to mobilize and organize for legalization and regulation.

One of the main organizational strategies of national and state-based pro-midwifery activism is to promote a look at the successes of so-called 'legal states' – those states where Certified Professional Midwifery is legal and well regulated. Midwives and activists in the illegal and unregulated states are encouraged to look to California, New Mexico, Oregon, Washington and other long-standing legal states for models of best practices and regulatory structure. National and statewide activists hold up these states as models for pro-midwifery legislation. Ultimately, however, the legality of the practice does not make as much difference as activists hope, precisely because the law has limited impact on norms and cultures of birth in a given locale.

The limits of law

As activists within, and scholars of, the Civil Rights, Disability Rights and Feminist movements would surely agree: legalization and legal status do not necessarily bring legitimation and cultural acceptance. The 'gap' between promise and implementation has been well documented (Calavita 2010). Law and society scholars have long been interested in this gap between law as it is written and intended, and law as it is practiced and implemented – what I am calling here the 'limits of law'. Scholarship in this area has proposed that reliance on law for social change proves futile for most social movements (Rosenberg 1991), and scholars have investigated flawed and failed implementation in the lower courts (Silverstein 2007, 1999; Kessler 1990; Burstein and Monaghan 1986; Sarat 1985; Pound 1910). There is excellent empirical work studying discretionary policy-making at the 'street-level' in bureaucratic and agency implementation (Barnes and Burke 2012; Nielsen 2004; Lipsky 1980), as well as state implementation of federal reform legislation (Keiser 2001; Haider-Markel 1998).

Studies focused specifically on the Civil Rights Movement, in particular, have attempted to deeply understand the limits and opportunities posed by strategies focusing on litigation (Klarman 2006). Clearly, the implementation of judicially mandated reforms, as well as reforms achieved through legislative action, can be stymied in multiple ways by 'powerful local interests' (Kessler 1990, 121), and by those who either willfully disobey, or are ignorant of, the reforms. This seems especially true when those reforms are meant to challenge dominant cultural norms regarding women and others seeking equality through rights mobilization (McCann and Silverstein 2008; Silverstein 2007; Marshall 2005; McCann 1994).

My interviews with midwives in varying regulatory regimes indicate that they experience the gap between law on the books and law in practice, and that disjuncture negatively impacts their professional lives. The extant sociolegal literature on legal implementation offers a way to understand the failure of pro-midwifery legislation and decriminalization to positively impact the practice of homebirth midwifery. Midwives are seeking *transformational laws* – laws meant to radically alter how institutions operate – and transformational laws require more than policy language to accomplish their goals (Kostiner 2003). They require deep cultural change and political action, in concert with legal mobilization (Beckett and Hoffman 2005). Absent significant cultural and social shifts, transformative legislation does not come with an enforcement guarantee, nor the ability to enable action on newly granted rights or modes of access. When midwives talk about their practice, they make this abundantly clear.

Practicing in legal states: what can we learn from California?

After periods of criminalization, decriminalization and recriminalization, Certified Nurse-Midwifery has been legal in California since 1960, and the scope of CNM practice includes legal attendance at homebirths. The state has had legislation enabling and regulating CPMs since 1993 (DeVries 1996); CPMs are permitted to attend homebirths, and the state's MediCal program makes them eligible for reimbursement.[3] It is very easy to find midwives – both CPMs and CNMs – in most areas of California, and even to get their services paid for by MediCal, or by insurance companies and HMOs. The state certainly appears to relatively friendly for midwives and to be a place where it is relatively easy to achieve a midwife-assisted homebirth.

Yet the state does extend its reach, primarily its administrative reach, into homebirth practices, and it does so in ways that constrain, and may seem to prohibit, practice. Midwives report a surprising level of threat of state or doctor interference. Even in California, with a relatively long history of legality, midwives experience themselves as under threat of prosecution, as operating in violation of regulation, and as facing social approbation of their profession. The five most onerous issue reported by midwives in legal states like California are: the requirement of a supervising physician; the necessity of procuring insurance; the ban on proctoring or having apprentices; the fear of selective oversight initiated by any one of the plethora of regulatory bodies to which they are answerable; and the practical need for a workable transfer relationship, made difficult by social and professional approbation of their practice. These five issues combine to make CPMs in even the most legal of legal states feel embattled.

Supervising physicians

It is not difficult to find CPMs that attend homebirth in California. During the 2 years I lived and researched in South LA and north Orange counties, I had no problem finding interview subjects: there were listings of midwives in the yellow pages, on line, at birth centers, at birthing classes, at the yoga studios where I practiced and at the natural food groceries where I shopped. My friends had used midwives, and even the nurse practitioner at my HMO could give me a referral or two.

So it was surprising to me when the first two interviews I conducted had moments like this:[4]

Interviewer: What are the legal and political issues facing midwives [in Southern California]?

Tova/Midwife: Well it's … it's very difficult. Written in the law is that we have to have a supervising physician, but they cannot legally write their names saying they're supervising us because of their insurance. And their insurance will drop them if they're involved with a home birth. So, therefore we're all practicing without a supervising position.

And like this:

Interviewer: You work with a doctor. Explain that relationship.

[Silence]

[Laughter]

Interviewer: You don't work with a doctor?

Angie/Midwife: Nobody can find doctor backup.

Interviewer: Which is required …?

Angie: Well, according to the law…

Clearly, these midwives, though afforded legal status under California code, understand themselves to be undertaking illegal practices.

Of the states where it is legal for direct entry and CPMs to attend homebirth, only four – California, New Jersey, New York and Delaware – have required written collaborative-practice agreements between the midwives and doctors.[5] Midwives, doctors and regulatory officials in these states widely acknowledge the problems with these agreements (Munz 2008).

Primary among the problems is the fact that physicians are increasingly unwilling to enter into supervisory relationships with midwives because of pressure from two powerful professional organizations: the American College of Obstetrics and Gynecology (ACOG) and the American Medical Association (AMA). In keeping with its formal policy stance that childbirth should occur 'in properly licensed, accredited, equipped and staffed obstetrical units', attended by 'qualified and licensed personnel' (American Medical Association H-420–998), the AMA has submitted *amicus curiae* briefs in support of state medical associations seeking to continue the criminal status of lay midwifery in states like Missouri.[6] ACOG has issued formal statements against home births for women attempting vaginal births after cesarean sections (VBACs) as well as vaginal deliveries for twins or breech births (ACOG Practice Bulletin, July 2004). As a result, the state of California (and several others) have made it illegal for CPMs to attend VBACs and require clients to write a formal right of refusal of care in order for their CNM to attend them in a home VBAC.

The formal statements of ACOG and the AMA not only inhibit midwives' ability to legally attend these births, they also propose to give the supervising physician a much broader, indeed truly supervisory, role in the pregnancy and birth. This is an unwelcome interpretation of the relationships for many midwives and their clients, in that it reinforces the hegemonic idea that the only appropriate personnel attending birth are medical personnel, an idea challenged by those planning out-of-hospital births.

The 2008 struggle in the state of Missouri has highlighted this difference in interpretation and helps us understand the plight of legal California midwives. Advocates of midwifery care in that state recently won a fight for legislation to decriminalize lay midwifery. An estimated 1000 home births occur every year in the state, the majority of them, prior to legalization in 2008, were attended by illegal midwives. Efforts to decriminalize initially failed when pro-midwifery advocates refused to agree to demands for written supervisory agreements with physicians. As the Missouri State Medical Association's government relations director, Tom Holloway, told a reporter, 'In the beginning of the process [of pregnancy], a patient needs to be screened by a physician. And more importantly, the physician needs to be knowledgeable about the patient and to be immediately available if something goes wrong' (Munz 2008). Obstetricians, gynecologists and nurse midwives are comfortable casting birth as a medical event; they view the pregnant and laboring woman as a 'patient', in need of medical care, supervision and perhaps intervention (Heimer 1999; McGregor 1998; Rooks 1997; Rooks et al. 1989; Luker 1984). However, many women seeking out-of-hospital births attended by midwives do so because they want to remove natural birth from the medical model: they seek an intervention-free birth, and view such a birth as a normal and natural occurrence. They view the supervisory-physician requirement as an unnecessary intervention of the medical model into normal, healthy birth as practiced by midwives. As Eve, a homebirth mom, puts it, 'I mean what midwives are trained to do is so *beyond* the actual medical, it's … so encompassing of *relationships*.'

Additionally, even those midwives who agree to follow the law in states where supervisory agreements are required find it very difficult to actually comply with legal demands. It is financially prohibitive for doctors in private practice to buy the malpractice and liability coverage necessary to carry a midwife on their plan, and hospitals routinely refuse to extend such insurance coverage to doctors wishing to have these relationships. As one California CPM told me:

> Written in the law is that we have to have a supervising physician, but they cannot legally write their names saying their supervising us because of their insurance. And their insurance will drop them if they're involved without a hospital birth. So, therefore we're all practicing without a supervising position.

The inability of doctors to cover midwives leads to a refusal to participate in supervisory relationships; oftentimes this refusal is a reluctant end to a long-standing and mutually beneficial relationship.

Fiona put it this way:

> Well, um, one of the, perhaps one of the most important things of the California law as it stands right now, is it says that licensed midwives must practice under the supervision of a physician. No midwife has physician supervision, because no physician is willing to take on the vicarious liability.

According to her, 'Physician supervision is not defined in the law, but it is generally taken to mean that there is an OB, uh, who is monitoring your care'.

> So almost, on a weekly basis or whatever you agreed on with this doctor, they're signing charts, going, "Yeah, that was a good decision. Yep, that's good." Literally taking, they're taking responsibility … for everything you do. In a homebirth situation, where malpractice, most malpractice insurance companies will forbid doctors …from even talking to a homebirth midwife. They will take away the malpractice insurance if you talk to a homebirth midwife.

So, midwives either go out of business, or practice in flagrant disobedience of the law. Michele Munz, a reporter for the *St. Louis Post Dispatch*, has covered the fight for decriminalization in Missouri. Of the supervisory relationship requirement, she writes, 'In California and Delaware, midwives flout the rule because so few doctors will work with them'. She then quotes Kathi Burns, the licensing program manager for the California Medical Board, 'We are aware that everyone is in a quandary on that point' (Munz 2008).

The additional quandary is that the law is difficult to enforce, which leads to both widespread disobedience and selective prosecution. Many midwives understand this combination as of prohibitive of their practice.

Insurance requirements

The question of insurance coverage, even aside from the role of mandatory coverage in making the supervisory relationship difficult to achieve, is paramount for midwives practicing in California. One Southern California woman, 'Fran', told me that her midwife (who had attended the births of both of Fran's sons, and was also the family's licensed chiropractor and homeopath) had closed the birthing part of her practice after the physician with whom she had a long-standing relationship told her he could no longer afford to carry her on his insurance plan. Rather than risk operating in violation of the law (without a supervisor) or without insurance coverage (and she could not afford to purchase her own for a coverage amount that made sense for her practice), this midwife abandoned that part of her practice.[7]

California law does *not* require CPMs to carry malpractice insurance; however, the regulations do require midwives to disclose their uninsured status.[8] As well, in order to rent office space, many landlords require the renter to be 'appropriately' insured. The disclosure requirement and demands of landlords are enough to motivate some midwives to seek coverage. Patti, quoted above, had just recently purchased malpractice insurance when I interviewed her:

> It was 2,600 dollars. … For, a year, for 50,000 dollars worth of insurance. It's nothing; it was a total, it was a total waste of my trip, of my time. And the only reason I got it was because the office I was working out of required me to have medical malpractice, so I found a place that sold it. … I had to go to Utah to get it. … Anyway, this insurance company was a smaller insurance company and the rule in Utah was you could go there to procure your insurance, but they couldn't come to you. Could not do it over the phone; you had to do it in person. … But anyway, so where I'm at, they want a million dollars. Well a million dollars is going to be like 30,000 or 40,000 dollars a year. … I've been practicing for 15 years, never been sued.

Patti bought the minimum insurance policy necessary, and she experienced the process as ridiculous; in her words she was 'jumping through hoops' to close 'loop holes, just loop holes'.

Many midwives in California are unwilling or unable to get coverage; those who are both unwilling to get coverage and unwilling to shoulder the perceived liability risk, close down.[9] This does not mean that homebirths end: Nancy, a mother in Los Angeles County, upon hearing that her midwife had gone out of business due to inability to afford coverage, told a group of women assembled for a La Leche League meeting,

'Women in the South Bay are going to start taking things into their own hands'.[10] She meant, as I soon found out, that women unable to find midwives for their homebirths were going to begin networks to give birth at home, unassisted.

Apprentice relationships

I had come to this research project with the understanding that the law was certainly structuring and informing practices of midwifery. However, I was surprised to find, through these interviews, that in a 'legal state' among well-established, long-practicing, easy-to-find midwives, there was such a sense of embattlement, such a self-identity of 'illegality', and such a worry about discretionary prosecution. I conducted many interviews at a time when circumstances might have raised those fears to the fore – the Hollywood Birth Center had been closed down, after a bad outcome in a birth attended by an apprentice operating without a preceptor present.[11]

The apprenticeship question was on the minds of many regulators and midwives, and it was evident from press reports that the status of the law was anything but clear. In fact, neither the 1993 law legalizing lay midwives, nor the 2000 amendment to the law, discussed the apprenticeship issue. This is an odd omission, as a primary difference between CNMs and CPMs is that the former often gain their knowledge and experience through apprenticeship relationships. Some interpreted the lack of wording about apprenticing in the California law as a tacit acknowledgement and endorsement of centuries of midwifery-training practice; others interpreted the lack of wording to mean that California midwives all needed to go through some sort of formal educational (and not apprenticing) process in order to obtain licensure and certification. In any event, California lawmakers rectified the confusion, at least temporarily, with clarifying legislation in 2005. That legislation allowed apprenticeship relationships, but placed constraints on the role apprentices could play in birth.

In 2006, though, even after legislative clarification, several California midwives cited the ambiguity in the law, and the prosecution of the apprentice and the preceptor at the Hollywood Birth Center, as strains on their practices. As my conversation with Patti revealed:

> There's a big deal about apprentices right now. ... Okay, the whole idea behind lay midwifery or traditional midwifery is that you learn it in the field. Yes, you're gonna take neonatal resuscitation or you might take IV therapy or you know, you might take an ob crisis class at a hospital or ... even a fetal monitoring class. ... You do take some classes and you read lots of books. But the main learning mechanism is learning with another midwife and learning on the scene. ... So, for a while there, there was a big brouhaha about midwives taking apprentices and how it's practicing medicine without a license. You're encouraging – you're aiding and abetting practicing without a license.

Interviewer: Which is criminal?

Patti: Yeah. It's criminal for me; it would be criminal...

Even though she, wrongly, interprets it as a criminal act to take on apprentices, she does so, both to enable her to manage a growing practice, and because, she says, 'this is a tradition we've been trying to preserve'. She and other midwives acknowledge that they are attempting to preserve this tradition in the face of competing professional interests. She continues:

> But a lot of the medical profession, sometimes even other midwives, they will say, "Well, let's make us more professional. Let's go to school. Let's not do it the old way. Let's do it the new way." Well, that's fine for them. If they want to go to school and get their little degree and their ego feels better about going to college, great. But, you know, there have been women for the last, I don't know how many thousands of years, that were midwives that couldn't write, couldn't read. And yet they knew the herbs, they knew the dosages and all that.

This implicit endorsement of non-professional knowledge is a direct challenge to the medical model of birth; it also challenges the move toward licensure and professionalism that is evident nationwide in the pro-midwife movement. Such a stance is extreme, and not reflective of many of the midwives I have interviewed; but it is interesting and important for the challenge it poses to perceptions about legal status as a panacea.

Transport arrangements

One of the most potentially stressful parts of a midwife's practice involves transfers of laboring women to a hospital setting. Some transports are, in Tova's words, 'smooth, smooth, smooth', and undertaken because of nonemergency conditions, like an extremely long labor ('failure to progress' in the medical model). In Tova's estimation, part of her success in smooth transfers is the relationship she forges with doctors and hospital staff:

> We have a backup doctor in place; I make a call, I say, "Here's what's going on," and they say, "Great." ... But you know... that's a large part of, of being able to transport in the current political climate, you know, it's being, it's having the people skills to deal with it.

However, she acknowledges fear accompanying even these nonemergency transports to 'friendly' hospitals:

> I think it's really important [to have people skills and build relationships], because *the law will not protect you*. 'Cause even if there's nothing wrong technically, I mean if, if I'm only transporting 'cause the mom wants an epidural, I mean, unlikely, but it happens, maybe she's tired – she wants an epidural, just because there is that supervision wording in the law, I can be arrested, 'cause I'm practicing illegally.

Interviewer:	So do you have a lawyer on retainer?
Tova:	[laughter]
Pamela (Tova's [unauthorized] apprentice, and a practicing attorney):	[laughter]: Well it's not that I do midwifery law, but I ... I would step in.

Patti was even more explicit in her discussion of the perils of transport when I asked her if she felt the threat of prosecution during a transfer:

> [sigh] There's different pockets of ... of ... areas where I feel a threat. If I have to transport to Orange County, I feel a threat. I'm very scared to take a woman into Orange County, any hospital ... any of them; because they will ... they call the police. And they write a report and they ... they report it to the state.

One of the primary arguments for licensure in unregulated states is that the interests of public health are better served by having transfer relationships in which midwives feel safe to stick around and brief the hospital staff on the needs of the laboring woman and her child. Many see this as preferable to the current situation in criminalized states, where a midwife will likely feel the need to drop a client off at the emergency room door, and leave to avoid potential prosecution. Certainly, legality is a central component of integration of care – and integration of care leads to better health outcomes for laboring people and babies (Vedam et al. 2018). Clearly, however, having a legal status does not completely solve the problems associated with risk of prosecution. Nor does it solve the problem of potential harassment of CPMs and laboring mothers.

Added to their fear of prosecution or state intervention as a result of the transfer is a deep distaste for the experiences some midwives and their clients have had at the hands of doctors and nurses in hospital settings. Kali, a midwife with a legal birth center practice, told me about her experiences:

> I've been a nurse for thirty-four years. I worked in a hospital. When I worked in labor and delivery, it was often, "Oh, here comes a granola family. They have a birth plan. They've been using a midwife. Why don't you take 'em? You like that stuff. And I would say, "Oh really? A birth plan? I, I'd love to work with these people! They know what they want!" And it would be troublesome for somebody else.

In her birth center practice, sometimes during a transfer, she would get:

> [a] belligerent nurse who's gonna make this case a statement of "You're double stupid already. You chose an out-of-hospital location. You chose a midwife. And I'm gonna make your life miserable from the day you walk in here," I've simply gone to her directly, you know, "Maybe you need to ask for a different assignment. If you can't work with me, if you can't work with my clients, believe me, it's gonna work for them because today is their day and if you and I can't work together… Find a new room."

Sometimes, though, the need to enter the hospital and submit to the medical model takes a chilling turn. Patti tells about a friend who had several homebirths before the one she describes below, in which the woman needed to deliver in the hospital:

> So she goes to the hospital let's say at one or two in the morning. I get there about two, and she's already got her epidural … so anyway, she's very comfortable and the little nurse comes in and says, "You know, doctor said to check you often." … Anyway, the doctor, it was two, three, four in the morning, the doctor was at home sleeping, but he had given her orders to call. Well, my friend kind of is a loud mouth; I want to put it like that. She's very bold and told them "Oh yeah, I had two homebirths and I'm only here for the epidural and we'd prefer to be left alone." Uh uh, that nursing staff did not like it. … So, anyway, I'm noticing that, you know, sometimes with an epidural you, you feel pushy, you can still feel pushy; sometimes you can't. Well, we are noticing that things are changing. And I said, "Theresa." I said, "Are you pushing?" She says, "I don't know."
>
> And I lift up the sheet and the baby's coming. So what do I do? I go out in the hall and I kinda wave down the nurse and I said, "The baby's coming." So – and – as a midwife I cannot practice in a hospital, right?
>
> Okay, so she comes in and the head nurse comes in and the nurse with the baby warmer comes in. Then stay against the wall. And the one nurse says, "Oh, you want a homebirth? Have a homebirth then." … My client is delivering her baby and of course as a midwife, you want to [help] … I looked her in the eye. I said, "Theresa, reach down and pick up your baby.

> [pitch changes] "Oh I can't. I can't." [pitch changes back] "Yes you can. You can." Something told me, the Holy Spirit told me, "Do not touch that baby." She picked it up and it, here this baby is against this gown and she tried to pull up her gown to cover it and she's yelling for a blanket and they're all just standing there.
>
> You talk about malpractice; breach of confidence, breach of care. ... The nurse that had the baby warmer handed somebody a blanket to put over the baby and handed her a bulb syringe so she could suction her own baby. ... So then the doctor comes in and starts yelling at her because she was like secretly planning a homebirth. Every time she started to say something, he cut her off because he had already heard the story from the nurses that "she didn't tell us that she was in labor" or she was, you know, pushing. ... They were waiting for me to [catch the baby], and later they came in with the birth certificate and they wanted me to sign it. And I said, "No, I'm not signing it." That would have been proof.

Patti continues:

> Same hospital, another doctor ... I brought my client in for failure to progress.
>
> They put her up in the bed, in the stirrups, and she's pushing. And this doctor comes in, and he-, this doctor knew me ... it is a very small hospital. And um, she [the laboring woman] says, you know, "I don't want an episiotomy." And he's like, "Well I'm a doctor, I'll decide." And she said, "I do not want an episiotomy." He took his two fingers ... and we're all-, I'm sitting-, I'm standing against the back wall, my assistant is next to me, and our eyes are about to bug out. He literally ripped her open. ... She got punished; you get punished for [trying to have] a homebirth.

Social approbation

This kind of treatment of women and their midwives from doctors and nurses isn't part of the technical legal and regulatory apparatus surrounding the practice of midwifery. But it is clearly a significant stress on their practice, and it contributes to their view of the law surrounding their practice. Midwives tell me that women feel 'punished' by doctors and nurses for pursing homebirth, and they understand that medical professionals, friends, and family members meet their birth choices with suspicion.[12] Midwives and their clients note that home birth in America is simply seen as 'odd', 'different' and 'crazy'.

Many women told me that long-standing friendships had been strained by their decision to have an out-of-hospital birth, and their friends' reaction to such a decision. As one told me, '[My friend] was mocking me – our decision. I didn't feel like I could share our plans with her anymore'. Internet sites devoted to birth and homebirth abound with stories from women whose in-laws, parents, friends, and co-workers are shocked and repelled by their decision to homebirth.

There is, indeed, tremendous social approbation against out-of-hospital birth – even in legal states with substantial pockets of subversive. Even doctors who agree to supervise midwifery face backlash from their peers. Bea, a midwife practicing in Missouri, told me:

> I remember one particular transfer that, um, she had been upfront with her doctors and told him that she was planning a homebirth and he agreed to be her backup. Which if his colleagues knew that, he would be in big trouble 'cause another, that happened a few years ago with another doctor. He was really raked over the coals by his colleagues when they found out that he had approved of this homebirth.

Many women who had or attempted homebirths reported to me during participant-observation that they had not told their 'normal' or 'mainstream' friends about their choice to give birth at home; many of them had not told immediate family members (mothers-in-law, siblings) of their decision to give birth at home with a midwife. They told me they didn't want to be looked down upon, seen as strange, or interfered with in their decision. They also may have had prenatal care with a physician, who they did not inform of their plans, for fear of patronizing, contentious and harshly judgmental conversations (Fisher and Todd 1993).

Social and cultural approbation certainly does trickle into doctor–midwife relationships, insurance company's coverage (or refusal of coverage) of procedures and practices, and tremendous oversight from state regulatory bodies. All of these constraints will ultimately negatively affect the availability of homebirth attended by a midwife. Dominant ideologies about birth that give primacy to ideas about risk, the necessity of medical intervention, and the role and interest of the state in these reproductive choices serve to make homebirth *de facto* illegal, or at the very least incredibly difficult to obtain, even in 'legal' states like California.

Activism in the face of limits

My research points to the limits of decriminalization and regulation in helping midwives and their clients feel safe, comfortable and empowered in their out-of-hospital practices and birth choices. These findings reinforce previous scholarship that points to the limits of law, and its implementation, to create transformational cultural change. Even though midwifery advocates focus on licensure as a regulatory reform, the primary goal of the movement is to facilitate out-of-hospital birth as a viable option for women; to accomplish this facilitation requires more than legalization, it will require a significant cultural shift, and a transformed cultural attitude toward birth. Adopting Krieger's understanding of an 'institution' as 'a web of interrelated norms, social meaning, implicit expectancies, and other 'taken-for-granted aspects of reality, which operate as largely invisible background rules in social interaction' (Krieger 2000, 480), we can indeed argue that pro-midwifery advocates are engaged in the struggle to *transform the institution of birth* in the United States.

Of course, such transformation is particularly difficult to achieve. This is true in part because humans – lawyers, judges, regulatory officials, doctors, nurses, clients, friends, mothers-in-law – are all engaged in the process of institutionalizing particular ideas and ideologies about birth. While law might in fact allow for out-of-hospital birth attended by a midwife, the everyday practices of people and interactions of folks do much to create hospitable, or inhospitable, environments for a legally available option. As Krieger's research on the implementation of the Americans with Disabilities Act shows, because transformative law is most often mobilized by 'social "outsiders" against social "insider" … insiders … are often better able than their outsider opponents to exploit the law's soft spots … and restrict the law's application' (Krieger 2000, 485). Doctors within hospital settings, and regulators for the Boards of Health and Nursing to which many midwives must answer, are insiders able to reinforce dominant culture's norms, even out-of-hospital midwifery practice is legal.

Midwives and their advocates are aware of the disjuncture between legal status and their ability to freely practice: they are aware of the limits of law. Flawed implementation of regulations meant to safeguard midwifery has not dampened midwifery advocates' enthusiasm for legal mobilization. And, though they often have a critique of the medical profession and professionalization in general, pro-midwifery advocates' critique of professionalism does not extend to the legal profession. Lawyers play prominent roles in the national movement for legalization, and their expertise in the process of writing legislation and regulation is of paramount importance. Activists are using law instrumentally, with great faith that legal status will have transformative power.

However, as Krieger reminds us, 'traditional norms and institutions do not vanish overnight ... norm competition does not end with the enactment of a transformative legal regime' (Krieger 2000, 488). The result of a solely instrumentalist focus on legalization might well be that many midwives will operate in legal states, with legal status – yet still be, and consider themselves to be, at risk for less-than-useful regulatory oversight, and impediments to practice like zealous prosecution and social approbation.

In order to be successful, then, birth option advocates may want to highlight those activities they are already undertaking which fall into what Kostiner calls a 'cultural schema' for activism. 'Activists operating within the "cultural schema" "mostly see the law as being marginal to activism". They do not view law as an important tool for social justice, nor do they see it as the "enemy" of social justice. Rather social justice in the cultural schema seems to be beyond the reach of law, as operating in a different realm of existence' (2003, 354). Examples of this sort of cultural activism abound, but they are seen primarily as ways to build grass-roots support for the legislative effort.

Beckett and Hoffman's analysis of advocacy for licensure of CPMs in Indiana shows clearly that the midwifery movement has had surprising success, even in the face of well organized medical interests arraying against them. Advocates have been successful in part because they have drawn on an already organized network present to help defend midwives in criminal prosecution and civil litigation (Beckett and Hoffman 2005, 127), and because of the organized presence of national advocacy organizations who are in a position to certify, license, study and develop best practices. In a way, pro-midwifery groups have fought science with science, and have mobilized professional ties and legal avenues to gain success in licensure (See Craven 2010; Hoffman 2008; Davis-Floyd and Johnson 2006).

However, midwives are also successful, Beckett and Hoffman note, because their advocates are able to mobilize symbolic and cultural claims. They write, 'the virtual, visual, and aural presence of an enthusiastic group of midwives and home birth consumers has had a powerful impact on these debates; in this case, the female identity of the resisters (and their association with a most powerful cultural icon, motherhood) has worked to their advantage' (2005, 127). Though it is not a focus of their work, Beckett and Hoffman also note that the midwives' and advocates' 'assertion of power through law' may further politicize them, and 'may trigger resistance to the social and legal hegemony upon which that [legal and medical] power rests' (2005, 126).

The present research suggests that this is the truly surprising and hopeful part of midwifery advocacy. Rather than resting on legislative success, midwives and their advocates might become radicalized in their politics of birth. As Kali explained it:

> If you're a CNM, in my opinion, you're still part of the medical model. You got the doctor and you got the CNM and she knows her place. Right? … Whereas licensed midwives and lay midwives are mavericks. They've always been mavericks and they'll continue to be mavericks. They think for themselves.

In celebrating their ability to 'think for themselves', these midwives may undertake to transform the cultural iconography of motherhood and the cultural institution of birth, in order to (re)normalize out-of-hospital, natural childbirth. In order to achieve true transformation, pro-midwifery advocates will need to wage a dual-pronged battle: one that asserts a demand for regulation and licensure, and another that refigures birth in America and the proper role of professionals in it. Midwives and their advocates will likely continue to use legal mobilization to achieve their goals, while also mobilizing politically and culturally to transform understandings of birth in their locale; an understanding of the limits of law in achieving their goals may contribute to their increased enthusiasm for working to change the cultures of birth in their locales.

Notes

1. Gender-inclusive language is an important part of evolving understandings of midwifery, and adopting it is an essential component to reproductive justice. Though this article will frequently refer to 'mothers' and 'women who give birth', I also adopt the terms 'parents', 'people who labor and deliver' and 'people who give birth'. These phrases are important correctives to gender normative constructions of pregnancy and delivery, and I adopt them frequently in this article. An excellent resource for this work is www.elephantcircle.net.
2. There is another category of midwife; those who are neither CPMs nor CNMs are referred to as 'direct entry' or 'lay' or 'traditional' midwives. Those midwives may be eligible, through their apprenticeship training, to sit for the CPM exam, but may choose not to because they have a different understanding of their calling to the practice of midwifery, and a different perspective on the role of certification, professionalization and credentialing.
3. California Code of Regulations Article 3.5 Section 1379.19; Licensed Midwife Practice Act 1993, amended CA SB 1479, 2000. See California College of Midwives, 'Standards, Guidelines, Protocols & Policies, and Minimum Practice Requirements' 2004.
4. None of my research subjects are identified by their given name; I use instead randomly generated pseudonyms for each midwife, in order to protect those who feel they are engaging in practices that run afoul of the law.
5. California's Business and Professions Code Section 2507 (a) sates that 'The license to practice midwifery authorizes the holder, *under the supervision of a licensed physician and surgeon*, to attend cases of normal childbirth and to provide prenatal, intrapartum, and postpartum care, including family-planning care, for the mother, and immediate care for the newborn.' 2507 (b) further states, 'As used in this article, the practice of midwifery constitutes the furthering or undertaking by any licensed midwife, *under the supervision of a licensed physician and surgeon who has current practice or training in obstetrics*, to assist a woman in childbirth so long as progress meets criteria accepted as normal'. And 2507 (d) further stipulates that 'the ratio of licensed midwives to supervising physicians and surgeons shall not be greater than four individual licensed midwives to one individual supervising physician and surgeon.' (All emphasis mine).
6. *Amicus Curiae* brief submitted by American Medical Association on behalf of Respondents (Missouri State Medical Association), 2007.
7. This phenomenon is well documented in the recent literature and not limited to CPMs by any means. Robinson found that malpractice insurance requirements put the profession of nurse-midwifery in a 'fight for survival' (1986, 1001). The American College of Nurse-Midwives responded quickly to the crisis, developing a plan to self-insure midwives through the

professional organization. Still, Jevitt and Johnson's (2007) study of Certified Nurse Midwives found that 'the price of private liability insurance is a disincentive for students to study midwifery and for clinical preceptors to work with students'. They further argue that 'Midwifery program directors and academic administrators must advocate for affordable liability coverage' (278). And, Judy Slome Cohain argues in the winter 2007 issue of Midwifery Today that medical malpractice coverage requirements decrease access to planned homebirth (2007). There are similar parallels to be made with other non-allopathic health care providers: chiropractors, naturopaths, homeopaths and massage therapists, for instance.

8. California State Law: Business and Professions Code, Section 2508 (a)(2).
9. This is not the only way in which insurance companies are impacting access to midwife-assisted homebirth: reimbursement for midwifery care is a contentious issue, and insurance coverage of the care is uneven.
10. Fieldnotes, March 2006.
11. Connie Rock, a co-founder of the birth center, used her blog to explain the closing of the Center at the time: http://morphogenesis.info/index.htm/__show_log/_p4/ Her plea was picked up by *Mothering* magazine, which included a discussion board thread on the incident here: http://www.mothering.com/forum/228-birth-professionals-archive/394726-revision-update-requesting-help-connie-rock-cpm.html Connie reached a settlement with the state medical board, and continued to be a leader in the California midwifery community.
12. Certainly, homebirth midwives are not the only alternative health care providers met with suspicion by members of the medical profession and the general public. Again, chiropractors, osteopaths, naturopaths and homeopaths are met with a similar mix of curiosity, suspicion and approbation.

Disclosure statement

No potential conflict of interest was reported by the author.

References

American College of Obstetrics and Gynecologists (ACOG). ACOG Practice Bulletin: Vaginal Birth After Previous Cesarean Delivery. Number 54. July 2004.

American Medical Association. *H-422.998 Obstetrical Delivery in the Home or Outpatient Facility.* Accessed on AMA website 20 May 2008. The American Medical Association.

Barnes, J., and T. F. Burke. 2012. "Making Way: Legal Mobilization, Organizational Response, and Wheelchair Access." *Law & Society Review* 46 (Spring): 167–198. doi:10.1111/j.1540-5893.2012.00476.x.

Beckett, K., and B. Hoffman. 2005. "Challenging Medicine: Law, Resistance, and the Cultural Politics of Childbirth." *Law & Society Review* 39 (1): 125–170. doi:10.1111/j.0023-9216.2005.00079.x.

Burstein, P., and K. Monaghan. 1986. "Equal Employment Opportunity and the Mobilization of Law." *Law & Society Review* 20 (3): 355–388. doi:10.2307/3053580.

Calavita, K. 2010. *An Invitation to Law and Society.* Chicago: University of Chicago Press.

Cohain, J. S. Winter 2007. "Mandatory Malpractice Insurance: Increases CS Rates and Profitability of Litigation, Decreases Planned Homebirths," *Midwifery Today* 84. doi:10.1097/01.opx.0000254035.39055.05

Cramer, R. A. 2009. "Creating Community while Interviewing Outlaws: Methodological Challenges and Opportunities." *The International Review of Qualitative Inquiry* 1 (4) :453–479. (February 2009).

Craven, C. 2010. *Pushing for Midwives: Homebirth Mothers and the Reproductive Rights Movement.* Philadelphia, PA: Temple University Press.

Davis-Floyd, R. 1993. *Birth as an American Rite of Passage.* Berkeley, CA: University of California Press.

Davis-Floyd, R., and C. B. Johnson. 2006. *Mainstreaming Midwives: The Politics of Change*. New York City: Routledge.

DeVries, R. G. 1996. *Making Midwives Legal: Childbirth, Medicine and the Law*. Columbus, OH: Ohio State University Press.

Fisher, S., and A. D. Todd. 1993. "Introduction." In *The Social Organization of Doctor-Patient Communication*, edited by A. D. Todd and S. Fisher, 1–16. NYC: Ablex Publishing Corporation.

Haider-Markel, D. P. 1998. "The Politics of Social Regulatory Policy: State and Federal Hate Crime Policy and Implementation Effort." *Political Research Quarterly* 51 (1, March): 69–88. doi:10.1177/106591299805100103.

Heimer, C. 1999. "Competing Institutions: Law, Medicine and Family in Neonatal Intensive Care." *Law & Society Review* 33 (1): 17–66. doi:10.2307/3115095.

Hoffman, B. 2008. "Minding the Gap: Legal Ideals and Strategic Action in State Legislative Hearings." *Law & Social Inquiry* 33 (Winter): 89–126. doi:10.1111/j.1747-4469.2008.00095.x.

Jevitt, C. M., and P. Johnson. 2007. "Liability Insurance in Midwifery Education: Faculty and Student Needs versus Academic Realities." *Journal of Professional Nursing* 23 (5): 278–284. doi:10.1016/j.profnurs.2007.01.020.

Keiser, L. R. 2001. "Street-Level Bureaucrats, Administrative Power and the Manipulation of Federal Social Security Disability Programs." *State Politics & Policy Quarterly* 1 (2): 144–164. doi:10.1177/153244000100100202.

Kessler, M. 1990. "Legal Mobilization for Social Reform: Power and the Politics of Agenda Setting." *Law & Society Review* 24 (1): 121–144. doi:10.2307/3053789.

Kitzinger, S. 2005. *The Politics of Birth*. London: Elsevier Books.

Klarman, M. 2006. *From Jim Crow to Civil Rights: The Supreme Court and the Struggle for Racial Equality*. New York City: Oxford University Press.

Kostiner, I. 2003. "Evaluating Legality: Toward a Cultural Approach to the Study of Law and Social Change." *Law and Society Review* 37 (June): 323. doi:10.1111/1540-5893.3702006.

Krieger, L. H. 2000. "Afterword: Socio-Legal Backlash." Berkeley Journal of Employment and Labor Law 21: 476.

Lipsky, M. 1980. *Street Level Bureaucrats: Dilemmas of the Individual in Public Services*. New York: Russell Sage Foundation.

Luker, K. 1984. *Abortion & the Politics of Motherhood*. Los Angeles: University of California Press.

Marshall, A.-M. 2005. "Idle Rights: Employees' Rights Consciousness and the Construction of Sexual Harassment Policies." *Law & Society Review* 39 (1): 83–124. doi:10.1111/j.0023-9216.2005.00078.x.

McCann, M. W. 1994. *Rights at Work: Pay Equity and the Politics of Legal Mobilization*. Chicago: University of Chicago Press.

McCann, M. W., and H. Silverstein. 2008. "Rethinking Law's Allurements: A Relational Analysis of Social Movement Lawyers in the United States." In *Cause Lawyering: Political Commitments and Professional Responsibilities*, edited by A. Sarat and S. Scheingold, 261–292. New York: Oxford University Press.

McGregor, D. K. 1998. *From Midwives to Medicine: The Birth of American Gynecology*. New Brunswick, NJ: Rutgers University Press.

Munz, M. 2008. "Midwifery Bill Runs into Issues in Senate." *St. Louis Post-Dispatch*, April 16. [Accessed on-line 19 May 2008].

Nielsen, L. B. 2004. *License to Harass: Law, Hierarchy and Offensive Public Speech*. Princeton: NJ: Princeton University Press.

Pound, R. 1910. "Law in Books and Law in Action." *American Law Review* 44: 12.

Robinson, G. A. 1986. "Midwifery and Malpractice Insurance: A Profession Fights for Its Survival." *University of Pennsylvania Law Review* 134 (4, April): 1001–1034. doi:10.2307/3312025.

Rooks, J. P. 1997. *Midwifery and Childbirth in America*. Philadelphia: Temple University Press.

Rooks, J. P., N. L. Weatherby, E. K. M. Ernst, S. Stapleton, D. Rosen, and A. Rosenfield. 1989. "Outcomes of Care in Birth Centers: The National Birth Center Study." *New England Journal of Medicine* 321: 1804–1811. doi:10.1056/NEJM198912283212606.

Rosenberg, G. N. 1991. *The Hollow Hope: Can Courts Bring About Social Change?* Chicago: University of Chicago Press.

Rothman, B. K. 1982. *In Labor: Women and Power in the Birthplace*. New York: W.W. Norton.

Sarat, A. 1985. "Legal Effectiveness and Social Studies of Law." *Legal Studies Forum* 9: 23.

Silverstein, H. 1999. "Road Closed: Evaluating the Judicial Bypass Provision of the Pennsylvania Abortion Control Act." *Law & Social Inquiry* 24 (1, Winter): 73–96. doi:10.1111/j.1747-4469.1999.tb00793.x.

Silverstein, H. 2007. *Girls on the Stand: How Courts Fail Pregnant Minors*. NYC: New York University Press.

Solinger, R. 2007. *Pregnancy and Power: A Short History of Reproductive Politics in America*. New York City: New York University Press.

Vedam, S., K. Stoll, M. MacDorman, E. DeClerq, R. Cramer, M. Cheney, T. Fisher, E. Butt, Y. Tony Yang, and H. P. Kennedy. 2018. "Mapping of Integration of Midwives across the United Sates: Impact on Access, Equity, and Outcomes." *PLOS One Medicine*. doi:10.1371/journal.pone.0192523.

Mothers do not make good workers: the role of work/life balance policies in reinforcing gendered stereotypes

Sarah Cote Hampson

ABSTRACT

'Family friendly' policies such as maternity leave allow millions of women in the United States to take some time off when they give birth or adopt a child in order to spend time physically recuperating and/or initiating a bond with their children. However, many working mothers report facing stereotypes that either negatively impact their decision-making about claiming their rights under work/life balance policies, or cause them to be the specific targets of discrimination in their workplaces. This article, which draws upon in-depth interviews with 48 women from 2 types of work environments (the U.S. military and academia), identifies stereotypes that have developed in these institutions. These stereotypes establish the identity of a working mother as the antithesis of an 'ideal worker'. I argue that the very policies that are aimed at easing the tension between work and family help to create and reinforce these stereotypes through discursive institutional processes.

Introduction

Millions of women in the United States take some time off when they give birth or adopt a child using 'family friendly' laws and policies in order to spend time recuperating and/or to initiate a bond with their children. Such allowances are grounded in federal law (The Family and Medical Leave Act of 1992), state and municipal laws (e.g. California's Paid Family Leave Law of 2002, or the City of Seattle's 2015 introduction of paid parental leave for city employees) and individual institutional policies. In recent years, another wave of policies aimed at improving the rate of breastfeeding among working mothers have also taken hold throughout various states. A provision in the Affordable Care Act has brought similar accommodation requirements to federal laws,[1] and many workplaces have gone above and beyond state and federal requirements and have implemented multiple lactation rooms and on-site support services.

Policies that aim to improve work/life balance are often created with the hope that changes in structural support for women in the workplace will allow for social changes to also take effect at work. Activists and policymakers hope that such policy changes will not only increase women's participation in the workplace, but also help women to

---

This article is adapted from Chapter 5 of *The Balance Gap: Working Mothers and the Limits of the Law* (Stanford University Press 2017).

experience greater overall equity as workers. These policies, however, have thus far fallen short of fully alleviating the tensions that women across the nation are still grappling with as they try to balance their work and their family responsibilities.[2] A recent Pew Research Center survey shows, for instance, that mothers are still far more likely to experience a career interruption than fathers in order to fulfill caregiving work. The study notes that 42 percent of mothers have reduced their working hours in order to care for a child or family member, compared with 28 percent of men, and 27 percent of women reported having quit their job to perform these caregiving tasks, compared with just 10 percent of men) (Cohn, Livingston, and Wang 2014). Another Pew survey shows that 41 percent of working mothers report that being a mother makes it harder to advance in their careers, compared with just 20 percent of working fathers who said the same (Pew Research Center 2015).

Women are also continuing to experience cultural stereotypes at work. Heilman and Chen find that in psychological experiments, women are viewed 14 percent less positively than men if they volunteer to stay late and work on a project and 12 percent more negatively than men if they do not (Heilman and Chen 2005). Moreover, Williams and Dempsey note that even women in high-earning professions such as law and medicine continue to be consigned to the 'office housework' that includes planning parties, ordering food and doing other undervalued, administrative tasks (Williams and Dempsey 2014). These studies reveal that there is essentially a gap between the changes in public policy over the last 25 years or so and the degree to which women feel the impact of these policies in their own lives.

Law and Society scholars have long interrogated the 'gap' between the law on the books and the law in action, and the role of the law in bringing about social change. It is therefore within the context of this literature that I expound on the disconnect between advances in 'family friendly' public policies and the lived experiences of working mothers. This article draws upon in-depth interviews with 48 women from 2 types of work environments: the U.S. military and academia. I apply Law and Society conversations about work and identity to the topic of working mothers. I explore the discourses that have arisen within institutional settings that are salient to the way that women think about their own identities as workers – and about their rights under federal, state and workplace work/life balance policies.

In what follows, I review the sociolegal literature that has already made significant headway in connecting law, discourse and identity – particularly within workplace settings – as a means of explaining gaps between the law on the books and the law in action. I then connect this discussion to a broader literature that has recognized and documented the significance of an 'ideal worker' construct within institutional settings. This discussion of the literature on law, discourse and identity and in particular the formation of an 'ideal worker' construct serve as the basis for what follows. I next introduce the empirical element of this analysis, which documents the existence of ideal worker-types in both academia and the U.S. military. I demonstrate that these ideal worker types within each workplace setting serve to establish and reinforce *stereotypes* of female workers within these institutions – stereotypes that set female workers in stark contrast to the ideal worker types. In the final section of this paper, I argue that these stereotypes – far from being allayed by work/life balance laws and policies – are often, in fact, reinforced and compounded by them. Indeed, this study reveals that the very policies aimed at increasing working mothers' workforce participation and retention can often reinforce damaging cultural stigmas of women as non-ideal workers.

Law, discourse and the 'ideal worker'

David Engel and Frank Munger's (2003) seminal work on the connection between rights and identity in the workplace traces the impact of the Americans with Disabilities Act (ADA) on individuals' legal consciousness. Their study reveals the complex relationship between law and the way that individuals think about, internalize and appropriate law. Through interviews with disabled workers, the authors demonstrate how these individuals engage with rights through their definition or re-definition of their individual *identities* – specifically in the context of work. Identity and paid employment are fundamentally linked, the authors claim, and laws such as the ADA seek to transform, not just the physical structure of the workplace for those with disabilities, but the social presumptions that undergird their very 'disabled-ness'. Rights, the authors argue, by permeating cultural norms and everyday discourse, can transform how individuals view themselves under the law, and also how others view them as individuals.

Legal consciousness, and its formation, is an important concept in Engel and Munger's work. Legal consciousness is essentially the way that individuals use the law and legal concepts to interpret the world around them, and their own lives and identities. Legal consciousness can impact individuals' thoughts, language and actions. Significantly, legal consciousness can also impact how individuals choose to use (or not use) the law (Engel 1984; McCann 1994; Ewick and Silbey 1998; Morgan 1999; Gilliom 2001; Haltom and McCann 2004; Marshall 2005). Therefore, the process by which individuals come to form this legal consciousness is a significant one, worthy of investigation. Engel and Munger define the development of legal consciousness as a two-way process, 'through which the self continually evolves and redefines the relevance or irrelevance of law' (2003, 13).

William Haltom and Michael McCann (2004) also examine the formation of legal consciousness using a process-based approach. In their study of the politics of tort reform, the authors look closely at the role of discourse in shaping legal consciousness. Haltom and McCann's study demonstrates the recursive role of media institutions, elites and ideology in shaping public discourse, and thus public consciousness around litigiousness in America. Other sociolegal scholars have also highlighted the significant role of discourse within institutional settings in shaping cultural norms and informal and formal legal systems (Ewick and Silbey 1998; Albiston 2010; Engel and Munger 2003; Marshall and Barclay 2003; Marshall 2005).

Discourse plays an important role within institutional settings in shaping both legal consciousness and individual identity. Its effect on legal consciousness and identity is important, because research has overwhelmingly shown the significance of individuals' subjective cognitive processes in the effective mobilization of rights. The impact of law and policies that establish individual rights, in other words, is limited by the power of informal norms, power relations, social interactions and institutional constraints (Albiston 2010; Quinn 2000; Scheingold 2004; McCann 1994; Bumiller 1992; Ewick and Silbey 1998; Marshall and Barclay 2003; Marshall 2005; Gruber 1998; Williams and Cooper 2004). Catherine Albiston, for instance, finds that women have difficulty mobilizing their right to FMLA leave, because 'workplace rights mobilization remains embedded within existing practices, deeply held beliefs, and taken-for-granted expectations about work, gender, and disability, all of which can create subtle but persistent resistance to these new rights' (2010, 181). In summary, sociolegal scholars have well documented the significant role that informal schemas and norms can play in nullifying rights or rights-granting polices. Furthermore, these scholars have shown in other contexts that such informal norms can often make it extremely difficult for individuals to claim their rights within institutional settings.

Several scholars, most notably Joan Williams, have documented the existence of an ideal worker concept within workplace contexts (Berns 2002; Williams 2000; 2009; Williams and Cooper 2004; Kessler-Harris 2001; Kelly et al. 2010). Williams (2000) in particular has argued for its detrimental effects on women's decisions to seek out or take up maternity leave rights. In *Unbending Gender*, she argues that both men and women face challenges posed by the notion of the ideal worker, which she claims is pervasive in American workplace culture. The ideal worker is childless or has an invisible caretaker at home, looking after domestic considerations and care needs so that the worker need not be concerned with these things. He or she is able to work full time and overtime, anytime. The ideal worker does not take maternity leave or need to pick up a sick child from school. The notion of the ideal worker, in other words, presents a dichotomy between 'good' workers as those who are entirely devoted to their jobs and 'bad' workers as those whose time and attention is consistently pulled to things outside work.

The ideal worker norm did not emerge from thin air. Rather, Williams argues, it is part of a larger ideology, which she calls an 'ideology of domesticity.' Williams documents how this ideology is both historically and still pervasive in American thought, culture and law.[3] Susan Moller Okin is a feminist theorist who tackles the history of this ideology head-on, arguing that liberal theorists have long ignored women, relegating them to a 'private' sphere that is irrelevant to the political or 'public' sphere. It is the ideological separation of these two spheres that is the primary source of continued injustice for women, argues Okin (1991).

Yet the ideology and practice of domesticity remain intimately connected in American culture and politics. Several feminist scholars point to the significant connection between gender and caregiving expectations in the American workplace. Martha Albertson Fineman's work, for instance, emphasizes cultural ambivalence toward the strong caregiving ties of many women in the United States, arguing that it is this bond that should in fact be recognized by law and society as the nuclear family rather than the sexual bond of man and wife (1995). Laura T. Kessler follows in Fineman's footsteps and looks specifically at the traditional role of caregiver that a large percentage of women still carry out in their private spheres, arguing that law and legal tradition have systematically ignored this role and the impact of its existence on women's equality of opportunity in the workplace (2001). Kessler suggests that a normative solution is needed to adjust this disconnect, because it is the ideological undervaluing of women's caregiving work that causes it to be overlooked and underaddressed in the workplace.

Complicating this literature on the overlooked private lives of women is the growing body of scholarship critiquing the active role that many work/life policies have played in further entrenching gendered roles. Fathering literature, in particular, has highlighted this critique, illuminating the problematic emphasis in institutional policies and culture on the need for *women* to have time to care for private needs, while men are expected to maintain their public identities without giving attention to private ones. As the fathering literature demonstrates, men are not only increasingly interested in being more involved in the development and raising of their children (Brandth and Kvande 1998; Doucet 2004; 2006; Wall and Arnold 2007); they can also make distinct and important contributions to child rearing (Doucet 2004; 2006; Featherstone 2003). Other studies have demonstrated the challenges that specific public policies and institutions pose to rectifying the imbalance of caretaking due to their contribution to perpetuating gendered identities (Hobson 2002; Jesmin and Seward 2011; Haas and O'Brien 2010; McKay and Doucet 2010).

The policies that have resulted from this historical and contemporary connection between women and caregiving roles, therefore, have emphasized the need to give *women* time away from work to care-give. This ideological connection is so strong that even when men are granted equal leave time for caregiving, women are still much more likely to take the time than men. According to the Bureau of Labor Statistics, women were 30 times more likely (3.2 percent of women taking leave, compared with .01 percent of men taking leave) to cite birth or adoption of a child as their reason for taking leave in any given week in 2011, even though they were only 3 percent more likely than men to take leave from work overall (U.S. Bureau of Labor and Statistics 2011).[4]

Not only is the construct of the ideal worker gendered, but it is also racialized. While white women struggle to meet the expectations of an ideal worker, they more easily meet the expectations of the ideal mother than women of color. Intersectional experiences of working mothers, therefore, lead to complex and contested issues that are often masked by homogenized discussions of 'women and work' that often assume a white subject. Heather MacPherson Parrott, for instance, demonstrates that white women have a larger 'motherhood penalty'[5] than women in other racial and ethnic groups. Parrott posits that this increased effect is due, not to white women's greater oppression in the workplace, but rather to greater variation in their ability to conform to the ideal worker construct. 'Motherhood may not further depress wages simply because their wages are already too low. These findings suggest that theorizing about the motherhood penalty and gender inequality may have limited applicability to minority women experiencing double jeopardy in the workplace' (Parrott 2014). In other words, the ideal worker may be attainable for white women without children, but it is already unattainable for women of color, regardless of their parental status. Policies such as maternity leave, therefore, are designed with a particular image of white motherhood in mind. The connection of this imagery to public policy, argues Parrott, is unhelpful for white women who experience large 'motherhood penalties' but also fundamentally unhelpful to Black and Hispanic women who would benefit far more from policies that aim to address racial and ethnic inequalities in wages and equal opportunity of employment.

This continued connection between the ideology of domesticity and public policy has unforeseen consequences for the experiences of all women hoping for workplace equality. Let us turn to the interview data to discuss ways in which the ideology of domesticity – and the ideal worker norm – have had a significant impact on the rights consciousness and rights claiming of women in both public universities and the U.S. military. Women who participated in this study identified two distinct workplace stereotypes tied to the ideal worker norm, and we will see the ways in which these women wrestled with the stereotypes when thinking through their rights.

Case selection and methods

Numerous scholars who look at rights claiming in the workplace have already highlighted the significance of institutional context in influencing rights consciousness and rights claiming (Marshall 2005; Albiston 2005; 2010; Reese and Lindenberg 2003; Zippel 2004; Munkres 2008; Seron, Pereira, and Kovath 2004; Hoffmann 2001). Yet these studies do not undertake a comparative analysis of institutional contexts. This paper therefore makes a conscious comparison of workplace contexts. This comparison allows me to make broader claims about the significance of discourse within institutional contexts, and its impact on rights mobilization.

Additionally, I choose to compare academic institutions and the U.S. military because each of these types of workplaces offers unique characteristics and cultures, which are also generally transferrable across specific institutions. For instance, the culture of academia may be said to transfer from university to university, and the culture of the U.S. military may be said to transfer from branch to branch, base to base. While each institutional site will have its own flavor, it is possible to make generalizations about the culture of these professions as 'institutions', while capturing a broad range of individual participants. Furthermore, both academia and the military have 'cultures' that have been documented to be deeply entrenched (e.g. For the academy, see: Mason, Wolfinger, and Goulden 2013; O'Brien Hallstein and O'Reilly 2012. For the U.S. military, see: Enloe 2014; Taber 2011; 2013). Since workplace culture is the primary focus of this study, these sites are ideal for exploring the questions I tackle in my work.

This paper draws on data from 48 in-depth interviews that I collected over a 1-year period from 2012 to 2013. Twenty-four of these interviews were conducted with academic faculty, and 24 of them were conducted with former and active duty service members from various branches of the U.S. military (Army, Navy, Air Force and Air Force reserves, Marines, and Coast Guard). The ages of the women interviewed range from 23 to 58. Some of the women who participated do not have children, but are thinking about becoming pregnant or adopting in the near future. Other participants have one or multiple children. Additionally, the levels of career achievement (and consequently income levels) vary widely among the women interviewed. Among military women, 15 of the women are enlisted members in ranks ranging from E-3 to E-7, and 9 of the women are or were officers, with the highest rank represented being a current colonel in the Air Force. Among faculty women, I spoke with 15 women at a small public university in the south, and 9 women at a large, multi-campus university in the northeast. Twelve women are visiting assistant professors still on the tenure-track, four women are tenured associate professors and six are adjuncts, instructors, or visiting assistant professors. Among all of the participants, race, ethnicity and sexuality does not vary considerably. Only three participants identified as 'non-white' and only one participant identified herself as being in a same-sex relationship. Most of the participants are married or living with a partner, with only six identifying as single or separated. Finally, 90 percent of the women interviewed also identified themselves as either the primary breadwinner or 'equal' in regard to wage earning in their households.[6]

Each woman interviewed was asked the same series of loosely organized questions about her experiences with taking maternity leave at her place of work, which included questions about her experiences with planning to have children, pregnancy and/or adoption, taking leave, finding information about policies, returning to work, and interactions with colleagues and/or supervisors regarding work/family issues. Each interviewee was also asked a series of questions about her opinions regarding maternity leave in the United States and at her place of work, and about how she might like to change policies if at all. These questions were all covered in each interview; however, the format and structure of each interview was unique, and certain follow-up questions differed based on each individual's related experiences.

In analyzing the interview data, I used interpretive methods to explore women's use of legal or rights-based language, and their formation of concepts and justifications for their actions in relation to the policies to which they are entitled concerning work/life balance. The choice of interpretive methods over something like content analysis here is appropriate, in that I was interested in a bottom-up development of concepts, rather than mapping preexisting terms and models onto these women's language and consciousness. Since I am interested in how women think about and interpret public policy, it was appropriate to use a method that would allow for inductive techniques for determining how women's knowledge of and interaction with these policies has been influenced (Schwartz-Shea and Yanow 2012). I conducted each interview myself, making note of major themes addressed at the time. I then reread each interview multiple times, noting major themes that emerged consistently throughout each case study. Finally, once I had identified several of the major themes I wanted to address in the analysis, I systematically coded each transcript for these themes.

Mothers are not ideal workers

Literature on both academia and the U.S. military documents to some extent what is expected of an ideal worker in these environments. In academia, for instance, faculty are expected to pursue tenure-track careers that lead to full professorship, which most often requires a grueling research and teaching schedule. These expectations are frequently coupled with an understanding that faculty must not have commitments that take their time and attention away from these expectations, particularly the research element. Recent studies of male and female academics, for instance, have demonstrated that the individuals in these careers who are most successful at maintaining a high level of research output are married men with children and the least successful are married women with children (Townsend 2013; Krapf, Ursprung, and Zimmermann 2014). These findings further emphasize the significance of unpaid domestic work in the ideal worker construct. Married men with children are successful, the authors of these studies suggest, because a female partner either fully or largely completes the 'second shift' of housework and child care within the home, allowing them to devote more time to their primary career. Married women with children are, conversely, doing a disproportionate share of the domestic work and are thus disadvantaged in the time they are able to devote to paid work (Hochschild 2001; Hochschild and Machung 2003; Mason, Wolfinger, and Goulden 2013; Townsend 2013; Krapf, Ursprung, and Zimmermann 2014).

In the military, the ideal worker is much more overtly masculine. As Cynthia Enloe notes, masculinity and the U.S. military are intimately connected. The ideal worker in the U.S. military is a 'warrior' – specifically, one who is male (2014). Yet in a volunteer military, recruitment of women soon became necessary in order to sustain its numbers.

In opening the military to women, Enloe argues, officials 'believe that they need to recruit and deploy women in only those ways that will not subvert the fundamentally masculinized culture of the military' (2014, 37). A woman in the U.S. military, therefore, is not an ideal worker simply by virtue of being female. Pregnancy and childbirth complicate this by reminding a woman's colleagues and superiors of her femaleness in very explicit ways. In both the U.S. military and public universities, my interviews demonstrate that institutional stereotypes have developed around women with children in these workplace settings as individuals who do not – and cannot – meet the expectations for an ideal worker.

The military mother who is avoiding deployment

In my interviews with military servicewomen, it became clear very quickly that a stereotype existed, and each of the women I spoke to was in some way reacting to it. In all but one of the interviews, the service member identified the stereotype explicitly. Essentially the stereotype is that women who become pregnant in the military do so in order to avoid her duties as a warrior in some way, though the duty most frequently referenced was overseas deployment. Mothers in the U.S. military therefore do not fit the ideal worker image in their workplace because the ideal worker in a military environment is one who is physically fit and always ready to do his or her duty when called on. A pregnant service member does not fit this model in that she receives 'special treatment' – which includes deferral from deployment for 4–12 months after childbirth[7] and exemptions from other typical duty requirements, such as uniform regulations or physical training exercises.

In detailing what the stereotype is, many of the women I interviewed were also careful to identify themselves as individuals who do *not* fit the stereotype. Grace, a 33-year-old sergeant first class in the Army, clarified that she was aware of the stereotype but that she wasn't deployable when she got pregnant:

> I mean there's a little bit of a stigma for people – especially women – that are staying behind [from a deployment]… . It's "Oh, did she get pregnant to get out of deployment?" I mean – which, I'd been pregnant before it was even known that we were deploying, but there's still always that little bit that, you know, the possibility of that chatter … it's more – I think, more of a gossip thing."

Grace goes on, however, to point out that she knows another woman who might better fit the stereotype:

> [A soldier under my supervision] was actually in Afghanistan when she found out she was pregnant… . From the view of the command, they were not out to do her any favors. You know, she got sent home; technically she could have been punished. I mean, it didn't happen, but it definitely leaves a bad taste in the command's mouth in a situation like that.

Similarly, Joyce, 58, currently serves as a colonel in the Air Force. As a captain, she left active duty for the reserves when she decided to start her family and reentered only when her children were school age. 'I separated [from active duty] what, a year and a half before the war [in Afghanistan] kicked off, so it wasn't like I did it because I had to go to war,' she explains, clearly indicating her knowledge of the stereotype and her own position outside its reach. She continues, though, to relate that

> a friend of mine was in a similar situation only she delivered her baby in August of 1990 … and her husband was already deployed to Desert Shield, and when she came back to our squadron, which is a deployable squadron, a flying squadron, she went over to a nondeployable squadron … and people talked about that. Even years later people talked about that, how she was given special treatment or that she didn't do what she should have done, which was deploy.

Sophia, a 23-year-old third-class petty officer in the Navy, had a harder time defending her position in relation to the stereotype. Sophia, who is not married, became pregnant unintentionally while on a deployable ship and had to leave her boat for shore duty as a result. She insists that she is not one of the 'girls who mess up' and 'put a stigma on all the rest of the pregnant girls'. Yet she felt as though she needed to hide her pregnancy from her fellow sailors when she left her ship, fearing that they would think she fit that stereotype:

> There were a few people like that, they were like, ah, yeah, I see what you're doing, you know. And I kind of tried to keep it really quiet that I was pregnant when I was leaving. I told a lot of people I was leaving because of a bad back. So I didn't want to be known as that girl who got pregnant or got knocked up and had to leave the boat.

Many of the servicewomen who were interviewed also went beyond simply mentioning the stereotype and defining themselves in opposition to it. A number of them also said that their decision-making, or that of other women they knew, has been influenced in whole or in part by the existence of this stereotype. For instance, some, like Gina, a chief petty officer in the Coast Guard, said that they consciously tried to work harder than their colleagues as a way of combating the image. Gina says:

> I feel like already because we're females we have to work twice as hard to earn the respect that the males are already given, and then when you have these impressions running around in everybody's minds, and then it just – it spurs me on even more. I moved up pretty quick in my advancement, and a lot of that is just my initiative and my drive to prove people wrong. I'm tired of hearing it.

Adrienne, a 38-year-old Air Force major, took a similar though slightly different approach to combating the stereotype. During her pregnancy, Adrienne took pride in doing tasks that were above and beyond those recommended by her military profile.[8] She talks about meeting wounded warriors on the flight line right up until delivery, and also braving a massive snowstorm to go into work at 8 months pregnant because she knew she would be able to get there before her supervisor to make sure that her work was being overseen at a critical time. She says she made these decisions because 'I just didn't want them to appear that I was using my profile to get out of work' – and that she was 'just doing what you're supposed to do as a leader'. She says of her profile:

> I think it recommended like you not stand for so many – for such a period of time or something like that – and then it allows you to wear tennis shoes if you wanted. Which is another thing: I never wore tennis shoes. I was so proud not to wear tennis shoes my whole entire pregnancy. I wore my boots – my combat boots the entire pregnancy. I guess I just didn't want them to think because I was on profile I was taking the easy way out.

Adrienne takes pride in wearing her combat boots while pregnant and performing other tasks that she would be within her rights under military regulation to forgo. In this way, she is signaling to herself and to others that she is an ideal worker. She does not fit the stereotype but rather is eager to show others that she does not need to claim her rights as a pregnant member of the Air Force. Adrienne's behavior reflects a consciousness that rights claiming would make her stand out as nonideal.

Like Adrienne, Liv, too, was quick to adopt behavior that would help her to stand out as an ideal worker in her new unit, stating her willingness to deploy earlier than required postpartum. Liv is a 26-year-old Army sergeant in an airborne unit who, at the time of our interview, had an 8-month-old baby. When Liv found out about her pregnancy, her unit had just returned from a deployment. 'There is no good or bad time to get pregnant in the Army,' she says, but notes that 'I was kind of in a good position because I did just get back from a deployment, so it's not like I looked like I was getting pregnant to get out of deployment'. When asked whether this impression concerned her, Liv replied, 'I mean, it's always in the back of your mind.... You know, my sergeant ... one time, you know, I went to the motor pool to go and help and he goes, "Ah, get out of here, you're useless," ... and I mean he was just joking, but he was also kind of like, you know, "You can't do anything for me because you're pregnant," so there is a stigma that's attached to it.'

When Liv was transferred to a new unit early in her pregnancy, she had to confront the stigma head-on, since this new unit was due to deploy soon and was not the same unit with which she had recently returned from deployment. Liv says that she was so worried about how being pregnant would look in this situation that she offered to waive her postpartum period of deferred eligibility for deployment:

> When I actually met the battalion commander ... he said, "Oh you getting ready to deploy with us?" and I said, "Well sir, I'm pregnant, you know, and I'm due in February," and at that time, they weren't supposed to deploy until a little bit later, so I said, "I could waive my postpartum time and I can deploy with you guys," and you know, he was all for that. He doesn't have any children.

Liv's immediate supervisor, a sergeant major, however, stopped her from doing this. 'He said that he wouldn't allow me to waive my postpartum time to meet them in Afghanistan.' Nevertheless, Liv's concern about how her pregnancy would look to her new lieutenant colonel and her fellow soldiers was concerning enough to her to consider relinquishing her right to defer deployment. For both Liv and Adrienne, waiving their rights to work/life balance policies aimed at improving their conditions in fact became a way for them to mark themselves as ideal workers.

Not all of the servicewomen felt that their decision-making due to the stereotype was a way to combat it. Some of them said that they knew that a lot of their colleagues simply accepted that children and the military do not go together. Gabrielle, a 36-year-old lieutenant colonel in the Air Force says, 'A good number of us [mothers in the Air Force] will punch[9] [leave the military altogether] at that ten-year point. Because at that point in time, you've either gotten married or you haven't and you want to, and you've had children and you're trying to balance and it just – something's gotta give basically'. Women who leave the military after 10 years of service lose out on significant benefits and compensation that can be attained only after 20 years of service. The existence of the stereotype, Gabrielle believes, causes many women to think that balancing a military career and family is simply not possible and so they leave, meaning that women are much scarcer in the higher ranks, where length of service is a prerequisite. This trend in the military is strikingly similar to the problem of the 'leaky pipeline' in academia, where women are also largely underrepresented at the higher ranks (Mason, Wolfinger, and Goulden 2013; Wolfinger, Mason, and Goulden 2009; Krapf, Ursprung, and Zimmermann 2014).

While not all of the servicewomen interviewed felt that they had been especially harmed by the existence of the stereotype, a few did. Zoe, a 29-year-old veteran who had served in the Air Force for three and a half years, cited the stereotype, and her supervisor's reaction to it, as the reason she decided to take the option offered by all branches of the armed forces – to leave service with an honorable discharge during pregnancy. Zoe says when she found out she was pregnant and would be a single mother, she had never intended to leave her career. 'I knew that it was gonna be a stressful experience, but I also knew that I was gonna have my schooling paid for, and that I would rise up in the ranks, and that this was what I had wanted to do since I could remember.' She says, though, that she decided to get out when a supervisor approached her after learning of her pregnancy, and threatened her.

> [T]he new NCOIC said to me, "mark my words, when you get back, as soon as your son is six months old, I'm deploying your ass." And I was like, what? Oh – what? And he was like, "yeah. You said you wanted to go on TCNs, and deployments and all this kind of shit when you got here. You're leaving when your son's six months old, so get your little family care plan together."

Six months postpartum is the earliest that women in the Air Force are required to be eligible to deploy again.[10] Zoe insists that she knew she would potentially have to deploy, but that it was the fact that her supervisor had made her feel as though she would be specifically targeted because he perceived that she was trying to get out of it that made her start to think about leaving.

> You know, I knew that it was a possibility… like my bucket comes up, or whatever, I want to go…but it would have been vastly different, because I knew the intention isn't to separate me from my child. You know, and that was his intention. And to cause me kind of like undo, you know, stress.

Even when more formal consequences are not evident, some of the women claim that the effect that the stereotype can have on relationships, with both their chain of command, and their colleagues, can also be significant. Brianna, a 34-year-old Army specialist with 2 children, whose husband is also serving in the Army, felt personally targeted because of the existence of the stereotype about mothers in the military. She says that not long after having her first child, she was deployed to Kuwait. 'Little did I know, I was pregnant with my daughter… . [My] first sergeant was irate. She was livid. She told me I should be a housewife. That the Army isn't for me. I'm a substandard soldier. She gave me 45 minutes of what she thought about me being pregnant'. Brianna said that she felt particularly hurt by being a target of this first sergeant, because prior to this incident, she had looked to her as a mentor for how to become a strong female leader in the military. 'She really got in my head, she really messed with me… . I joined the military to serve my country. I come from kind of like a rich background of military in my family. And so for me to deploy, I was very proud… . So a lot of me felt like I let my unit down, I let myself down, I let my family down'. Their relationship remained strained, and Brianna was relieved when she was later transferred and no longer required to work with that supervisor.

It is clear that the stereotype of a mother in the military who gets pregnant to avoid deployment or in other ways 'shirk' her duty is one that stands in direct contrast to the 'ideal worker' notion of the service member who is always ready to do their duty. Yet it is also important to note at this point that the very policies aimed at recruiting and retaining mothers who serve may be directly feeding into this stereotype. By keeping female service members from deployment, allowing them time away to breastfeed, and time away from other requirements such as uniform codes and PT exercises, these 'family friendly' policies serve to offer confirmation of the existing stereotype (or perhaps even fed its creation) – that military mothers are not ideal workers.

The academic mother who is not a serious scholar

Women faculty working in public universities identified a stereotype with features unique to academia but nonetheless strikingly similar to that faced by U.S. military servicewomen. Most of the women interviewed referred to an explicit stereotype: that women who have children at an academic institution are not serious scholars. In addition, the minority of these women who did not explicitly reference a stereotype still talked about how having a family could cause them professional difficulties, but their discussion of this tension was more implicit.

Some of the women faculty referred to interactions with colleagues in their workplaces where the stereotype and how to counteract it were discussed outright. Valerie, for instance, a visiting assistant professor with a 2-year-old son, discusses how this stereotype was related in stark terms to her by another female colleague:

> It was like Labor Day or something, that we had classes, but none of the local public schools had classes. A couple of the parents brought their kids to the office. But I did have someone tell me – I didn't bring my son – but I did have someone tell me, you know, "As a woman I wouldn't do that if I were you. People have trouble taking moms seriously, and they won't take you seriously if they see you walking around with your son. They won't think you take the job seriously."

Carol, a 39-year-old associate professor with a young child, says that she also had an interaction with a colleague that made her aware of the stereotype.

> [My colleague] is a woman who is not – does not have a partner and does not have kids, and … she is a person who – the excessive energy around – "Oh let's talk about your kids, oh it's so exciting that you're pregnant" – felt suspicious to me… . I mean, it was very nice of her … but I just remember feeling like she was wanting to peg me as, okay, now she's a mom. Like, she's not really a scholar, she's a mom, and so I'm gonna talk to her in a baby voice about the kids… . I don't think that this was intentional. I don't think that this was, you know, some sort of consciously hostile thing. But it felt to me like I'm being stereotyped.

Overall, the women employed at the public universities seemed less concerned than the servicewomen had about needing to distinguish their own position outside the stereotype. Though some women, like Carol, indicated that they have made conscious choices to avoid being stereotyped, not every individual interviewed made this distinction as starkly or as comprehensively as the servicewomen did. Furthermore, none of the female faculty felt a need to point out that while she did not fit the stereotype, other female faculty did. Instead, the faculty who identified the stereotype explicitly went on to deny its validity.

Nonetheless, each woman interviewed discussed the difficulties that she had faced in trying to be do her job well while balancing it with her family demands. Therefore, the phrase *work/life balance* (and a concern for achieving it) was a consistent theme across these interviews. What seemed to be a trend among academic women was to discuss the choices that they had made in response to these demands. Many of the female faculty interviewed said that their knowledge of the stereotype had caused them to feel conflicted or anxious about navigating work/life balance policies. Additionally, some faculty admitted that a consciousness of the stereotype had some serious effects on their decision-making. Therefore, while female faculty members, on the whole, were not as willing to openly acknowledge that the stereotype correctly characterized some women in their profession as the servicewomen were, they nevertheless struggled to define themselves in opposition to it, indicating its significant impact on their rights consciousness.

Several of the academic women, like the servicewomen, talked about feeling the need to work harder to counter the narrative that they are somehow shirking their duties. Louise, for example, an assistant professor at Oak University with four children, says that she feels anxiety about appearing to be a good worker. 'I mean … I don't want people think that I'm just cashing it in – taking advantage of people's goodwill'. Louise talks about feeling guilty for not making her time on bed rest with her latest pregnancy count more in terms of working toward her publishing record. 'I mean, I read tons of stuff online, you know … like, everybody dreams of having seven weeks where you're sitting on your bed doing nothing but that … but it doesn't ever work out that way'. Louise goes on to say that even though she worked on article revisions and read during this time, and despite being 'on track' with her publication record, she felt that 'I lost that summer'.

Additionally, Vicky, a mother of two at Elm who is in her forties, says that she worked from home during her entire maternity leave with her second child:

> I was one of those really awful people who knew that they could take the time away, but would sit on the computer and do the work. Because [my son] had been born … early, I hadn't finished some of those projects that I was supposed to finish, I felt really compelled to do them, and so a week after he was born I was probably getting back on the computer and trying to do the work.

These stories are consistent with a recent national study of U.S. mothers, which reported that 43 percent of women surveyed did at least some work for their employer while on maternity leave (Declercq et al. 2013).

Other academic mothers felt that they had to make some difficult personal choices in order to respond to the stereotype. Constance's story, for instance, provides a clear example of engaging in personal sacrifice to conform to ideal worker norms. Constance is a 39-year-old assistant professor in her first year of a tenure-track position at a small public university in the American South. While on the academic job market in the year prior to our interview, Constance admits to having struggled with whether to get pregnant. 'I'm probably in a little bit of an unusual situation because of my age… . We've had some difficulty – not getting pregnant, but I had some losses, so I knew I was going to have to start work pregnant'. When I spoke with her, Constance had just given birth. She says she timed her pregnancy so that she would give birth during the summer months, thereby hoping to avoid any impact on her teaching. This timing was also important because 'I knew, because I had calculated all of this out, that I would not have maternity leave or modified duties because I hadn't been employed here for a year... . I thought maybe they would kind of swing it, or maybe they would help me out with something, but I didn't know, and so that's why I had to – I timed it so I would have the baby in summer'.

Constance says that she struggled considerably with the implications that starting a family would have on her career. She recounts feeling the dual pressure of trying to become a first-time parent at her age while at the same time starting a new job. Constance says she felt comfortable trying to get pregnant only in the window of time that would have allowed her to have her baby in the summer before she started her job, because 'I was worried about how it would look at my job... . I mean, I am a good worker, right? I'm a responsible person, and I didn't want to start off on ... what seemed like they would think of as an irresponsible thing'. Terrified of becoming pregnant at the 'wrong' time in her career, Constance chose to undergo physically demanding hormone therapy in order to conceive within a certain window of time.

Marie, too, made a personal choice that for her was extremely difficult. Marie is a 31-year-old visiting assistant professor who does not yet have children and is waiting to do so until she secures a tenure-track job. She feels that the stereotype is particularly acute for her as a visiting assistant professor. Although she wants to ask about policies available to her, she says, 'It's this question you're told you cannot ask because it'll work against you in the job evaluation, and they'll assume that you're about to go out and have a whole litter of babies, so – yeah, I feel very silenced about [it]. I couldn't ask if just in case, what are my rights, how would you handle it – nothing'. In addition to this tension, Marie also feels conflicted because she is a Catholic and until recently was not using birth control. As a married woman, Marie faced a potentially impossible situation: 'The choice I was looking at was not so much contracept as not contracept, although that was my solution. The choice I was looking at is abortion or my career ... that's not a choice.'[11] Marie made a difficult decision for her to go against the teachings of her religion and use birth control in order to counteract the stereotype that she faces in her career.

Most commonly, however, the academic women who were in faculty roles mentioned making career sacrifices in order to be able to better balance the demands of their jobs and the demands of their families. This decision seems to be a way of trying to take ownership of the stereotype and nullify its significance by discussing it in terms of personal choice. Alex, for instance, says:

> Yeah, I think at some point I decided, am I going to be the most aggressive publisher in the world, or am I going to be okay with not being the most aggressive publisher in the world, and spend more time with my kids? And I made that decision, and, you know, I was a little worried. I did fine with tenure – I was a little worried with tenure, I think everybody is – but I certainly at that point, when I was turning in my packet[12] I was like, I wish I had, you know, been a little bit more productive at least, you know, somewhere in there. But at the same time, it was a decision I made.

Alex takes responsibility for her decision to make some career sacrifices to attain a better work/family balance. At the same time, the stereotype of her as someone who is not as serious about her career seems to have caused her some doubt about her choices when she was going up for tenure. Therefore, although her personal decision-making was a way of voicing her autonomy from the stereotype, she was not entirely able to escape its power to cause her anxiety.

As was the case with the servicewomen, not all of the women faculty members interviewed said that they had felt personally targeted because of the stereotype. A few, however, did witness or experience personal attacks or discrimination because of their decision to have children. One assistant professor interviewed, who does not yet have children but is thinking about having them in the near future, was not affected herself, but she had a friend who she felt had been targeted, and this experience made her wary of having children before tenure:

> One of my colleagues went up for tenure, and she had stopped the clock, and she was just really, really worried about tenure, because – she ended up getting it, but I guess at her panel interview, what she told me was that people had said like, "You know, you had that whole extra year. What were you doing?" And she said, "Well, you know, I had an infant at home. I wasn't really – I just didn't have the opportunity to focus on my research. It wasn't like a sabbatical year," and just even having to defend that just seems really shortsighted to me.

Other women felt more directly targeted. Danielle, a 32-year-old visiting assistant professor with a young child, says that she felt singled out by a fellow faculty member while pregnant. Her job involves fieldwork, so she was frequently out in the field working rather than in her office. 'I had a particular faculty member contact the dean telling the dean that I'm not in my office, that I'm not doing my job, because I'm not face-to-face. And so I got an e-mail that was forwarded from my dean, asking where am I, and I simply replied, "I'm in the field."' Danielle expressed, like many of the other women interviewed, that she had been working extra hard during her pregnancy to make up for the fact that she was going to take time off. That was why this colleague's behavior seemed especially perplexing to her. When asked why she thought that colleague had targeted her to report to her dean, Danielle, who also identifies as African American, said, 'She was very, very conservative in her beliefs, and [my] being at the time unmarried and pregnant, probably added to her personal views toward me'. In Danielle's opinion, the institutional construct of the ideal worker reinforced and heightened other ideological constructs that this coworker held in her mind about who is a 'good mother'. Danielle thus found herself unable to meet the expectations of this colleague for *either* an ideal worker or an ideal mother.

Nora, a mother of two children, felt even more explicitly targeted because of the stereotype. Nora is an associate professor and administrator. When she was applying for an advanced administrative position a few years prior, Nora recounts that her interviewer said something surprising to her: 'She said she was concerned about my ability to do the job because I had a child… . So at that point in time I was like … you've got to be kidding me'. Nora was not chosen for the position. Nora says that she feels her job and the stereotype that exists in her place of work is counterproductive. 'There's nothing enlightened about that'. The first reaction when someone has or adopts a child, says Nora, 'ought to be, "Congratulations! How can we make it so that you can enjoy and have a healthy experience for you and your child, and then embrace you so that you come back to us ready to go," and that's just never happened that I've seen.'

Eve, a 33-year-old mother of two who is an assistant professor, said that she almost didn't to return to her job in the year that she was interviewed because of an experience where she had felt targeted as a mother at work. She said that at first, her supervisor and her colleagues had been excited and happy for her when she returned to work from maternity leave with her most recent child:

> And then as we started to get into the evaluation process of my work, those conversations kind of started to change a little bit. Like my evaluation, my midtenure review. I started getting comments. I had my lowest annual review the year that I [took maternity leave], with the comment written that my personal life was affecting my work… . Comments being made perhaps I should consider getting a nanny instead of using child care if I wanted to be successful in my job. Have I ever thought about working part time, so that I can spend more time at home with my children? Comments like that from my colleagues and from my immediate supervisor that I was not expecting… . It made me start to think that maybe I couldn't do it. Like, wow – maybe I can't be the mom that I want to be and be the professional that I want to be at the same time, and it really kind of started to weigh heavily on me, reconsidering my options for employment. Maybe I needed to go part time; maybe I needed to do different things. I almost didn't come back this year.

Paradoxically, when asked whether she personally felt that her performance at her job had suffered because of having her second child, Eve emphatically denied it: 'No. Not at all. Not at all. I felt like I was able to balance it. I had a great support system at home, and so I thought I … was doing fine. I really did… . I actually felt – hey I can do this! Like, this is really manageable. So I was really surprised with the outcome'.

As with their counterparts in the U.S. military, policies aimed at recruiting and retaining academic mothers by offering to allow them to stop their tenure clock, and to take time away from their research and teaching duties, may in face be feeding into a preexisting expectation (or helping to *construct* the expectation) that academic mothers are not ideal workers. In both public universities and the U.S. military, each of the women interviewed had either an explicit or an implicit understanding of the ideal worker norm as it exists within her institution. The expectations of their individual jobs are drastically different, but the ideological construction of gender identities, which set expectations on women that they should be primary caregivers and in charge of the domestic sphere, leads to similar expectations of an ideal worker within each workplace setting. Ideal workers are not meant to be focused on what is going on at home, and women in these workplace settings are constantly struggling with that expectation. These women are also often doing battle in their workplaces with stereotypes that expect them to underperform in their jobs because they have domestic commitments. Although each woman in this study combats these constructs and the larger ideologies behind them differently, it is possible to see a clear connection between the ways that ideal workers are conceived within these institutions. Larger ideological constructs such as the ideal worker therefore permeate workplace cultures and take on unique institutional flavors. Yet the core of the construct remains and clearly affects how women think about and act on their rights in these cases.

The role of policy in creating and reinforcing stereotypes

Most sociolegal scholarship has treated stereotypes as norms that operate in the 'shadow of the law', governing attitudes and behavior in ways that are not governed by the law or are norms that perhaps have grown out of an absence of law. Norms that exist in the shadow of the law may even be in conflict with laws or policies themselves. Catherine Albiston discusses the power of such stereotypes to regulate women's abilities to bargain for their rights under the Family and Medical Leave Act. She notes that

> over time, the interconnected and mutually reinforcing systems of meaning among, and work have come to form an invisible cognitive framework that gives meaning to leave for family or medical purposes. In particular, seemingly neutral features of work, such as attendance and time invested in work rather than productivity, have come to define "good workers". (Albiston 2005, 17. See also Albiston 2010)

The narratives presented here illustrate the relevance of Albiston's observation in broader context. The power of normative constructs such as the ideal worker (and the stereotypes that emerge around them) goes beyond what is possible to regulate with policy. Attitudes and behaviors such as those described in this article may be discouraged by the policies in place in these institutions, but hearts and minds cannot be effectively changed by policies alone, and in fact cultural change must often happen before policies can be truly effective. Indeed, this is one of the fundamental points made by the critical legal studies movement: 'Liberal rights rhetoric ordinarily fails to consider that fundamental social changes are necessary to allow people to exercise their rights' (Tushnet 1984, 1390).

While this observation alone is interesting and important, another significant finding emerges from this research. The opportunity for institutional comparison provided by these interviews – the ability to look at two very different workplaces, with very different policies and nonpolicy normative ordering – reveals connections that go beyond institution-specific norms. The stereotypes that are visible in the military and academia are all connected to values associated with being an ideal worker (with what is 'ideal' having specific institutional characteristics in each case). Furthermore, the stereotypes that are present in these institutions indicate that mothers are being defined as antithetical to the ideal worker. They are in fact workers who shirk their responsibilities.

What is even more unsettling about these findings is that they indicate a close connection between the existence of institutional stereotypes of mothers and the policies aimed at protecting mothers in the workplace. Policies such as maternity leave, breast-feeding accommodations and duty, or uniform modification all offer important contributions to the health and well-being of mother and child. Yet the fact is that maternity and other work/family balance policies create a legal environment in which mothers *are* receiving exemptions from workplace duties that other workers are not entitled to. The stereotype in the military is that military mothers are trying to get out of deployment, an essential duty, potentially required of anyone at any time. While it may not be true that an individual is trying to avoid deployment, a pregnant woman or new mother does not deploy with her unit. Pregnancy or childbirth and the subsequent deployment deferral make mothers an exception to that duty, putting them in stark contrast to the ideal male warrior who is able to do his duty at any time. Likewise, in academia, faculty members must 'publish or perish', and in many other ways are expected to demonstrate devotion to the job. Mothers are exempted from the expectations of their jobs in academia to have children, if only for a time, when they stop the tenure clock, or take 6 weeks or more of maternity leave that keeps them out of the office and exempts them from teaching and service requirements. Furthermore, though less observable in the data presented above, it is also likely that many women face intersectional stereotyping that makes these workplace stereotypes more or less relevant for them. For instance, the expectations around white notions of domesticity and 'good mothering' may mean that women of color face a double stereotype – a situation in which, as working mothers, they are unable to meet the expectations for ideal workers *or* ideal mothers.

The stereotypes observed in this research are important to record and wrestle with, not simply because they hold power in and of themselves to shape attitudes and behaviors (often in negative ways) but they also reflect the inherent problems in the current structure of work/family policies themselves. Work/family policies may often be implemented without taking into account how an institutional culture might react, and begin to shape norms and attitudes around those policies. Indeed, through an examination of the ideological discourse in two workplace-specific cultures, it is evident that as long as workplace policies are structured to exempt mothers from work for family needs in ways that other workers are not permitted to be exempt (or do not ordinarily opt to be exempted), then mothers will continue to struggle against stereotypes that paint them as workers who are (intentionally or not) shirking their responsibilities.

The ideology of domesticity – and its pervasive ideal worker norm in the context of two specific institutions – is incredibly salient. The ideal worker norm operates within these institutional settings, taking on distinct institutional flavors that are either explicitly or implicitly referenced by all of the interview participants, indicating their internalization to some degree or another. Each participant reacted to these stereotypes in different ways, and rights-claiming was not uniformly affected by the internalization of these norms. However, what factors affect how these women gain legal knowledge about work/life balance policies in their workplaces becomes clearer. By understanding the pervasiveness of these norms, their origins, and how they are communicated within an institution and internalized by individuals, it becomes obvious that public policy, born within a particular historical and ideological context, can both assist with and complicate rights claiming.

Conclusion

This article presents a particularly difficult problem by critiquing a set of public policies that have been hard-won and are cherished by most U.S. women. Indeed, women in my interviews often cited the existence of work/life balance policies such as maternity leave and other 'special accommodations' as having been essential to helping them stay in their jobs. Louise, an associate professor at Oak University, put it this way: 'I needed those policies … those policies saved my ass'. Yet it is also clear from this analysis that the current state of work/life balance policies is inherently problematic. Such policies rely heavily on an ideology of domesticity that perpetuates norms of women's caregiving. The persistence of this ideology within institutional policy then reinforces that ideology within workplace norms and cultures, which also creates additional tensions for women to navigate if they want to claim these policies. This analysis begs a larger societal discussion about how policies might be better designed and implemented to take these ideological and structural complexities into account.

Notes

1. After the passage of the Affordable Care Act, Section 7(r) of the Fair Labor Standards Act was amended to require that employers with 50 or more employees give their employees 'reasonable break time' to express breast milk for the first year after a child's birth 'each time such employee has need to express' as well as the provision of 'a place, other than a bathroom, that is shielded from view' to express milk (https://www.dol.gov/whd/nursing

mothers/Sec7rFLSA_btnm.htm). Breastfeeding policies such as these are cited by women as important for their ability to follow the advice of healthcare professionals that it is ideal to provide infants with breastmilk for the first 6 months of their life (American Academy of Pediatrics 2012).

2. It is for this reason that I focus on 'mothers' in contrast with non-mothers in this research. While not wishing to provide an essential definition for 'woman' or 'mother' in this study, I do think that the data which points to an ongoing marginalization of 'women' and 'mothers' in U.S. society means that an emphasis on 'mothers' rather than 'parents' is warranted. However, I also acknowledge that by homogenizing the term 'mother' these data and others are masking the very real differences between and among women and others who identify as doing the care work often described as 'mothering'.
3. For instance, Williams (2000) cites a *Washington Post* poll from 1998 indicating that two-thirds of Americans believe it would be better for women to stay home and care for family and children. Yet this ideology is not time-bound. In a Pew Center study 12 years later, 37 percent of respondents said that 'mothers of young children working outside the home' is a 'bad thing for society' while only 27 percent of respondents said it is a 'good thing for society' (Taylor et al. 2010).
4. It is worth noting, however, that men were 1.4 times more likely than women (2.6 percent of those taking leave, compared to 1.9 percent of women taking leave) to cite child or elder care (other than for illness) as their reason for taking leave.
5. This is a term that is used to refer to the phenomenon that occurs when working women have children and experience a greater gap in their wages compared to women without children. This 'penalty' increases with the birth of each child.
6. Only one-third of the women in this study identified as being the primary breadwinner in her household. On a national level, by comparison, 40% of all households with children under 18 include mothers who are the sole or primary breadwinner (Wang et al. 2013). However, the majority of women in my study (22 out of 48) responded that they and their partner were 'equal' breadwinners, which masks minor income differences that may bring my sample closer to the national average.
7. The length of time depends on the service branch and whether the mother is breast-feeding. The Air Force recently expanded this time to 12 months for breast-feeding mothers, but at the time the interviews were conducted, the women in this study were eligible for 4–6 months of postpartum deferral. In early 2016, the Pentagon announced that all branches would now extend their maternity leave to 12 weeks for women and 14 days of paid leave for fathers (Ferdinando 2016).
8. A profile is a system used by the military to determine what a service member should be expected to do mentally, physically and medically for certain jobs and for their particular circumstances. A pregnancy changes an individual's profile temporarily.
9. 'Punch out' is slang for ejecting from a military aircraft.
10. That was the case at the time of my interview with Zoe. It is worth noting, however, that the Air Force changed its policy in 2012 to extend this time period to 12 months post-partum for breastfeeding mothers. Until recently, the Army required postpartum mothers to be eligible to deploy as early as 4 months after giving birth (http://breastfeedingincombatboots.com/military-policies/).
11. Both the use of contraception and abortion are forbidden under the teachings of the Catholic Church. Marie chose to use contraception because she felt that if she were to become pregnant, she would have to give up her career because the constraints of being a mother in academia would be too great. Additionally, because of her religion, abortion is an unthinkable option for Marie.
12. 'Packet' refers to the packet of materials a tenure-track professor is required to put together in order to support a case for tenure. These materials include published materials, teaching evaluations and other evidence of meeting the tenure criteria specified by the tenure-granting institution.

Acknowledgements

Thanks to Johanna Hopper and the School of Interdisciplinary Arts and Sciences at the University of Washington Tacoma for providing research support for this article.

Disclosure statement

No potential conflict of interest was reported by the author.

References

Albiston, C. 2010. *Institutional Inequality and the Mobilization of the Family and Medical Leave Act: Rights on Leave*. New York: Cambridge University Press.

Albiston, C. R. 2005. "Bargaining in the Shadow of Social Institutions: Competing Discourses and Social Change in Workplace Mobilization of Civil Rights." *Law and Society Review* 39 (1): 11–50. doi:10.1111/j.0023-9216.2005.00076.x.

American Academy of Pediatrics. 2012. "Breastfeeding and the Use of Human Milk." *Pediatrics* 129 (3): 827–841. doi:10.1542/peds.2011-3552.

Berns, S. 2002. *Women Going Backwards: Law and Change in a Family Unfriendly Society*. Aldershot: Ashgate.

Brandth, B., and E. Kvande. 1998. "Masculinity and Child Care: The Reconstruction of Fathering." *Sociological Review* 46 (2): 293–313. doi:10.1111/1467-954X.00120.

Bumiller, K. 1992. *The Civil Rights Society: The Social Construction of Victims*. Baltimore: Johns Hopkins University Press.

Cohn, D., G. Livingston, and W. Wang. 2014. *After Decades of Decline, A Rise in Stay-at-Home Mothers*. Washington, D.C.: Pew Research Center's Social & Demographic Trends project. Apr.

Declercq, E. R., M. P. Carol Sakala, S. A. Corry, and A. Herrlich. 2013. *Listening to Mothers III: New Mothers Speak Out: Major Survey Findings*. New York, NY: Childbirth Connection.

Doucet, A. 2004. "Fathers and the Responsibility for Children: A Puzzle and a Tension." *Atlantis: Critical Studies in Gender, Culture and Social Justice* 28 (2): 103–114.

Doucet, A. 2006. *Do Men Mother? Fathering, Care, and Domestic Responsibility*. Toronto, ON: University of Toronto Press.

Engel, D. M. 1984. "The Oven Bird's Song: Insiders, Outsiders, and Personal Injuries in an American Community." *Law and Society Review* 18 (4): 551–582. doi:10.2307/3053447.

Engel, D. M., and F. W. Munger. 2003. *Rights of Inclusion: Law and Identity in the Life Stories of Americans with Disabilities*. Chicago: University of Chicago Press.

Enloe, C. H. 2014. *Bananas, Beaches and Bases: Making Feminist Sense of International Politics*. 2nd ed. Berkeley: University of California Press.

Ewick, P., and S. S. Silbey. 1998. *The Common Place of Law: Stories from Everyday Life*. Chicago: University of Chicago Press.

Featherstone, B. 2003. "Taking Fathers Seriously." *British Journal of Social Work* 33 (2): 239–254. doi:10.1093/bjsw/33.2.239.

Ferdinando, L. 2016. "Carter Announces 12 Weeks Paid Military Maternity Leave, Other Benefits." *DOD News*. accessed Oct 7, 2016 http://www.defense.gov/News/Article/Article/645958/carter-announces-12-weeks-paid-military-maternity-leave-other-benefits

Fineman, M. A. 1995. *The Neutered Mother, the Sexual Family and Other Twentieth Century Tragedies*. New York, NY: Routledge.

Gilliom, J. 2001. *Overseers of the Poor: Surveillance, Resistance, and the Limits of Privacy*. Chicago: University of Chicago Press.

Gruber, J. E. 1998. "The Impact of Male Work Environments and Organizational Policies on Women's Experiences of Sexual Harassment." *Gender and Society* 12 (3): 301–320. doi:10.1177/0891243298012003004.

Haas, L., and M. O'Brien. 2010. "New Observations on How Fathers Work and Care: Introduction to the Special Issue-Men, Work and Parenting-Part I." *Fathering* 8 (3): 271. doi:10.3149/fth.0803.271.

Haltom, W., and M. Michael. 2004. *Distorting the Law: Politics, Media, and the Litigation Crisis*. Chicago: University of Chicago Press.

Heilman, M. E., and J. J. Chen. 2005. "Same Behavior, Different Consequences: Reactions to Men's and Women's Altruistic Citizenship Behavior." *Journal of Applied Psychology* 90 (3): 431–441. doi:10.1037/0021-9010.90.3.431.

Hobson, B. M. 2002. *Making Men into Fathers: Men, Masculinities, and the Social Politics of Fatherhood*. Cambridge: Cambridge University Press.

Hochschild, A. R. 2001. *The Time Bind*. New York, NY: Owl book.

Hochschild, A. R., and A. Machung. 2003. *The Second Shift*. 2nd ed. New York, NY: Penguin Books.

Hoffman, E. A. 2001. "Confrontation and Compromise: Dispute Resolution at a Worker Cooperative Coal Mine." *Law and Social Inquiry* 26: 150–170. doi:10.1111/j.1747-4469.2001.tb00189.x.

Jesmin, S. S., and R. R. Seward. 2011. "Parental Leave and Fathers' Involvement with Children in Bangladesh: A Comparison with United States." *Journal of Comparative Family Studies* 42 (1): 95–112.

Kelly, E. L., S. K. Ammons, K. Chermack, and P. Moen. 2010. "Gendered Challenge, Gendered Response Confronting the Ideal Worker Norm in a White-Collar Organization." *Gender and Society* 24 (3): 281–303. doi:10.1177/0891243210372073.

Kessler, L. T. 2001. "The Attachment Gap: Employment Discrimination Law, Women's Cultural Caregiving, and the Limits of Economic and Liberal Legal Theory." *University of Michigan Journal of Law Reform* 34: 371–468.

Kessler-Harris, A. 2001. *In Pursuit of Equity: Women, Men, and the Quest for Economic Citizenship in 20th-Century America*. New York, NY: Oxford University Press.

Krapf, M., H. Ursprung, and C. Zimmermann. 2014. *Parenthood and Productivity of Highly Skilled Labor: Evidence from the Groves of Academe*. St. Louis: Federal Reserve Bank of St. Louis.

Marshall, A.-M. 2005. "Idle Rights: Employees' Rights Consciousness and the Construction of Sexual Harassment Policies." *Law and Society Review* 39: 83–124. doi:10.1111/j.0023-9216.2005.00078.x.

Marshall, A.-M., and S. Barclay. 2003. "In Their Own Words: How Ordinary People Construct the Legal World." *Law and Social Inquiry* 28 (3): 617–628. doi:10.1111/j.1747-4469.2003.tb00209.x.

Mason, M. A., N. H. Wolfinger, and M. Goulden. 2013. *Do Babies Matter? Gender and Family in the Ivory Tower*. New Brunswick, NJ: Rutgers University Press.

McCann, M. W. 1994. *Rights at Work: Pay Equity Reform and the Politics of Legal Mobilization*. Chicago: University of Chicago Press.

McKay, L., and A. Doucet. 2010. "'Without Taking Away Her Leave': A Canadian Case Study of Couples' Decisions on Fathers' Use of Paid Parental Leave." *Fathering: A Journal of Theory, Research, and Practice about Men as Fathers* 8 (3): 300–320. doi:10.3149/fth.0803.300.

Morgan, P. A. 1999. "Risking Relationships: Understanding the Litigation Choices of Sexually Harassed Women." *Law and Society Review* 33 (1): 67–92. doi:10.2307/3115096.

Munkres, S. A. 2008. "Claiming 'Victim' to Harassment Law: Legal Consciousness of the Privileged." *Law and Social Inquiry* 33 (2): 447–472. doi:10.1111/j.1747-4469.2008.00109.x.

O'Brien Hallstein, L., and A. O'Reilly. 2012. "Academic Motherhood in a Post–Second Wave Context: Framing the Conversation." In *Academic Motherhood in a Post–Second Wave Context: Challenges, Strategies, and Possibilities*, edited by L. O'Brien Hallstein and A. O'Reilly, 1–46. Bradford, ON: Demeter Press.

Okin, S. M. 1991. *Justice, Gender, and the Family*. New York, NY: Basic Books.

Parrott, H. 2014. "Housework, Children, and Women's Wages across Racial–Ethnic Groups." *Social Science Research* 46: 72–84. doi:10.1016/j.ssresearch.2014.02.004.

Pew Research Center. 2015. *Raising Kids and Running a Household: How Working Parents Share the Load*. Nov. http://www.pewsocialtrends.org/2015/11/04/raising-kids-and-running-a-household-how-working-parents-share-the-load/

Quinn, B. A. 2000. "The Paradox of Complaining: Law, Humor, and Harassment in the Everyday Work World." *Law and Social Inquiry* 25 (4): 1151–1185. doi:10.1111/j.1747-4469.2000.tb00319.x.

Reese, L. A., and K. E. Lindenberg. 2003. "The Importance of Training on Sexual Harassment Policy Outcomes." *Review of Public Personnel Administration* 23 (3): 175–191. doi:10.1177/0734371X03253214.

Scheingold, S. A. 2004. *The Politics of Rights: Lawyers, Public Policy, and Political Change*. 2nd ed. Ann Arbor: University of Michigan Press.

Schwartz-Shea, P., and D. Yanow. 2012. *Interpretive Research Design: Concepts and Processes*. New York, NY: Routledge.

Seron, C., J. Pereira, and J. Kovath. 2004. "Judging Police Misconduct: 'Street-Level' versus Professional Policing." *Law and Society Review* 38 (4): 665–710. doi:10.1111/j.0023-9216.2004.00063.x.

Taber, N. 2011. "<Th>'You Better Not Get Pregnant while You're Here': Tensions between Masculinities and Femininities in Military Communities of Practice." *International Journal of Lifelong Education* 30 (3): 331–348.

Taber, N. 2013. "A Composite Life History of A Mother in the Military: Storying Gendered Experiences." *Women's Studies International Forum* 37: 16–25. doi:10.1016/j.wsif.2013.01.007

Taylor, P., K. Parker, W. Wang, R. Morin, J. M. Horowitz, D. Cohn, and G. Livingston. 2010. *The Decline of Marriage and Rise of New Families*. Washington, DC: Pew Research Center. http://www.pewsocialtrends.org/files/2010/11/pew-social-trends-2010-families.pdf.

Townsend, R. B. 2013. "Gender and Success in Academia: More from the Historians' Career Paths Survey." *Perspectives on History* 51 (1). Accessed Oct 7, 2016. https://www.historians.org/publications-and-directories/perspectives-on-history/january-2013/gender-and-success-in-academia#.

Tushnet, M. 1984. "A Critique of Rights: An Essay on Rights." *Texas Law Review* 62 (8): 1363–1404.

Wall, G., and S. Arnold. 2007. "How Involved Is Involved Fathering? An Exploration of the Contemporary Culture of Fatherhood." *Gender and Society* 21 (4): 508–527. doi:10.1177/0891243207304973.

Wang, W., K. Parker, and P. Taylor. 2013. *Breadwinner Moms: Mothers are the Sole or Primary Provider in Four-in-Ten Households with Children; Public Conflicted about the Growing Trend*. Washington, DC: Pew Research Center.

Williams, J. 2000. *Unbending Gender: Why Family and Work Conflict and What to Do about It*. Oxford: New York: Oxford University Press.

Williams, J. 2009. "Reconstructive Feminism: Changing the Way We Talk about Gender and Work Thirty Years after the PDA." *Yale Journal of Law & Feminism* 21 (1): 79–117.

Williams, J., and R. Dempsey. 2014. *What Works for Women at Work: Four Patterns Working Women Need to Know*. New York, NY: New York University Press.

Williams, J. C., and H. C. Cooper. 2004. "The Public Policy of Motherhood." *Journal of Social Issues* 60 (4): 849–865. doi:10.1111/j.0022-4537.2004.00390.x.

Wolfinger, N. H., M. A. Mason, and M. Goulden. 2009. "Stay in the Game: Gender, Family Formation and Alternative Trajectories in the Academic Life Course." *Social Forces* 87 (3): 1591–1621. doi:10.1353/sof.0.0182.

Zippel, K. 2004. "Implementing Sexual Harassment Law in the United States and Germany." In *Equality in the Workplace: Gendering Workplace Policy Analysis*, edited by H. Gottfried and R. Laura, 183–214. Lanham, MD: Lexington Books.

Embedded exclusions: exploring gender equality in Peru's participatory democratic framework

Stephanie McNulty

ABSTRACT

Do participatory institutions facilitate gender empowerment? As these institutions spread around the world, we still know very little about the gendered nature of participatory democratic spaces. Through the case study of state-mandated participatory budgeting in Peru, this article employs original data on participation to explore gender and inclusion. The study suggests that participatory institutions are not promoting gender equality. Instead, state actors have created new political spaces that exclude women and women's organizations and reify traditional gender norms. Like representative democratic institutions, gender inequities are embedded in these very spaces that are meant to empower all citizens.

Latin America has become the epicenter for participatory governance since the majority of the countries in the region have adopted democratic procedures as part of what Samuel Huntington (1991) called the 'third wave of democratization.' However, representative democracy has not solved many of the problems facing the region, such as pervasive corruption, a lack of transparency, clientelism, and the exclusion of historically marginalized constituencies in the public policy-making process. Participatory institutions have emerged around the region in response to these perceived failings of representative democracy. Government officials are formally codifying a number of institutional innovations, among them citizen councils and participatory planning processes, to engage citizens more actively in the policy-making processes.

Participatory budgeting (PB) represents the most prominent institutional response in the repertoire of policy reforms that now exists in Latin America.[1] Born in Porto Alegre, Brazil in the late 1980s, PB is a process that allows residents of particular localities to have voice and vote in their capital investment spending (i.e., infrastructure or public works projects). It now takes place in thousand of cities and states (and even one nation – Portugal) around the world. Several Latin American governments have mandated or incentivized PB through legislation, including Peru, Colombia, and the Dominican Republic.

Even given the rapid spread of PB around the world – with a growing number of national legal frameworks governing it – we still know very little about the gendered nature of participatory democratic spaces. This void in the literature on gender and participatory democracy is surprising because there is an extensive literature about women's participation in representative institutions around the world. Scholars generally analyze gender and representation through the lens of both descriptive and substantive representation (Pitkin 1967). Using this same framework, described below, this study suggests that participatory institutions are not promoting gender equality. Instead, state actors have created new political spaces that exclude women and women's organizations and reify traditional gender norms. Like representative democratic institutions, gender inequities are embedded in these very spaces that are meant to empower all citizens. In sum, the legal framework mandating PB nationally does not overcome embedded exclusionary practices in Latin American countries.

This finding is explicated through the case study of PB in Peru. An extensive legal framework exists in this particular country to promote gender equality and mandate several participatory institutions, including participatory budgets, in every subnational government in Peru. One of the goals of these institutions is to include traditionally underrepresented groups, including women, in policy decisions that affect their everyday lives. As such, some reform agents hoped for improved public policy as well as genuine gender empowerment to emerge through these new public spaces. The data clearly demonstrate that these outcomes are not taking place. After documenting that result, the article then asks why. Four factors explain this disappointing outcome, including shortcomings of the law itself, the gendered character of organizational life in Peru, and inherent deficiencies of the dominant neoliberal paradigm within which PB emerged.

The paper unfolds in six sections. The first section discusses gender in Peru, documenting the exclusion that women face in the social, political, and economic spheres and briefly noting some of the national legal initiatives that exist to tackle these problems. Next, the paper outlines the national-level participatory legal framework in Peru, codified as part of a decentralization reform in 2002. After a brief discussion of the methodology employed, the paper presents data regarding descriptive representation and substantive outcomes for PB at the regional and district levels of government in Peru. The data clearly demonstrate a lack of inclusion in these forums; therefore, the subsequent section explores why the PB legal framework in Peru does not achieve its goals. The paper concludes with a brief discussion of the implications of this case.

Gender and participation in Peru

Before providing a snapshot of gender in Peru, a caveat is in order. Historically, 'gender' has been operationalized in public policy using the binary categories of male/female. This does not capture the spectrum of gender identifications that exist, and gender fluidity and transgender representation in the public sphere are therefore rendered invisible. The existing data also do not capture intersectionality. We know that indigenous, rural, and Afro-Peruvian women do face more social, political, and economic barriers than their urban, white or *mestiza* counterparts. LGBTQ+ citizens also suffer from severe discrimination in schools, the public sphere, and the workforce.-[2] Because this study relies on government data and observations, it does not overcome this limitation. When subnational governments document participation in the PB or other participatory institutions, they use a binary measure of male/female and data about race or ethnicity are not available. This standard is adopted in all government documents and programs that track the implementation of participatory institutions and public spending. Therefore, while flawed, this study follows the lead on the current (albeit problematic) public policy operationalization of 'gender' that the state currently employs in Peru.[3]

The data that exist clearly demonstrate that women are under-represented in most political spaces in Peru. Women make up 50% of the population in Peru and vote in elections, which is mandatory in Peru, at the same rate as men. The gender make-up of elected positions, however, provides a stark glimpse into the lack of women's representation.[4] Twenty-one percent of parliamentarians are female, a percentage that has increased over time due to electoral quotas for party lists; however, this does not come close to parity. In the most recent regional and local election (2015–2018), women won 40% of the elected regional council seats, 3% of the mayoral positions, and 4% of the regional governorships (1 of 25 seats).

Are gender inequalities effectively addressed in public policies? Not really. The National Statistics Institute documents several gender gaps in state services. As of 2014, women and men completed primary education at mostly the same rate around the country, however only 61.5% of women complete secondary education while 82.7% of men do. 64.4% of women participate in the national labor force compared to 82.7% of men. Women make 16% less than men in public sector jobs and 29% less in the private sector ('Esta es la brecha salarial entre hombres y mujeres en el Perú' 2017). Peru has high levels of femicide as well (see Table 1). All of these gender gaps are exacerbated for rural, indigenous, and Afro-Peruvian women.

There are multiple national initiatives that exist to attack these problems. Peru is a signatory to the Beijing Platform, and the national government created the Ministry of the Woman in 1996 (currently the Ministry of Women and Vulnerable Populations). A major step forward for Peruvian feminists took place with the passage of an Equal Opportunity Law (Law 28,983) in 2007. The law is meant to 'guarantee men and women the right to equality, dignity, freedom for development, health and autonomy' and applies to legal, institutional, and policy arenas in all levels of government (Article 1). In 2012, a National Plan for Equal Gender Equality was approved (DS 004–2012-MIMP), with several strategic objectives, including incorporating gender into all public policies in a transversal way, reducing gender gaps in health, education, and the economy, reducing rates of gender-based violence, and '*increasing the participation of men and women in decision making and citizen and political participation*' (emphasis mine).

Despite these initiatives, gender inequities persist in electoral institutions and in social and economic spheres. However, we know much less about the role of gender in participatory institutions. This paper seeks to fill that void by exploring efforts to promote gender equality in decision-making and political participation in the PB process.

Table 1. Potential and confirmed cases of femicide in Peru, by year.

Year	# of Femicide Cases	# of Potential Femicide Cases	Total Number of Cases
2009	139	64	**203**
2010	121	47	**168**
2011	93	66	**159**
2012	83	91	**174**
2013	131	151	**282**
2014	96	186	**282**
2015	95	198	**293**
2016	124	258	**382**

Source: Ministerio de la Mujer y Poblaciones Vulnerables, https://www.mimp.gob.pe/contigo/contenidos/pncontigo-articulos.php?codigo=39

Peru's participatory institutions

Peruvian participatory institutions have a long history; however, they became formally codified in the national legal code as part of a sweeping decentralization reform that began in 2002.[5] The decentralization reform empowered several levels of government – departmental, provincial, and district (or municipal) – and collapses them into two administrative categories: regional (the former departments) and local[6] (provinces and district/municipal) levels of government. The reform created 25 regional governments (the 24 original departments and one 'special region,' the Province of Callao), which are like states in the United States. With the exception of Callao, each region has a capital city and elected regional officials (a governor and a regional legislative council). Each region has several provinces (196 as of 2014), which also have elected mayors and legislative councils. Finally, the reform gave additional powers to district governments, which existed prior to the reform but were relatively weak. Districts are led by mayors and city councils, and as of the end of 2015 there were 1,867 districts in Peru (the number fluctuates based on shifting demographic patterns).

Peru's decentralization reform is extremely participatory on paper. For example, the reform mandates that regional and local governments set up civil society 'coordination councils,' with elected members serving with mayors to make decisions about development planning and budgets. In addition, the reform states that the subnational governments shall 'formulate their budgets with the participation of the population and publicly disclose their execution annually according to the law.' This led to the 2003 Participatory Budgeting Law (Law 28,056), which mandates that all regions, provinces, and districts undertake PB annually. The PB law is guided by a principle that 'considerations of equity are a constitutive and orienting component of local and regional management, without discrimination.' The law states that the Ministry of Finance and Economics (MEF) should oversee the process and provide instructions to all subnational governments regularly regarding the specifics of PB. The original participatory budget law outlined eight phases that occurred over the course of the year, including a call for participation, registration of participants, a training period for participants – called 'participatory agents' or PAs – the formation of a technical team, and several meetings during which participating agents prioritize and vote on investment projects. The final phase consisted of setting up an oversight committee, made up of civil society organizations (CSOs), to monitor spending and progress on prioritized projects. In 2009, the Peruvian government reformed the original Participatory Budget Law to reduce these eight steps to four. Law 29,298, outlines the phases for PB at the regional, provincial, and district levels of government (see Figure 1[7]), and the MEF further outlined the process in its 2010 Instructions sent to all subnational government (see Instructivo 001–2010-EF-76.01).

To what extent is this legal framework gendered? As part of the Equal Opportunity Law, regional and district governments must develop Gender Equality Plans to incorporate gender into all aspects of their policymaking, including citizen participation mechanisms. Further, the National Plan for Gender Equality states that subnational governments should promote women's participation in all participatory spaces (Strategic Objective 7, Result 5). Also, the PB feeds into the larger national budget process, which is, since the passage of the Equal Opportunity Law, explicitly meant to incorporate policies that promote gender equality (see Law 29,083). This mandate has

Figure 1. Phases of the participatory budget process.

been translated, at least on paper, to the national system for evaluating public investment spending (*Sistema Nacional* de *Presupuesto*, or SNIP) and Results based Budgeting (*Presupuesto por Resultados*, or PpR), which began in 2007.[8] The PpR is a strategy that links spending to measureable results (originally eight results that have now expanded to more than 50). Furthermore, the law dictates that all tracking of spending outcomes must be broken down by gender using a male/female binary.

As long as the legally mandated process is followed, each subnational government can organize its PB process autonomously. Generally, Phases One and Two consist of one or two workshops during which participating agents are trained, go over the regional or local development plan to prioritize spending efforts, learn what has been approved and funded in previous years ('*rendición* de *cuentas*'), prioritize the capital investment projects for the next fiscal year, and elect an oversight committee. After the training and prioritization workshops, the subnational government asks for project proposals from the participants, which are delivered to the subnational government officials. A technical team then meets to score the proposals using a scoring matrix. Ideally, at the final workshop, participants should review the proposed investment projects and approve them. In reality, what usually happens is the government presents the projects with the highest scores and participants 'approve' them.

Participating agents are defined as representatives from civil society, members of the coordination council, and government officials. CSOs should register in advance with the subnational government's office that runs the process, and each regional, provincial, and district government can determine the registration process. As such, registration criteria vary around the country. It is common to mandate that the organization should have legal status. Some governments are flexible about the criteria to allow more informal groups and individuals to participate. Regional processes are supposed to include CSOs with regional (or at least provincial) reach and local processes engage representatives from neighborhood organizations.

How is a project proposal submitted? Again, a registered participant, representing a CSO can submit a written proposal for a public works project. Each government determines how much information has to be submitted in the proposal files (called '*fichas*'). Once a proposal is submitted, the technical team reviews it using a scoring matrix, also developed by each particular governmental office. Generally, the proposals with the highest number of points are presented to participants at the final prioritization workshop.

Once a proposal makes it to the list of prioritized projects, however, there is still a long process to follow before the public works project is actually funded and executed. In fact, interviewees told me that a project takes about two to three years minimum to move from the idea phase (usually the proposal that is presented in the PB forum) through completion. Once an idea moves ahead in a PB process, the government has to do a costly pre-investment feasibility study using contracted experts (usually engineering firms) who have to go through a public bidding phase. Municipal officials told me that these studies have to come from proposal budgets, participating agents rarely correctly work them into their proposed budgets. Thus, almost immediately the project budget needs to be reworked. In some cases, the project might die at this point because the study may uncover additional costs or problems that cannot be overcome. If the project does move ahead after this study, it then needs to be added to the national government's investment project tracking system (called SNIP until 2017 and currently called the *Sistema Nacional* de *Programación Multianual y Gestión* de *Inversiones* or INVIERTE.PE). Again, municipal and national government authorities stressed to me in interviews that there are multiple steps that must be followed when entering a project into the system. The bottom line is that investment projects in Peru demand a long and highly technical process to be executed.

Thus, there are several formal policies and laws in place that promote gender inclusion and equality in participatory institutions through public spending efforts. Is the PB following through with these myriad legal stipulations? After a brief description of the study's methodology, this question is explored.

Methodology

This article employs Pitkin's typology of representation, e.g. descriptive and substantive, in a previously unexplored political arena – participatory spaces. Descriptive representation refers to the concept that a public forum should reflect the make-up of the population that participates in it. For example, if women make up 50% of the population, than an institutional setting should reflect that. However, scholars also point out that mere presence in a meeting or institution is not enough. We need to strive for substantive outcomes that emerge to address the needs of that population. Thus, scholars also often explore substantive representation in terms of policy outcomes of the same political processes.

This article builds on years of research on Peru's PB, including a book project that documented six regional PB processes from 2004 to 2010 (McNulty 2011). Since then I have also documented descriptive representation of women in the regional PB process from 2007 to 2015, partly using an online portal that the MEF hosts to track the PB process (McNulty 2015).[9] To better understand who is participating in these forums as well as the nature of their participation, I recently followed the 2018[10] PB process in five municipal districts in Lima. I chose the districts to capture variance in socio-economic status and geographic location (e.g. rural/urban) as elucidated in Table 2.

Table 2. Demographic statistics for districts under study.

Location	Population	HDI	Life Expectancy	% Population with Secondary Education Completed	Per Capita Family Income in New Sols/month
Peru	30,135,875	.5058	74.31	67.87	696.9
Lima Metropolitan	8,481,415	.6417	79.02	79.09	1049.2
Miraflores	85,000	.7574	76.5	N/A	953.4
Surco	326,928	.7371	79.45	87.05	1324.3
Pueblo Libre	77,038	.7532	79.44	87.19	1415.9
Villa Maria	426,462	.5879	78.97	74.15	877.8
Chincha Alta	63,000	.5144	N/A	73.89	N/A

Sources: Muncipalidad de Miraflores 2016, Municipalidad de Pueblo Libre 2016, Muncipalidad de Surco 2016, Municipalidad de Villa María del Triunfo 2016, Provincia de Chinca 2014.

The district-level research design consists of two methods: non-participant observation and semi-structured interviews. For the observations, I received permission from municipal authorities to attend and observe PB meetings that unfolded during the workshops. While in meetings, I documented the following aspects:

- Time, length, place, and agenda.
- Number of participants every 30 min, broken down by rank (municipal official or neighborhood representative) and gender.
- General estimate of the age of participants, including percent over 50 and the number of accompanied children.
- Person who spoke, noting their position (municipal official or neighborhood representative), what kind of intervention (presentation, question, comment, response), gender, and how long they spoke.
- Qualitative observations regarding the meeting process and the gender dynamics as the meeting progressed.[11]

In total, I attended 10 district PB meetings and documented speaking patterns for a total of 867 min.

During the first half of 2017 I also conducted a series of semi-structured in-person interviews with a total of 40 people familiar with PB in Peru. I first interviewed scholars and activists in Lima who have followed PB since it began in the early 2000s, then leaders of neighborhood groups, municipal officials, and former mayors and/or mayoral candidates in the districts.

Gender and PB in Peru

In order to understand the extent to which Peru's PB promotes gender equity or empowerment, we can explore the process at the regional and district level of government. By looking at both descriptive and substantive aspects of gender and representation. Scholars have argued that women's representation in the public sphere is important in both descriptive and substantive ways. Descriptive representation refers to the idea that a public forum should reflect the make-up of the population that participates in it (Htun 2004). Therefore, if women make up 50% of the population, then the institutional settings should reflect that make up. Scholars also point out that women's presence alone in a meeting or institution is not enough. We need to strive for substantive representation, or 'the expression and implementation of women's preferences' (Karpowitz and Mendelberg 2014, 16). In some cases, the presence of women in an institutional setting has led to substantive outcomes that promote gendered policy choices (Htun 2003; Schwindt-Bayer 2010; Thomas 1991; Thomas and Welch 1991; Wangnerud 2000). For example, Leslie Schwindt-Bayer's work (2010, 188) shows that 'women in Latin American legislatures do place a special priority on promoting a feminist agenda and are able to translate this priority into legislative action.' However, not all women promote feminist policies and some male politicians certainly promote gender and family friendly public policies. Thus, descriptive representation does not necessarily lead to substantive representation.

As noted earlier, most of what we know about women's representation in political spaces is based on representative democratic institutions, such as legislative and executive offices. This study explores women's descriptive and substantive representation in PB forums to explore the extent to which participatory institutions can engage and empower women in Peru.

Descriptive representation

Who participates in the PB processes around the country? The two levels of government have different legal frameworks (i.e., the General Regional Law and the General Municipal Law) and, by nature, attract different participants. Regional governments should invite legally registered organizations that have regional (or at least provincial) reach. District processes mostly include neighborhood organizations. All organizations send their leaders to represent them in meetings.

This section explores the gender breakdown of these participants at the district level to examine the descriptive representation of women in PB.[12] It is very difficult to document gender indicators at the district level in Peru due to the sheer number of districts. Thus, this section documents gender dynamics in the five district PB processes that I observed in 2017. At first glance, descriptive data suggest that women and men are participating in equal rates in these forums. At the beginning of the meetings the gender breakdown is mostly equal, with female participants making up 51% of the participants. Because I documented the number and gender of participants in 30-min intervals (T) in each meeting, it is also clear that this percentage stays relatively stable throughout the meeting (see Table 3). Thus, in terms of attendance patterns, it would appear that there is gender parity.

In sum, women do participate in equal numbers in the district PB forums when measured as presence in a meeting.

Substantive representation

Does this descriptive representation translate to the substantive empowerment of women? As several scholars have noted, we must move beyond merely counting women to fully understand the extent to which Peru's participatory institutions are gendered (Allegretti and Falanga 2015; Cornwall 2003; Frey 2015; Pape 2014; Su 2017b). We must explore whether women can express their ideas and preferences freely in PB meetings, and, if so, whether these ideas and preferences are then translated into

Table 3. Percent female and male participants over time in PB meetings.

Time	Male (%)	Female (%)
T1	49	51
T2	47	53
T3	46	54
T4	46	54
T5	47	53

concrete investment projects that challenge existing gender hierarchies and power relations. Thus, two ways to analyze substantive representation are to explore speech patterns during PB meetings and determine if the approved and funded projects effectively address the gender gaps noted above.[13]

a. Speech Patterns

Are men and women's voices valued equally in PB? One way to understand this is to document who is speaking in these forums. There is a large and suggestive literature about gender and discourse in decision-making that suggests that speaking in a meeting is a sign of power (e.g. Karpowitz, Mendelberg, and Shaker 2012; Mansbridge 1983; Sanders 1997). Participant speech patterns tell us much about who holds discursive power and who does not.

In terms of actual speaking patterns, the PB meetings are very much dominated by males, and especially males in positions of authority. When counted, males speak 61% of the total times (see Table 4). However, it is important to disaggregate this percentage by a person's role in the meeting. The two roles are neighborhood representatives and municipal officials. Neighborhood males speak 58% of the time that all neighbors spoke combined. However, male municipal officials speak 73% of the combined number of times that municipal officials spoke. In other words, male municipal officials are dominating the meetings when measured in terms of the number of times people speak.

In contrast, how long do women speak? This indicator gives us an even deeper glance into the nature of the discursive power of the participants. Men speak 79% of the time in all meetings combined, which means women are speaking 21% of the time (see Table 5). However, again it is useful to break this number down by role. Neighborhood male representatives speak 65% of the time that all neighbors spoke. Municipal males spoke 84% of the time that all municipal officials spoke.

What kind of interventions are participants making? I tracked several kinds of interventions including: presentations, questions, and comments. Again, the data provide several insights into who holds discursive power in these meetings.

Table 4. Number of times (and percentage of times) agents spoke in a meeting, by gender and rank.

Role	M	F	Total
Municipal Officials	22 (73%)	8 (27%)	30
Neighborhood Representative	68 (58%)	50 (42%)	118
Total	90 (61%)	58 (39%)	148

Table 5. Number of spoken minutes, by gender and rank.

	Number of Minutes	M	F
Municipal Official	600	502 (84%)	98 (16%)
Neighborhood Representative	227	145 (64%)	82 (36%)
Total	827	647 (79%)	180 (21%)

In almost all of the meetings that I observed, municipal officials presented information for the majority of the time (65%). Table 6[14] demonstrates that, again, municipal males dominated presenting time, speaking 89% of the time allotted for presentations by the municipal government. Of the total time that neighbors spent asking questions, 60% was used by men.

Exploring the gender breakdown of comments, arguably the time when expressions of preferences would be made, is extremely illuminating in terms of both general power and gender dynamics. Comments were only part of the meeting for 12% of the times where interventions were tracked. During that time, male neighbors spoke 76% of the time. Clearly, female neighbors are not being heard if we assume that making comments would allow for that kind of intervention to take place.

These observations reveal important gender and power hierarchies in participatory forums. Municipal officials generally are speaking many more times and for much longer than the neighborhood representatives. Municipal males are dominating that discourse. They barely let their female colleagues speak in these meetings. Further, it is primarily men who present, ask questions, and comment on the business at hand. Thus, these forums should not be considered truly 'participatory' or empowering for women.

Qualitative observations provide another way to explore gender dynamics in the meetings. In every meeting that I attended, municipal officials ran the meeting. The men, overwhelmingly, presented information as the women signed people in and handed out food during breaks. Sometimes, municipal officials would make overtly sexist remarks, such as the following announcement by the mayor in a meeting in Pueblo Libre, a middle class district in the center of Lima:

> If you have any questions at all, please contact our office. In fact, my assistant [younger female next to him] would like to create a WhatsApp group for the neighbors. So please, send her your number at [states number]. Now, [laughs] don't just text her to flirt with her since she is so attractive. [Audience laughs.]

These examples, combined with the data on who is actually speaking in the meetings, suggest that although women are present in equal numbers in urban district PB processes, they are not treated as equal participants.

b. Project Spending

Are women's preferences and needs being met through project spending? The best systematic study of this is Miloslavich Túpac's (2013) analysis of regional investment projects from 2008 to 2011. Miloslavich categorizes all prioritized and approved infrastructure projects in regional and local governments using three public spending categories: social promotion, education, and health. She finds that of 81,114 projects prioritized in regional and local PB processes, only 153 addressed women. Of the 13,008 projects that were later approved (not all prioritized projects make it through the

Table 6. Number of minutes by kind of intervention.

Kind of intervention	M	F	Total
Presentation (municipal official)	317 (89%)	42 (11%)	359 (65%)
Question (neighbor)	78 (60%)	51 (40%)	129 (23%)
Comment (neighbor)	51 (76%)	16 (24%)	67 (12%)
Total			555

technical approval process), 28 addressed women (Miloslavich Túpac 2013, 14). According to Miloslavich Túpac (2013), most of these projects are women's shelters, women's centers, and productive centers (for job training, etc.) and make up less than 1% of total investment spending. Calling the participatory budget in Peru a 'discriminatory mechanism,' Miloslavich Túpac (2013, 9–10) is extremely critical of PB, writing:

> Women have intervened in these processes at an average rate of 30%. They have presented projects, yet these projects have been left aside by *machismo* and a lack of professionalism in the technical team and by the National Public Investment System (SNIP) that only allows construction of women's centers, shelters, and community spaces for workshops.

Miloslavich, one of the original architects of decentralization and participatory institutions has determined that PB does very little to attack gender discrimination in this country. In fact, when interviewed, Miloslavich called PB a 'waste of women's time.'

Anecdotes from feminist organizations that have worked to promote projects that challenge gender norms add interesting details to the finding. An interviewee who had fought for a regional investment project that would help all district governments incorporate gender into their public policies in a transversal way made the following observations:

> In 2009, we won a project for 9 million soles. We had worked hard to form several alliances to finally get this project funded. Once it was prioritized and put in the queue of approved projects, the regional government started decreasing the annual budget. The next year the regional government would only give us 4 million. The regional government kept cutting funds every year. Then, we also noticed that the project was not being implemented well. We asked to see the budgets, no one from the government ever responded. We did do some training and have had some success. However, later, when the regional president changed most of these gains were erased.

Her story suggests that, even if 'gendered' projects are funded, they may not be implemented well or have long-term impact.

Exploring limitations

Several key findings emerge. First, in descriptive terms women are participating in equal numbers. This corresponds to rates of voting among women, which, again, is mandatory, and is higher than in electoral spaces. However, the presence of women is not translating to gender equality or women's empowerment. Why are Peru's participatory institutions failing to meet their purported goal of improving gender equality? This section explores three factors that explain this outcome.

Limits of the law

The first important explanation for the lack of gender empowerment in Peru's PB lies in the several shortcomings in the law. It is not uncommon for laws to exist on the books in Peru and to be implemented in a way that does not comply with the original intent. This discrepancy occurs in many countries in Latin America, including Peru. For example, although all 25 regions had drafted Equal Opportunity Plans, as of 2016 only seven had actually institutionalized them (Prodescentralización 2011). This is just one example of the general absence of implementation of many existing legal initiatives. However, parts of the PB law are being implemented; therefore, a general disregard for the legal framework is not a satisfactory explanation for PB's inability to empower women in Peru.

There are several opportunities throughout the process to promote gender equality. District, provincial, or regional development plans can incorporate a gender analysis, the registration of agents can stress parity or include gender quotas, workshops can provide opportunities for men and women to participate, and the approved projects can attack gender inequalities (Centro de Estudios y Promoción de Desarrollo (DESCO) 2007). However, officials are not taking these steps in the districts that I observed.

One example lies in technical scoring process of PB projects. The law states that all public spending *should* take gender into account. However, in practice the technical team's scoring matrices hardly do so, if at all. Gender is either completely absent as a criterion for funding (as in Villa Maria del Triunfo's scoring matrix in Annex 2) or makes up a small percentage of the points and puts all 'vulnerable populations' into one box (as in the Miraflores scoring matrix in Annex 2). Technical teams make most of the decisions and are often dominated by men; team members of both sexes are rarely trained in gender analysis. And, as Diana Miloslavich notes, the SNIP does not effectively stress gender impact, even though several laws mandate that it should. Thus, although women make up one-third to one-half of the participating agents, they benefit from less than 1% of the outcomes.

Gendered spaces: neighborhood organizations in Lima

A second factor that helps us to understand the data presented above lies in the organizational dynamics embedded in the kinds of CSOs that participate in PB in these districts in Peru. Women are actually participating in high numbers in this particular civic and political space. However, this quantitative observation obscures systemic gender inequalities embedded in the nature of neighborhood and domestic life in Peru. To understand them, we need to look at the history of neighborhood groups ('*juntas vecinales*') and neighborhood participation in urban Lima. Neighborhood groups have a long history in Peru, emerging in force during the economic crisis in the 1980s as 'survival' organizations. There is very little written about these organizations, probably because there are literally hundreds of thousands of distinct organizations, each representing several blocks in a neighborhood. They mostly deal with extremely local issues, like security, sidewalks, street lamps, and potholes.

The Organic Municipal Law (Law 27,972) formalizes the role of these organizations in local government. Chapter Four of the law states their functions, which include proposing investment priorities, monitoring the execution of public works and development plans, and improving citizen security. Leaders are elected each year and each organization should hold at least four meetings per year. They should participate in all local citizen participation processes (Title Eight), and every municipal government should have a 'Neighborhood Participation' team to register the organizations with the municipal government. Thus, after the decentralization reform, these organizations started to play a more active role in local governments.

Women are very active in neighborhood organizations in Lima. Again, exact numbers would be impossible to document; however, when I interviewed neighborhood activists about their particular organizations, they all said that their leadership is comprised of at least 50% women. This could be interpreted as surprising, given the general lack of women's representation in most elected positions discussed above. However, when I asked municipal officials and neighborhood activists why women are more active in these spaces (when compared to regional and national political spaces), the responses indicated that women's participation is often linked to deep-rooted gender norms and viewed as non-threatening to existing power structures.

For example, male officials and activists responded to my question, without fail: 'They are home, they have more time.' I asked one president of a neighborhood organization why women are so active in these groups and his response illustrated this belief. 'They don't have anything to do [laughs]. Time, they usually have more time. Some say women can get more done than men.' A female president of another neighborhood organization in the same district gave me a more nuanced answer:

> *Question: Tell me about your organization.*
> Well, the moms in the neighborhood got together to organize ourselves and work on security. We would meet in the park. Our husbands were working and we were professional women, we had our own ideas but were staying at home with the kids. We started a women's organization (*comité de damas*) and even had one man [laughs]. Our first project was to get a fountain with a Virgin Mary in our park. This district has a lot of parks and each one has a Virgin. Slowly the group started to be more formal.
> Question: Why do you think women are so active in neighborhood organizations?
> President: In Lima, there is so much to do. The men are working. This gives me a way to stay involved. Now that my husband is gone and my kids are grown, I participate in many different institutions now.

Another neighborhood activist spoke to me about her experience:

> Question: Why did you get involved in your neighborhood organization?
> I started because we needed new pavement on my block of the street. I said I would participate until I got my street fixed. I have been participating for several years and I still don't have my street [laughs]. Honestly, I consider it to be my service to the community. Now, neighbors come to me and tell me about their neighborhood problems.
> Question: Why are women so involved?
> We are better organized, we get along better, we know what we need because it is our house. We are seeking order, like in our houses.
> Question: Would you ever want to get involved in other forms of politics?
> No, politics is too corrupt. This is where we live; we have to take care of the spaces.

The responses provide insight into why female participation is higher in this particular space than in most political institutions. First, the neighborhood, which in most cases is really a few blocks, is seen as the natural extension of the domestic sphere. It is 'apolitical.' Participation in these organizations is seen as a way to keep their domestic spheres tidy and safe. As a result, these organizations are seen as relatively nonthreatening and weak.

This perception is not always valid, and, in some ways, these organizations wield a lot of political power in local governments. For example, one ex-mayoral candidate told me: 'Neighborhood organizations manage a lot of information, they have power with the mayor. Each president of the zone has the mayor's direct number. When I was running, everyone told me to meet them; they have a lot of power.' Candidates seek endorsements from the leaders of neighborhood organizations during elections and mayors stay in close contact with the leaders.

Embedded neoliberalism

A final important explanation for the gender hierarchies that clearly exist in these processes lies in the larger political context in which PB emerged in this particular country. Notably, the decentralization reform was passed in the context of a hegemonic neoliberal discourse that dominated the country. This neoliberal philosophy that underlies PB in Peru has reinforced gender hierarchies and imbalances.

The neoliberal stress on citizen participation, especially strong during the wave of second generation reforms in the 1990s, has been criticized by feminist scholars as inherently gendered (see, for example, Benería 2011; Dawson 2000). Neoliberalism stresses the role of supposedly objective and neutral 'markets' that generate economic growth. The role of the state is minimized, therefore calling into need citizen participation in institutions like the ones discussed above. However, markets are not neutral. They reinforce existing hierarchies, including gendered hierarchies. For example, women's domestic labor is generally of little formal economic value in the neoliberal paradigm (Benería 1997). Further, because women often hold jobs in the lower paid sectors of society, they are disproportionately affected by the reforms.

The importance of the context in which the reforms have been implemented is better understood when we look at the origins of PB. PB began in Porto Alegre, Brazil as a radical democratic initiative. The institution was meant to incorporate citizens into government decision-making priorities to allocate public resources in a way that embraced social justice. Gender inclusion was an explicit goal of many of the PB programs that later spread around Brazil as part of the Worker's Party ideological commitment to leftist ideals. While not perfect, these goals were embedded in the Workers' Party's PB programs.

As PB spread around Latin America, the social justice component has been dropped. Instead, PB and other participatory institutions have emerged as a policy instrument often promoted, or at least supported by, neoliberal reformers and international donors (Baiocchi and Ganuza 2014; Goldfrank 2012). This is the exact context in which Peruvian reformers set up the participatory governance framework in the early 2000s.

The data presented above suggest that participatory institutions, embedded in neoliberal reform efforts, are not engaging women and men equally, and, in some cases do reinforce traditional gender norms. Those in authority often discount women's work in district level PB processes. Women are not given an equal chance to participate during meetings. In regional processes, women's organizations are not participating at expected rates, due to organizational weaknesses. The social justice efforts that were so integral to the original PB experiences have mostly been ignored in Peru. As a result, gender equality will never emerge from these forums unless major changes are made.

Concluding observations

Several important conclusions emerge from the careful analysis of gender and PB in Peru. The study provides evidence of persistent gender inequalities in so-called participatory forums. These dynamics exist despite several laws that purport to eliminate gender discrimination in participatory institutions, subnational governments, and public spending. We can infer from the analysis of PB that additional participatory institutions in Peru, such as the coordination councils mentioned above, are undoubtedly also failing at promoting gender equality. These failings are part of the larger political context of gender exclusion and discrimination that exist in representative democratic institutions and through public policy failings that exist in this country. None of the policy 'solutions' that are discussed above, such as Peru's Equal Opportunity Law, appear to be effectively tackling these deep-rooted historical trends. Legal efforts to mandate participation are not able to effect change in this particular public policy effort.

Examining PB in Peru also reveals the deeply rooted gender biases that exist in second-generation neoliberal reform efforts such as these. This finding echoes Andrea Cornwall's argument that participatory institutions are not necessarily inclusive. She writes that '[t]he very projects that appear so transformative can turn out to be supportive of a status quo that is highly inequitable for women' (Cornwall 2003, 1329). Even when mandated by national governments, participatory institutions can be spaces permeated by inequalities and gender discrimination. Of course, more research is needed to fully understand these biases. However, this case clearly suggests that the Peruvian state is not eradicating gender inequalities by setting up participatory institutions around the country. Instead, neoliberal policies embedded in gendered praxis have reinforced the exact exclusions that they claim to erase.

Furthermore, the case clearly demonstrates that we cannot assume that the number of women in a meeting translates to real power in these spaces. In Peru's PB, gender biases are not immediately apparent if we measure gender in terms of mere presence in a meeting. The analysis of speech patterns clearly shows that women attend these forums, but they do not speak at the same rate. Exclusionary trends become visible when we explore speaking patterns in the meetings and the policy outcomes that emerge. In other words, this study clearly demonstrates that achieving parity in descriptive terms does not translate to actual gender empowerment. This is especially important to keep in mind in an era of empowerment solutions that sometimes focus on the presence of women in meetings and forums. We must dig deeper and do more to achieve the goal of empowerment.

Finally, more research on inclusion in participatory spaces is needed. Much less is known about this issue than gender and participation in representative democratic spaces. This research also highlights the void in our knowledge about grass-roots, neighborhood organizations in and around Lima (and by extension many other urban centers in Latin America). By failing to study these spaces, we fall into the trap of dismissing them as insignificant political arenas. Questions that demand further exploration include: Why are women participating in these organizations and meetings? What are their preferences in terms of project outcomes? How do they perceive meeting dynamics?

In sum, the case of Peruvian district PB suggests that participatory institutions are not inclusive. Careful attention to this problem, including changes to the legal framework, can rectify this outcome. This attention will necessitate policy change and additional research. Without these changes, we will not see meaningful gender empowerment in participatory democratic spaces.

Notes

1. There is an enormous literature on PB around the world. For a sample see Sintomer, Röcke, and Herzberg (2016); Su (2017a); Wampler and Hartz-Karp (2012). Also visit https://www.participatorybudgeting.org/. According to the Latinno database, at least 15 countries in Latin America have experimented with or continue to use PB as a tool for engaging citizens in decision making. For more on PB in Latin America, see Wampler, McNulty, and Touchton (2018) and Sintomer, Hershberg, and Allegretti (2013).
2. For example the Global Barometer of Gay Rights gives Peru an 'F' when measured using 29 indices that examine constitutional protections of sexual minorities, the level of gay rights advocacy, socio-economic rights, and societal persecution of sexual minorities. See Dicklitch-Nelson, Thompson, and Yost (2016).
3. There are many feminist organizations and reformers who are advocating for a more nuanced analysis of gender in all aspects of public policies. However, to date these efforts have not been translated to the formal legal framework.
4. Statistics about political representation and education are from: http://www.inei.gob.pe/estadisticas/indice-tematico/brechas-de-genero-7913/.
5. For more on Peru's decentralization reform, (see Controlaría General de la República (2014); McNulty (2011); Prodescentralización (2016); Zas Friz Burga (2004)). For more on participatory institutions in Peru, (see McNulty (2011); Remy (2016, 2011); López Ricci (2014)).
6. In this paper I use the terms local and district interchangeably.
7. Adapted from Prodescentralización (2010).
8. See Chapter IV of Law 28411 (*Ley General del Sistema Nacional* de *Presupuesto*).
9. http://ppto-participativo.mef.gob.pe/entrada.php.
10. The process takes place one year before the next fiscal year. In other words, participants vote on the 2018 participatory budget in 2017.
11. To gather this data I adapted an observation tool used by Frank Bryan (2004) when observing town hall meetings over a period of 30 years in Vermont. I am grateful to him for sharing his tools. To see the tool visit: https://stephaniemcnulty.net/data-and-methods/.
12. For more information on gender and participation in the regional PB process, see McNulty (2015).
13. Determining the extent to which investment spending attacks gender inequalities is problematic. One way that is often used in Peru is to look at social spending, i.e. projects that work to improve health and education, as opposed to 'grey' infrastructure projects. The assumption here is that women and children will naturally benefit more from social investments, therefore they are 'gendered' projects. This distinction is not perfect, in that it falls pretty to reinforcing traditional gender norms, however, this is the standard currently used in Peru.
14. The number of minutes do not total 827 because not all kinds of interventions (which also include group work, responses, and some moments of disagreement expressed in general outbursts) are included here.

Acknowledgments

I would like to thank Kabir Hossain for his assistance with reviewing the literature for this project and Amy Largacha Cedeno for her assistance with data collection in Lima. I am also grateful to the participants of Drake University's Gender, Sexuality, and the Law Workshop, especially Renee Cramer, Sarah Hampson, and Mollie Clark, for their comments on an earlier draft. Finally, I am grateful to Franklin and Marshall College for providing funding for this research.

Disclosure statement

No potential conflict of interest was reported by the author.

References

Allegretti, G., and R. Falanga. 2015. "Women in Budgeting: A Critical Assessment of Participatory Budgeting Experiences." In *Gender Responsive and Participatory Budgeting: Imperatives for Equitable Public Expenditure*, edited by C. Ng, 33–54. Springer Briefs in Environment, Security, Development and Peace 22. New York: Springer.

Baiocchi, G., and E. Ganuza. 2014. "Participatory Budgeting as if Emancipation Mattered." *Politics and Society* 42 (1): 29–50. doi:10.1177/0032329213512978.

Benería, L. 1997. "Accounting for Women's Work: The Progress of Two Decades." In *The Women, Gender, and Development Reader*, edited by N. Visvanathan, L. Duggan, N. Wiegersma, and L. Nisonoff, 112–117. New York: Zed Books.

Benería, L. 2011. "Globalization, Labor, and Women's Work: Critical Challenges for a Post-Neoliberal World." In *Harvesting Feminist Knowledge for Public Policy: Rebuilding Progress*, edited by D. Jain and D. Elso, 70–92. Los Angeles, CA: Sage Publishers.

Bryan, F. 2004. *Real Democracy: The New England Town Hall Meeting and How It Works*. Chicago: University of Chicago Press.

Centro de Estudios y Promoción de Desarrollo (DESCO). 2007. "Agenda política de la mujer de San Juan de Miraflores: 10 demandas urgentes. Presupuestos participativos con enfoque de género." *Equipo técnico del Programa Urbano*. Lima: DESCO - Programa Urbano. 2.

Controlaría General de la República. 2014. *Estudio de proceso de descentralización en el Perú*. Lima, Peru: Controlaría General de la República.

Cornwall, A. 2003. "Whose Voices? Whose Choices? Reflections on Gender and Participatory Development." *World Development* 31 (8): 1325–1342. doi:10.1016/S0305-750X(03)00086-X.

Dawson, G. 2000. "A Feminist Economic Perspective." In *Market, State, and Feminism*, edited by G. Dawson, L. Brown, and S. Hatt, 1–13. London: Edward Elgar Publishing.

Dicklitch-Nelson, S., S. Thompson, and B. Yost. 2016. "Human Rights and the Global Barometer of Gay Rights: A Multi-Year Analysis." Paper prepared for the 57th Annual International Studies Conference.

"Esta es la brecha salarial entre hombres y mujeres en el Perú." 2017. *Perú21*, June 3. https://peru21.pe/economia/brecha-salarial-hombres-mujeres-peru-68082

Frey, R. 2015. "Interlinking Gender Responsiveness and Participation in Public Budgeting Processes." In *Gender Responsive and Participatory Budgeting: Imperatives for Equitable Public Expenditure*, edited by C. Ng, 19–31. SpringerBriefs in Environment, Security, Development and Peace 22. New York: Springer

Goldfrank, B. 2012. "The World Bank and the Globalization of Participatory Budgeting." *Journal of Public Deliberation* 8 (2). http://www.publicdeliberation.net/jpd/vol8/iss2/art7/.

Htun, M. 2003. "Women and Democracy." In *Constructing Democratic Governance in Latin America*. 2nd ed. edited by J. I. Domínguez and M. Shifter, 118–136. Baltimore: Johns Hopkins University Press. Chapter.

Htun, M. 2004. "Is Gender like Ethnicity? The Political Representation of Identity Groups." *Perspectives on Politics* 2 (3): 439–458. doi:10.1017/S1537592704040241.

Huntington, S. 1991. *The Third Wave: Democratization in the Late Twentieth Century*. Norman, OK: University of Oklahoma Press.

Instituto Nacional de Estadistica e Informatica (INEI). 2009. *Perú: Población empadronada de beneficiarios del programa del Vaso de Leche, 2006–2008*. Lima, Peru: INEI.

Karpowitz, C. F., and T. Mendelberg. 2014. *The Silent Sex: Gender, Deliberation, and Institutions*. Princeton: Princeton University Press.

Karpowitz, C. F., T. Mendelberg, and L. Shaker. 2012. "Gender Inequality and Deliberative Participation." *The American Political Science Review* 106 (3): 533–547. doi:10.1017/S0003055412000329.

López Ricci, J. 2014. *"Presupuesto Participativo 11 años después*: *¿Cambio de rumbo o más de lo mismo?*." In *Cuadernos Descentralistas*. Vol. 30. Lima, Perú: Grupo Propuesta Ciudadana.

Mansbridge, J. 1983. *Beyond Adversary Democracy*. Chicago: University of Chicago Press.

McNulty, S. L. 2015. "Barriers to Participation: Exploring Gender in Peru's Participatory Budget Process." *The Journal of Development Studies* 51 (11): 1429–1443. doi:10.1080/00220388.2015.1010155.

McNulty, S. 2011. *Voice and Vote: Decentralization and Participation in Post-Fujimori Peru*. Stanford, CA: Stanford University Press.

Miloslavich Túpac, D. 2013. *Escasa inversión del estado en las mujeres: Observatorio Presupuesto Participativo 2008–2011*. Lima, Peru: Flora Tristan.

Muncipalidad de Miraflores. 2016. "Plan De Desarrollo Local Concertado Del Distrito De Miraflores 2017 – 2021." www.miraflores.gob.pe

Muncipalidad de Surco. 2016. "Plan de Desarrollo Concertado de Santiago de Surco 2017–2021." http://www.munisurco.gob.pe/segunda_portada/municipalidad/index.asp?pagina=Politicas_Planes/index.html

Municipalidad de Pueblo Libre. 2016. "Plan de Desarrollo Local Concertado Pueblo Libre 2017–2021." www.muniplibre.gob.pe/assets/docs/pp/pdlc_2017_2021.pdf

Municipalidad de Villa María del Triunfo. 2016. "Plan de Desarrollo Local Concertado Villa María del Triunfo 2017–2021." www.munivmt.gob.pe/PDLC_2017–2021.pdf

Pape, M. 2014. "Participatory Budgeting for Whom? A Feminist Perspective." M.S. Thesis, University of Wisconsin-Madison.

Pitkin, H. 1967. *The Concept of Representation*. Berkeley: University of California Press.

Prodescentralización. 2010. *Guía del Presupuesto Participativo Basado en Resultados*. Lima, Peru: Programa ProDescentralización.

Prodescentralización. 2011. *Proceso de descentralización: Balance y agenda a Julio de 2011*. Lima, Peru: Programa ProDescentralización.

Prodescentralización. 2016. *Informe Anual sobre el estado del proceso de Descentralización – A enero de 2016*. Lima, Peru: Programa ProDescentralización.

Provincia de Chinca. 2014. "Plan De Desarrollo Local De La Provincia De Chincha 2014–2029." http://www.municipalidadchincha.gob.pe/webchincha/Muni-Chincha-2015/menu.html

Remy, M. I. 2011. "*Participación* ciudadana y gobiernos descentralizados." *Cuadernos Descentralistas 28*. Lima, Peru: Grupo Propuesta Ciudadana.

Remy, M. I. 2016. "La participación y representación política desde las regiones." In *Participación, Competencia, y Representación Política: Contribuciones para el Debate*, edited by J. Aragón, 147–158. Lima, Peru: Jurado Nacional de Elecciones.

Sanders, L. M. 1997. "Against Deliberation." *Political Theory* 25 (3): 347–376. doi:10.1177/0090591797025003002.

Schwindt-Bayer, L. 2010. *Political Power and Women's Representation in Latin America*. Oxford: Oxford University Press.

Sintomer, Y., C. Hershberg, and G. Allegretti. 2013. *Participatory Budgeting Worldwide (Dialog Global No. 25)*. Bonn: Engagement Global.

Sintomer, Y., A. Röcke, and C. Herzberg. 2016. *Participatory Budgeting in Europe: Democracy and Public Governance*. Abingdon, UK: Routledge.

Su, C. 2017a. "From Porto Alegre to New York City: Participatory Budgeting and Democracy." *New Political Science* 39 (1): 67–75. doi:10.1080/07393148.2017.1278854.

Su, C. 2017b. "Beyond Inclusion: Critical Race Theory and Participatory Budgeting." *New Political Science* 39 (1): 126–142. doi:10.1080/07393148.2017.1278858.

Thomas, S. 1991. "The Impact of Women on State Legislative Policies." *The Journal of Politics* 53 (4): 958–976. doi:10.2307/2131862.

Thomas, S., and S. Welch. 1991. "The Impact of Gender on Activities and Priorities of State Legislators." *The Western Political Quarterly* 44 (2): 445–456. doi:10.2307/448788.

Wampler, B., and J. Hartz-Karp. 2012. "Participatory Budgeting: Diffusion and Outcomes across the World." *Journal of Public Deliberation* 8 (2), Article 13. http://www.publicdeliberation.net/jpd/vol8/iss2/art13.

Wampler, B., S. McNulty, and M. Touchton. 2018. "Participatory Budgeting: Spreading across the Globe." http://www.transparency-initiative.org/uncategorized/2626/participatory-budgeting-spreading-across-globe-2/

Wangnerud, L. 2000. "Testing the Politics of Presence: Women's Representation in the Swedish Riksdag." *Scandanavian Political Studies* 23 (1): 67–91. doi:10.1111/1467-9477.00031.

Zas Friz Burga, J. 2004. *La insistencia de la voluntad: El actual proceso Peruano de descentralización política y sus antecedentes inmediatos (1980–2004)*. Lima, Peru: Defensoría Del Pueblo.

Gender, the workplace and the limits of the law: a reply to Cramer and Cote Hampson

Stephanie McNulty

ABSTRACT

This reply discusses two articles that explore the limits of legal initiatives that attempt to rectify gender imbalances. The two articles tackle different issue areas (birthing and parental policies), yet come to similar conclusions: legal initiatives cannot necessarily change deeply entrenched cultural norms about women's bodies and choices. The articles also point to the problematic conclusion that policies meant to improve women's experience and expand their choices are ultimately restricted by societal norms about a woman's imagined role in the home and workplace. The articles push the boundaries of debates about gender empowerment and the law, and suggest a series of questions that remain to be answered.

This is a reply to:

Cote Hampson, S. 2018. "Mothers Do Not Make Good Workers: The Role of Work/Life Balance Policies in Reinforcing Gendered Stereotypes." *Global Discourse*. doi: 10.1080/23269995.2018.1521129

and

Cramer, R. A. 2018. "The Limits of Law in Securing Reproductive Freedoms: Midwife-Assisted Homebirth in the United States." *Global Discourse*. doi: 10.1080/23269995.2018.1521122

This article serves as a reply to Renée Ann Cramer's 'The Limits of Law in Securing Reproductive Freedoms: Midwife-Assisted Homebirth in the United States' and Sarah Cote Hampson's 'Mothers Do Not Make Good Workers: The Role of Work/Life Balance Policies in Reinforcing Gendered Stereotypes'. Both articles point to the limits of legal initiatives that attempt to rectify gender imbalances. The articles tackle different issue areas (birthing and parental policies), yet point to similar conclusions: legal initiatives cannot necessarily change deeply entrenched cultural norms about women's bodies and choices. They both provide rich narratives about women's experiences, gathered through interviews with women who have lived at the boundary of these norms and the laws that are simply not achieving their goals.

These findings might be counter-intuitive to some. Shouldn't laws protect and empower women in the absence of cultural changes? However, law and society scholars have a long history of documenting that fact that 'legalization and legal status do not necessarily bring legitimation and cultural acceptance' (Cramer 2018, 3). These articles further these findings in previously under-explored realms, including the regulation of homebirths and the implementation of 'family friendly' workplace policies in the military and higher education. By delving into two of these articles, we can further illustrate why this disconnect exists.

Cramer's (2018) piece explores the issue of 'legalizing' homebirth midwives by giving them professional status and decriminalizing their work. Currently, 28 states allow regulated Certified Professional Midwifery (CPM) and 22 states do not. The midwifery movement in many of those 22 states is advocating for legal status. However, Cramer's (2018) ethnographic research in California suggests that the particular details of the legislative 'protections' matter. Even in California, a progressive state with a long history of homebirths, Certified Professional Midwifes must work under the supervision of a physician, be insured and be able to transfer patients safely to hospitals in certain situations. In their in-depth interviews with midwifes, the professionals make it very clear that these requirements simply can't be met. Physicians are hesitant to take on the supervisory relationship, and insurance is extremely costly to obtain. Thus, many CPMs operate outside of the law in this supposedly 'legal' environment.

All of these factors show that ultimately the CPMs (and the families doing homebirths) are beholden to a series of institutions (the medical profession, insurance companies and the hospital industry) that are not particularly prone to supporting what some view as alternative or non-traditional birthing practices. Further, all of these institutions are deeply embedded in patriarchal norms that include stereotypes about midwifes, nurses and doctors. Cramer (2018) does not argue that efforts to legalize CPM in the remaining states are futile; rather, she makes the point that to be successful, activists must also take into account the need to shift cultural norms about birthing in the United States.

Cote Hampson (2018) makes very similar arguments about the limitation of what are called 'family friendly work policies', focusing on how they directly challenge the culturally embedded norm of the 'ideal worker'. Cote Hampson (2018) explores these questions in two highly structured, patriarchal and hierarchical sectors of employment: the military and higher education. Both sectors have long-held norms about the 'ideal worker'.

Cote Hampson (2018) observes that the ideal military worker is always available to serve and physically fit. However, military women can defer deployment for several months after giving birth (as well as opt into other exemptions from uniform requirements and training). As a result, they are sometimes viewed as using childbirth as a way to avoid their obligations. The military woman who Cote Hampson interviews often spoke about their experience in light of these stereotypes, sometimes defensively explaining how their experience is unique and other times talking about hiding their pregnancies to avoid being penalized for stereotypical behavior. Others consciously act against the stereotype in an effort to be seen as equal, which problematically goes against what may be best for the woman and child in the long term. Next, Cote Hampson (2018) explicates that the 'serious scholar' ideal in the academy, i.e. a person who is driven to research and does not take long breaks from their research agenda by spending time at home with their families. Cote Hampson's interviewees recognized that women who take parental leave after childbirth, for example, may be viewed and treated differently as well as suffer negative consequences to their careers.

Another conclusion that emerges in Cote Hampson's (2018) work is that the workplace policies that now exist, hard won by activists, are inadvertently reinforcing the image of the ideal worker as inherently masculine (read: able to spend ample time outside the home serving their institutions). This same tension emerges in Cramer's (2018) piece and is ultimately unresolved. Policies meant to improve women's experience and expand their choices are restricted by societal norms about a woman's imagined role in the home and workplace.

For this reason, both articles leave us with several questions. Can any policy initiative eradicate the tensions inherent in these (and other) employment sectors? If so, what policies might be best? If not, where does this leave us? Can cultural changes take place without legislative initiatives? These questions are beyond the scope of the articles in this section but do demand more attention. Every worker will benefit when these questions are resolved.

Disclosure statement

No potential conflict of interest was reported by the author.

References

Cote Hampson, S. 2018. "Mothers Do Not Make Good Workers: The Role of Work/Life Balance Policies in Reinforcing Gendered Stereotypes." *Global Discourse*. doi: 10.1080/23269995.2018.1521129

Cramer, R. A. 2018. "The Limits of Law in Securing Reproductive Freedoms: Midwife-Assisted Homebirth in the United States." *Global Discourse*. doi: 10.1080/23269995.2018.1521122

Law's promises and its limits: a reply to Cramer and McNulty

Sarah Cote Hampson

ABSTRACT
Cote Hampson discusses the ways in which Cramer and McNulty's pieces are linked to her own article in terms of their focus on the law's failure to live up to its promises. She highlights the tensions raised in each piece between seeking cultural versus legal remedies to social inequities, and argues that critical scholarship may offer one of the best "solutions" to the problems posed by the law's limits.

This is a reply to:

Cramer, R.A. 2018. "The Limits of Law in Securing Reproductive Freedoms: Midwife-Assisted Homebirth in the United States." *Global Discourse*. doi:10.1080/23269995.2018.1521122.

and

McNulty, S. 2018. "Embedded Exclusions: Exploring Gender Equality in Peru's Participatory Democratic Framework." *Global Discourse*. doi:10.1080/23269995.2018.1521137.

All three of the articles in this cluster wrestle with the question of how marginalized voices can best be heard. Stephanie McNulty (2018) explores the impact of women's voices in participatory democracy in Peru; Renee Cramer (2018) captures the voices of midwives (mostly women) who are caught up in a battle for legal recognition, and my article (Cote Hampson 2018) highlights the voices of working mothers who are deciding whether or not to claim their rights to work/life balance policies. All of these pieces are therefore not only focusing specifically on the significance of women's voices, but on how those voices are struggling to be heard within the limitations established by legal frameworks. 'The limits of the law' therefore, can be understood in one sense as the boundaries within which these women must work in order for their voices to be granted legitimacy – to join a larger, legally recognizable, conversation.

Yet 'the limits of the law' can also refer to the ways in which the law's *promise* to recognize voices – to lend them legitimacy – can itself be limited. Here is where I think the most interesting, and disheartening, contributions of these pieces lies. McNulty (2018), for instance, calls into question the promise of policies aimed at increasing women's participation in democratic governance, such as participatory budgeting requirements, demonstrating that increased participation does not necessarily lead to increased *voice* for women in these processes. Cramer (2018), too, finds that the promises of legalization of their practices have not been fulfilled, as many midwives in so-called 'legal states' find non-legal or quasi-legal barriers to their practices, including difficulty with insurance coverage and relationships with other healthcare professionals. Why this failure of the law to achieve its promises? Both Cramer (2018) and McNulty (2018) in their own ways point to cultural norms having a more substantive impact on whether or not these women are heard than the formal legal protections they seek/are mobilizing. Cramer (2018) refers to the hegemony of the 'medical model' of birth impacting the ability of the alternative messages of midwives to be heard. McNulty (2018) captures a sexist culture in her observations of participatory budgeting meetings wherein women's voices do not carry the same weight as men's – despite their 'equal' participation in terms of numbers. In my own research, I also find informal norms are often more significant in the lived experiences of working mothers than their formal rights under law/ policies aimed at protecting them.

It is particularly striking that in both of these articles, despite the failure of the law to live up to its promises, the women in question still seek formal legal remedies to their problems with achieving equal voice. All three of the authors in this cluster are somewhat at a loss to explain exactly *why* the belief in formal law's promises persists, in the face of its many failures alongside strong cultural counter-norms. Cramer (2018), perhaps, does the best job of wrestling with this problem, arguing that activism within a 'cultural schema' – rather than within a legal-centric framework – may be the best way forward for activists looking to make more meaningful social change. I think that this makes sense, and is certainly consistent with what I argue in my own piece (Cote Hampson 2018) – that only through a focus on *cultural* change can legal change be meaningful. Yet I am also reluctant to leave readers with a sense of security as to the way forward. I do think, as Stuart Scheingold (2004) says, there is political and symbolic value to the 'myth of rights' but there is also a danger to their symbolism, for which each of these articles offers evidence. There is a danger that formal legal recognition can provide a cover – 'window dressing' as Lauren Edelman (2016) calls it – that masks continuing inequalities with the veneer of legal recognition. It is this tension – between law's mobilizing and legitimizing power, and its propensity to fail in its promises – with which all marginalized voices seeking to be heard must wrestle. Though I have sometimes been criticized in my own work for not having clearly proposed 'solutions' to the problems I uncover with work/life balance policies and the inequities that they often mask and perpetuate, I think that there is an important role for the critical work of scholars such as Cramer and McNulty, who highlight the limits of the law to bring about meaningful social change, and who do not necessarily offer direct solutions to these problems. It may be that simply discovering, recording and discussing the disconnect between the law's promises and its failure to deliver on those promises is the best we can offer, promoting an ongoing cultural and legal self-reflective process that may (or may not) lead to change.

References

Cote Hampson, S. 2018. "Mothers Do Not Make Good Workers: The Role of Work/Life Balance Policies in Reinforcing Gendered Stereotypes." *Global Discourse*. doi:10.1080/23269995.2018.1521129.

Cramer, R. A. 2018. "The Limits of Law in Securing Reproductive Freedoms: Midwife-Assisted Homebirth in the United States." *Global Discourse*. doi:10.1080/23269995.2018.1521122.

Edelman, L. B. 2016. *Working Law: Courts, Corporations, and Symbolic Civil Rights*. Chicago: University of Chicago Press.

McNulty, S. 2018. Embedded Exclusions: Exploring Gender Equality in Peru's Participatory Democratic Framework." *Global Discourse*. doi:10.1080/23269995.2018.1521137.

Scheingold, S. A. 2004. *The Politics of Rights: Lawyers, Public Policy, and Political Change*. 2nd ed. Ann Arbor: University of Michigan Press.

Process is insufficient: a reply to Cote Hampson and McNulty

Renée Ann Cramer

ABSTRACT

This reply explores the implications raised by a scholarly conversation among the pieces by Cramer, Cote Hampson, and McNulty in this special issue of *Global Discourse*. Cramer's piece argues that midwives and women living in states where home births are legally attended by Certified Professional Midwives continue to experience confusion about legal status, and chilling social approbation that constrains access to reproductive choice. Cote Hampson argues that women in hierarchical professions in the United States, as typified by academia and the military, often refuse to avail themselves of policies meant to facilitate work-life balance, in large part because they understand accessing maternity leave to be a stereotyped behavior that weakens employers' perception of them as ideal workers. And, McNulty's research shows that procedural changes meant to facilitate – indeed mandate – women's participation in participatory-budgeting regimes in Peru may increase the presence of women in these meetings, but do not increase their actual, meaningful participation. In light of the findings of all three pieces, that women's access to rights is not meaningfully expanded by procedural changes, this comment asks whether legal venues and procedural changes are the best ways by which women can assert claims to equality, equity, and justice.

This is a reply to:

Cote Hampson, S. 2018. "Mothers Do Not Make Good Workers: The Role of Work/Life Balance Policies in Reinforcing Gendered Stereotypes." *Global Discourse*. doi:10.1080/23269995.2018.1521129.

and

McNulty, S. 2018. "Embedded exclusions: exploring gender equality in Peru's participatory democratic framework." *Global Discourse*. doi:10.1080/23269995.2018.1521137.

The articles in the research cluster on policies intended to achieve gender equality and access to rights, for the special edition of *Global Discourse* on gender, sexuality, and the law each highlight the limits of law to achieve meaningful social change, absent attention to cultural norms. These three articles are written about very different types of policies: maternity leave (Cote Hampson 2018), access to options in childbirth (Cramer

2018), and participatory budgeting (McNulty 2018) and cover very specific and different cultural contexts: academia and the military, homebirth families in the United States, and local governing structures in Peru. Cramer's (2018) piece argues that midwives and women living in states where home births are legally attended by certified professional midwives continue to experience confusion about legal status, and chilling social approbation that constrains access to reproductive choice. Cote Hampson (2018) argues that women in hierarchical professions in the United States, as typified by academia and the military, often refuse to avail themselves of policies meant to facilitate work-life balance, in large part because they understand accessing maternity leave to be a stereotyped behavior that weakens employers' perception of them as ideal workers. And, McNulty's (2018) research shows that procedural changes meant to facilitate – indeed mandate – women's participation in participatory-budgeting regimes in Peru may increase the presence of women in these meetings, but do not increase their actual, meaningful participation.

That these articles all offer a sobering view of the role of legal reform to achieve desired outcomes related to gender equity and justice should give scholars and activists pause, and cause us to question whether it is a limitation of law per se or a limitation of law *as it relates to women's equality* in particular.

Sarah Cote Hampson's (2018) article, 'Mothers Do Not Make Good Workers: The Role of Work/Life Balance Policies in Reinforcing Gendered Stereotypes', investigates the reticence of women in academia and the military to take the maternal leave provided to them by employer policy. Using data gleaned from interviews with women who take, and do not take, advantage of leave policies, Cote Hampson's (2018) article makes a significant contribution to the literature in socio-legal studies, which stresses the significance of attending to 'bottom up' approaches to legal and social change. Such scholarship has long theorized that if reforms are comprised of 'top down' policies, they are unlikely to be successful; Cote Hampson's (2018) article clearly demonstrates the disconnect between maternal leave policies and the lived experience of women workers (2), resulting in women who refuse to take the leave afforded them by policy. Cote Hampson's (2018) article offers the additionally disturbing finding that, as maternal leave policies become more progressive, women experience even greater stereotyping that limits their access to policies.

McNulty's (2018) research, and my own, also offer support for this finding about the limits of progressive policies to achieve equity, in very different contexts. In 'Embedded exclusions: exploring gender equality in Peru's participatory democratic framework', McNulty finds that the presence of women in participatory-budgeting processes does not ensure their meaningful contributions. My article, 'The Limits of Law in Securing Reproductive Freedoms: Midwife-Assisted Homebirth in the United States' (Cramer 2018), shows that the presence of legal status for midwives in the United States does not ameliorate cultural approbation that results in constrained access to birth options. Though laws legalizing midwifery and policies mandating women's presence are progressive interventions into gender equality, our research shows that institutions and disciplines like medicine and science, budgeting and economics, both prove resistant to changes meant to ensure women access to their preferences.

McNulty's (2018) study clearly shows that policies meant to facilitate women's participation in democratic decision-making do work, if 'working' is measured as women's mere presence at these meetings and in these venues. Women in Peru are indeed more present in budgeting and planning meetings than they previously had been. However, as we know, and as her analysis demonstrates, mere presence is insufficient to achieving the goals of increased participation. Indeed, McNulty's (2018) article shows us clearly that presence doesn't equate to power, parity doesn't equate to equity, and process doesn't equate to substance. McNulty (2018) shows that men talk more, and present more frequently, even in spaces meant to equalize voice; this indicates gender inequity in the ways that people envision what is appropriate for women's roles and contributions. The state in Peru is unable to effectively promote gender equality through participatory institutions, simply because gender inequality is rooted much more deeply than procedural norms.

Recently, women in political science have successfully organized a campaign to get women included on panels, in press reports, and on important committees. Frustrated that women's expertise was so frequently overlooked in these venues, a group of scholars organized around the hashtag #WomenAlsoKnowStuff to highlight the dearth of women's voices (Beaulieu et al. 2017). Their successful mobilization underscores one of McNulty's key points, women's presence – while important – is not sufficient. Women's voices must be heard, in order to make an impact on policy discussions and such hearing depends on skillful facilitation, mentoring, and systemic institutional change.

McNulty's (2018) article clearly demonstrates that participatory institutions are not necessarily inclusive – progressive reforms are constrained by deeply ingrained gender norms and contemporary practices of neoliberal governance. Her work further demonstrates that the provision of women's participation in planning processes allows the illusion that their participation is meaningful and robust; in other words, progressive policies meant to facilitate participation instead may operate to constrain it. My work with midwives finds that progressive and enabling legislation meant to facilitate access to midwifery care is often implemented or interpreted in ways that do the opposite. In states where their practice is legal, midwives and their clients experience alienation from, and confusion about, the law that results in their feeling that they are transgressing. In states where their practice is legal, midwives and their clients experience social approbation and harassment so strong as to rise to the level of obstetric violence and assault. Women in states where midwifery is legal continue to experience near constant threat of prosecution, and worry about their ability to practice their professor and access care. McNulty and Cramer both points to limits of law to achieving meaningful social change for women.

The data provided in the articles by McNulty, Cramer, and Cote Hampson all indicate that the women in question in these various contexts are well aware of the constraints they operate within, and that they take steps to mitigate against those constraints, even to their own detriment. Cote Hampson (2018), for example, shows clearly that women avoid being stereotyped, by avoiding taking leave. Cramer (2018) shows that midwives will avoid particular hospitals, to avoid particularly bad experiences. And McNulty's (2018) data indicates that women are aware when their contributions are marginalized. These constraints may all be a failure of contemporary law to get at root causes of gender oppression and women's inequality. We might read them and believe that the key to success is the crafting of better and more inclusive policy, coupled with a more vigorous and substantive framing of rights claims.

However, a close reading of Cote Hampson's piece raises the possibility that rights claiming *itself* is problematic for women hoping to achieve justice via law. In previous iterations of her work, Cote Hampson (2017) has seemed to indicate that norm of the ideal worker, and stereotypes of women who access leave, combine to make women less-than-eager to claim access to policies meant to aid them in balancing work and family life. The current article, though, offers an even more nuanced investigation of rights claiming; in this piece, rights claiming itself becomes one of the stereotyped behaviors that women engage in. Rights claiming, for women in Cote Hampson's article, appears to be a sign of weakness. Rights claiming, for women in Cote Hampson's study, is what you do when you need something; and, as an ideal worker, you're not supposed to need anything. In this vein, policies become framed as 'rights of workers' who access them when they need them, rather than as 'obligations of employers' to provide to all workers. This perception of 'needfulness', then, additionally impacts women in their willingness to access rights – which indicates that the problem with access might be as deep as how citizens construct 'rights', something a policy fix will not suffice to remedy. While the articles by McNulty and Cramer do not explicitly address the rights claiming aspects of gender equity embedded within the policies they investigate, women hoping to access equity via the processes in these studies may be similarly plagued by perceptions of 'needfulness' and stereotypes about their presence, as opposed to perceptions of their competency to participate in decision-making about their own lives, their maternity care, and the governance of their bodies and communities.

The seeming paradox evident in all three articles – that more progressive policies have not resulted in more robust equality for women – is a problem for law and society, and gender and law scholars, to work out. These three articles certainly do not stand alone. They stem from and contribute to scholarship from others concerned about the disconnect between policy and lived experience as they pertain to gender equity, among them those provided in this special issue as well as in the work of Helena Silverstein (2007) on minors' lack of access to abortion and Rose Corrigan (2013) on women's lack of access to adequate support and prosecution after sexual assault. Given decades' worth of work pointing to this disconnect, and the limits of law, we might fruitfully ask why women's rights are particularly intractable. Do progressive policies fail to live up to their promise arise because of cultural constructions of women, femininity, and gender? Or, as Catharine MacKinnon wrote nearly 30 years ago – is it law itself that is particularly intractable, given law's roots in patriarchal systems of oppression (MacKinnon 1989)? In either instance, as the pieces in this research cluster all suggest, perhaps it is the case that women's rights will best be located in political, not legal, processes of social change and cultural transformation.

Disclosure statement

No potential conflict of interest was reported by the author.

References

Beaulieu, E., A. E. Boydstun, N. E. Brown, and K. Y. Dionne. 2017. "Women Also Know Stuff: Meta-Level Mentoring to Battle Gender Bias in Political Science." *PS: Political Science & Politics* 50 (3): 779–783. doi:10.1017/S1049096517000580.

Corrigan, R. 2013. *Up against the Wall: Rape Reform and the Failure of Success*. New York City: New York Univeristy Press.

Cote Hampson, S. 2017. *The Balance Gap: Working Mothers and the Limits of Law*. Palo Alto: Stanford University Press.

Cote Hampson, S. 2018. "Mothers Do Not Make Good Workers: The Role of Work/Life Balance Policies in Reinforcing Gendered Stereotypes." *Global Discourse*. doi:10.1080/23269995.2018.1521129.

Cramer, R. A. 2018. "The Limits of Law in Securing Reproductive Freedoms: Midwife-Assisted Homebirth in the United States." *Global Discourse*. doi: 10.1080/23269995.2018.1521122.

MacKinnon, C. 1989. *Towards a Feminist Theory of the State*. Cambridge: Harvard University Press.

McNulty, S. 2018. "Embedded exclusions: exploring gender equality in Peru's participatory democratic framework." *Global Discourse*. doi:10.1080/23269995.2018.1521137.

Silverstein, H. 2007. *Girls on the Stand: How Courts Fail Pregnant Minors*. New York City: New York University Press.

Policymaking for gender equality: a reply to Cramer, Cote Hampson, and McNulty

Sara Feldman

ABSTRACT

This paper is a response to articles by Renée Ann Cramer, Sarah Cote Hampson and Stephanie McNulty. These articles examine the role of stereotypes and culture in perpetuating traditional gender norms and beliefs about women, as well as the limits of laws and policies created with the intention of supporting gender equality. These articles find that in each area of research, policies intended to support women and their specific needs in their professional, governmental, and reproductive lives are failing to promote equality. Each article examines a different area in life that a woman may experience. However, overlapping themes such as culture, masculinity, stereotypes, as well as institutions and limitations in law and policies all contribute to the lack of success in policies regarding gender equality.

This is a reply to:

Cramer, R.A. (2018). 'The Limits of Law in Securing Reproductive Freedoms: Midwife-Assisted Homebirth in the United States.' *Global Discourse*. doi: 10.1080/23269995.2018.1521122.

and

Cote Hampson, S. (2018). 'Mothers Do Not Make Good Workers: The Role of Work/Life Balance Policies in Reinforcing Gendered Stereotypes,' *Global Discourse*. doi: 10.1080/23269995.2018.1521129.

and

McNulty, S. (2018). 'Embedded exclusions: exploring gender equality in Peru's participatory democratic framework.' *Global Discourse*. doi: 10.1080/23269995.2018.1521137.

In these articles, Cramer, Cote Hampson, and McNulty investigate the role of stereotypes and limitations of law that exist in policies created to promote gender equality and how they perpetuate traditional gender norms and beliefs about women. McNulty's (2018) article, 'Embedded exclusions: exploring gender equality in Peru's participatory democratic framework', elaborates her findings regarding women's participation in participatory institutions and representation in the participatory budget (PB) process. McNulty's

(2018) work suggests that the institutions and legal frameworks that exist with the intention to promote gender equality are failing to do so. In a study of six regional PB processes from 2004 through 2010, she has found that in terms of attendance patterns, gender is parity. However, when it comes to how frequent and long men and women spoke, there was a clear domination by men. One of the major consequences of this is the fact that women's concerns and preferences are not being heard.

McNulty (2018) articulates the shortcomings and limits of the law and legal framework itself and the political context in which the law emerged as reasons for this failure. McNulty (2018) explains that there are several ways to incorporate and promote gender equality in development plans, such as including gender quotas and workshops that can provide opportunities for both men and women to participate in and address gender inequalities. Another limitation lies in the technical scoring process of PB projects that rarely have gender as a criterion. Finally, the neoliberal political context from which these initiatives stemmed from has reinforced existing gender hierarchies and imbalances.

McNulty's (2018) article about participatory institutions in Peru highlights the deeply ingrained culture of machismo, which is seen in the gendered participation of women in specific areas, such as their neighborhoods, rather than regional politics. The neighborhood, which encompasses a few blocks, is seen as a natural extension of the domestic sphere. Therefore, women's participation in neighborhood organizations is seen as a way to keep the domestic sphere clean, while also coding some neighborhood organizations as non-powerful and nonthreatening to the existing power structures.

Similarly, Cote Hampson's (2018) article, 'Mothers Do Not Make Good Workers: The Role of Work/Life Balance Policies in Reinforcing Gendered Stereotypes', investigates the 'deeply-rooted construct', of the 'ideal worker' in academic and military life in the United States. Cote Hampson (2018) explains that the ideal worker is childless or has someone else looking after domestic concerns, is able to work full time and overtime, anytime, and does not take maternity leave or need to leave work for child-related reasons. Women often complete the 'second shift' of housework and childcare within the home, doing a disproportionate share of the domestic work, and limiting the amount of time they can devote to paid work. The traditional role of caregiver that a large percent of women still carry out in their private lives, and its impact on women's equality of opportunity in the workplace, has been systematically ignored and overlooked during the creation of work/life policies.

In academia, Cote Hampson (2018) argues that women are unable to be 'idea workers' due to their multiple obligations in life and inability to devote their lives solely to their work. Due to the 'second shift', women in academia are not considered serious scholars, as their time is often divided between domestic and professional work. As a result, women must seriously consider the familial and professional choices they have to make in order to meet the demands of both work and life. Several women discussed how they felt the need to work harder to counteract the belief that they were somehow neglecting their duties or feeling anxiety about appears to be a good worker. Whether it be personal sacrifices, such as working while on maternity leave, to conform to ideal worker norms or struggling with the decision to become pregnant, or the pressure to continuously publish without interruption, women in academia struggle with being able to meet the expectations of an 'ideal worker' when facing institutional beliefs and norms about what that entails.

The U.S. military has an even more rigid and overtly masculine construction of the ideal worker. The 'ideal worker' in the U.S. military is inherently male, as they are able to deploy without thought or consideration and potential of pregnancy or small children at home. Women are, inherently, unable to be ideal soldiers because of their capacity to become pregnant. Due to its close relationship to masculinity, there is a stereotype that women who become pregnant in the military do so in order to avoid their duties as a warrior, specifically referencing overseas deployment, making them unable to fit the criteria of an ideal warrior always ready to do her duty when called on. Many women interviewed by Cote Hampson were careful to identify themselves as individuals who did not fit that stereotype. Similar to women in academia, some servicewomen were quite ready to adopt behavior that would help them stand out as an ideal soldier, such as willingness to deploy earlier than required, postpartum.

Cote Hampson (2018) discusses how normative constructs such as the ideal worker, and the stereotypes created and associated with them, goes beyond what is possible to regulate with policy, and argues that often, cultural change must occur for policies to truly be effective. Cote Hampson (2018) notes that there is a close connection between the existence of institutional stereotypes of mothers and policies aimed at protecting mothers in the workplace, exempting mothers in ways that other workers are not permitted to be exempt. These work/family policies may often be implemented without taking into account how an institutional culture might react and begin to shape norms around those policies, resulting in the further perpetuation of stereotypes painting mothers as workers who are shirking their responsibilities. As a result, laws and policies intended to help mothers are limited by the fact that they operate within institutions that historically and culturally have not included women and their unique needs.

In 'The Limits of Law in Securing Reproductive Freedoms: Midwife-Assisted Homebirth in the United States', Cramer (2018) discusses culture and stereotypes with regard to birth and medical professionalism and social approbation. Two powerful medical professional organizations, the American College of Obstetrics and Gynecology (ACOG) and the American Medical Association (AMA) both continue to pressure medical professionals to play a supervisory role in pregnancy and birth and the belief that the only appropriate place for birth is in a hospital. As a result, midwives face a number of obstacles that hinder their ability to practice, such as a supervising physician, procuring insurance, the fear of selective prosecution, and the need for a workable transferable relationship. The requirement of a supervising physician and insurance results in midwives undertaking illegal practices as it is financially prohibitive for doctors to carry a midwife on their plan or hospitals routinely refuse insurance coverage to doctors wishing to have that type of relationship. As a result, women who want midwife-assisted homebirths, and midwives themselves, are constricted by the culture of medical professionalism that seek to prohibit birth in nonhospital settings.

Furthermore, midwives explained that women feel 'punished' by doctors and nurses while they are also met with suspicion from medical professionals, friends, and family members. The culture in America is simply that midwives and their clients are 'odd', 'different', and 'crazy'. Some women described strained friendships due to the decision to have an out-of-hospital birth, while others chose not to tell certain people in their lives, not wanting to be looked down upon or seen as strange for their decision. Others said they did not want others to interfere with their decision. Clearly, the dominant culture surrounding birth and the necessity of medical intervention has made women apprehensive about telling others about their decision to have an out-of-hospital birth, while also significantly limiting women's access to alternative birth choices by making the practice of midwifery nearly impossible or illegal.

Cramer (2018) discusses the gap between legalization and legitimation and cultural acceptance. Midwives are seeking transformational laws – laws meant to radically alter how institutions operate – which require deep cultural change and political action. Though Certified Nurse-Midwifery (CNM) and Certified Professional Midwives (CPM) are legal in California, the state's administrative reach into home birth practices constrain and prohibit its practice. As a result, midwives are under threat of prosecution, operating in violation of regulations, and face doctor or state interference in their practices. Many midwives understand themselves to be undertaking illegal practices when practicing, even though they are afforded legal status under California code. Cramer's (2018) research, like Cote Hampson's assertion, argues that a cultural change must occur for midwifery practice to be accepted. Though it is legal in California for CNMs and CPMs to practice and operate, the government, medical institution, and culture surrounding midwifery limit its practice to the point where midwives are practicing illegally, even though their status is legal.

McNulty's (2018) findings are quite interesting regarding the lack of female voice in participatory institutions. Further research could examine and analyze the speaking contributions women do make at PB meetings, and how that is received by their male colleagues. Additionally, different types of data collection – such as interviews – with women engaged in participatory institutions to learn how they understand and interpret their experiences and whether they believe their voices are heard in participatory institutions. Would including gender in the scoring and criterion of projects help bring about change? McNulty (2018) suggests further changes to the legal framework as a way to include women, however, was not successful the first time: Could a cultural change, especially regarding machismo, be more impactful in women's participation in participatory institutions? In addition, further research into more regional governments in Peru that differ in population size, life expectancy, education, and income would help to gain a better understanding of how female participation varies by region.

Cote Hampson (2018) identifies a deeply ingrained culture of masculinity in the U.S. military and powerful construct of the 'ideal worker' in academia. Could a change in the culture of masculinity occur in a society that it is so deeply intertwined with? Would a culture change be more beneficial than enacting more policies specifically address women and maternity? To what extent would expanding family policies create real change? What would be the cultural and legal/policy impact if men started taking paternity leave? Can a culture change occur if women are inherently unable to be ideal soldiers because of their capacity to become pregnant and give birth? Further research that interviews a more diverse group of people, including race, ethnicity, socioeconomic status, sexuality, gender identity, and more could help to better understand how people with multiple identities prevent them from being 'ideal workers' experience and engage with these stereotypes.

Cramer (2018) argues that both a cultural and legal change must occur to create and maintain access to midwifery. To what extent are masculinity and medical professionalism related? Can medical professionalism be influenced by a cultural change with organizations like ACOG and the AMA putting significant pressure on the medical institution to keep birth medicalized? How and can legal mobilization and cultural and political mobilization work together to support midwifery? Further research of public opinion of midwifery and out-of-hospital birth would be interesting to examine to gauge public support for legalization of midwifery. In addition, examining the accessibility of midwives as an option that people of all races, ethnicities, socioeconomic statuses, gender identities, sexualities, and regional locations could be another interesting topic of research.

These three articles all make important contributions to understanding how women experience their work environments, experience with birth, and participation in government. Though they all bring new voices to the conversation about women's experiences in these areas, there are still voices of people who have been left out, and continue to be left out of the conversation. These three pieces highlight the how culture and stereotypes influence women's experiences and conflicts between their work and personal lives, while also highlighting the limits of the law. Clearly, changes in policy are not enough to change the experiences of women in these areas of their lives, and policies intended to include or aid women end up further perpetuating negative stereotypes of women and enforce gender inequality in these spaces.

Disclosure statement

No potential conflict of interest was reported by the author.

References

Cote Hampson, S. 2018. "Mothers Do Not Make Good Workers: The Role of Work/Life Balance Policies in Reinforcing Gendered Stereotypes." *Global Discourse*. doi:10.1080/23269995.2018.1521129.

Cramer, R. A. 2018. "The Limits of Law in Securing Reproductive Freedoms: Midwife-Assisted Homebirth in the United States." *Global Discourse*. doi:10.1080/23269995.2018.1521122.

McNulty, S. 2018. "Embedded exclusions: exploring gender equality in Peru's participatory democratic framework." *Global Discourse*. doi:10.1080/23269995.2018.1521137.

Index

Note: **Bold** page numbers refer to tables, *italic* page numbers refer to figures and page numbers followed by "n" denote endnotes.

www.ingramcontent.com/pod-product-compliance
Lightning Source LLC
LaVergne TN
LVHW011131300926
849160LV00008B/610

9780367730840